Can you spit across the street?

The memoirs of a boy growing up in Mid-America
in the middle of the twentieth century

BY
Joe M. Welling

To order more copies of this book, or for more information
about Joe Welling, please go to

joewelling.com

WELBROOK  PUBLISHING

FOREWORD

"Why don't you write a book?" many people have asked me. They think I have led an interesting life (in what I feel is a very limited way) and have met fascinating people and observed or participated in a multitude of experiences worth passing on to others—some poignant, some enlightening, some nostalgic and most humorous, even hilarious. While I certainly agree with this, my experiences pale by comparison with those of the truly interesting people of our time. From my perspective, my experiences and the aspects of my life aren't sufficient to make even an interesting magazine article to most people, much less a book. "Why in the world would anyone be interested in reading about anything concerning my life?" I ask myself (or respond to others). How egotistical or arrogant I would be to think otherwise.

However, what would we have missed if Jean Shepherd felt this way? Or S.E. Hinton? Or Neil Simon? Or Bill Cosby? Or Willie Morris? Or others who have set stories of their personal experiences or life to paper. I certainly don't mean to put myself in the same category with these icons. But I've come to realize that writing about personal experiences doesn't necessarily have to do with telling reluctant readers about one's self, but rather about the experiences, the fascinating people and the interesting occurrences, no matter how simple or uneventful they may seem.

I'm one of those who believes that movies of the twentieth century have been one of the most valuable (and often accurate,

i

but sometimes horribly inaccurate) reflections of the best and the worst of our civilization and life in America. One of my favorite film genres is that which does an accurate job of portraying nostalgia and life in America in the mid-twentieth century, when times were simpler (or at least seemed to be) and values were somewhat lofty and uncomplicated. What I'm talking about are the movies whose primary focus is recapturing some of these times—not just stories which took place years ago or historical movies, but true depictions of events or everyday life in the middle third of the century when the era and the nostalgia was as important to the movie as any of the characters. Some of those which come to mind for me are movies such as "To Kill a Mockingbird", "Lost in Yonkers", "My Dog Skip", "American Graffiti", some of the Woody Allen films and of course the wonderful movies "Tex", "Rumble Fish" and "The Outsiders", based on books written by S.E. Hinton, a girl who followed me at Will Rogers High School by a few years. The first of her books, The Outsiders, was written while she was still in high school. All three of these books were based on events in and around Tulsa, my high school and my hangouts. (Incidentally, I admire and appreciate director Francis Ford Coppola for sticking close to the books, the spirit of the stories and filming the movies on location in Tulsa, where the stories took place, rather than taking the easy way out and filming them in Los Angeles or at some studio's backlot.)

At the top of my list would be the movies created by Jean Shepherd. The best of these (in my humble opinion) is "A Christmas Story", which has become a classic and is shown numerous times each Christmas season—nearly as often as "It's a Good Life" and "Miracle on 34th Street". In Shepherd's movies he narrates stories and anecdotes that took place during his childhood in the forties. As a contemporary, I totally identify with these stories.

In this regard, Shepherd's books and movies have been an

inspiration to me and to my writing of this book.

I don't know how many others found Ralphie's quest for a Red Ryder B-B Gun as significant as I, but there must be quite a few owing to the success of the movie. Like Seinfeld, the most successful (and arguably the best written) comedy series in the history of American television, many of the nostalgic movies, such as "A Christmas Story" are stories about "nothing".

So, I decided to add my book about nothing to the stack of others already written. It may be that no one will be interested in reading it. . .probably not even my family. I may be the only one who gets anything out of this exercise through my resurrection of a pot full of memories about times when life was simple, the country was, for the most part, at peace, (and even when we were at war, there was something unifying and cathartic which came from the tragedy), Happy Days really did exist and terrorism was something at which Boris Karloff and Bela Lugosi were quite good but it never touched us after we walked out of the movie theater.

My childhood was one which reflected much of what a lot of people like to remember about the forties and fifties. I was a child of the times. I did nothing to create the times, change the times or even help mold the times. All I did was go along with them and ride the wave. My hope is that those who lived through those times will find some events or passages which will take them back to some of their own, pleasant memories. And for those who were born after this era, such as my children, I hope they can get a small glimpse of a truly magical period.

I would like to emphasize that everything I present in this book, for the most part, is true, to the best of my memory. In some cases I created or recreated dialogue in situations which I did not actually hear or experience the words spoken (such as in the Elvis story). But I was told or have a good idea of what transpired. This is done in the interest of readability and giving the reader a greater sense of experiencing the situation.

I didn't even change any names to protect the "innocent" in the book. Occasionally I use full names of some of the people concerned. However, to save embarrassment for some, I used only first names for most of the people involved, including my family members—but they are the actual first names. This does little to disguise who they are for those who know them or may be familiar with the events. If I offended anyone, I sincerely apologize. It is not my intention to embarrass anyone or to hold anyone up for ridicule, except myself in many of the stories. I am not one who is normally into self-deprecation. However, as with many people, the funniest things that happened to me during those uncertain times of youth were of my own doing. Some are still too painful or embarrassing to relate or laugh about. Others are too good to keep to myself, no matter how stupid, foolish or ill-advised they were. All I can say about most of my actions is: "Seemed like a good idea at the time".

Acknowledgements

The author wishes to express his appreciation to many people who contributed to the writing of this book. Of course, the greatest thanks go to those who participated in the events which comprise the anecdotes related.

But during the composition of the book, the author is especially grateful to the following, for their help:

Stephanie Hill, Managing Editor, KOTV Channel 6 in Tulsa

Certain individuals (whose names escape me) with the Chamber of Commerce in Chickasha, Oklahoma

Judge James Peter Messler (ret.), the best batboy the Tulsa Oilers ever had

My good friends John and Betsey Owen and John's invaluable help in the publishing and artwork for the book

My high school buddy, Dick Risk, who not only provided invaluable help in guiding the publishing, but kept a fire built under me until I did it.

Numerous classmates, friends and others who helped jog my memory or clarify certain points, including:

Tom Scoggins

Glenda Davis and the late Stanley Davis

Daryl Lansdale

Ron and Carole Woods

The late James Kerby

Joanne and Be-Bop Bob Moses

Alex MacLean

CONTENTS

PART ONE

The Pre-School Years

Morningside Hospital

Chapter One
BC (Before Conscious-memory)

I think my life-long love for bread and all bakery goods was instilled in me from birth. I was born at Morningside Hospital in Tulsa (which was later changed to Hillcrest Hospital and is now known as Hillcrest Medical Center). In 1940 there was no air conditioning and it was August. In Oklahoma, August temperatures can be stifling—running over 100 degrees on most days when rain does not offer relief. New mothers were generally kept in the hospital for at least a week, not kicked out the next day as they are now. My mother's room was on the fourth floor with window opened wide over the Rainbo Bread bakery, located just next door. They baked their fresh bread twice a day and the aroma is unbelievable. I know the nurses must have purposely picked the baking times to bring me to my mother's bed where I undoubtedly encountered my first real frustrating moments of indecision—go for the breast or hold out for the bread, whose tantalizing aroma carried promises of dietary delights that I could only dream about. The breast won. (It might still be a close contest today.) But I think I must have known even then that whatever produced that smell would probably build strong bodies at least eight ways.

We moved quite a bit in those years before I started to school, but I really don't remember much about it. My father was a piping system design engineer, which is just a fancy term for "draftsman". So, we lived in places where there were new facilities being built, such as refineries and plants, and the engineering company he worked for would send us to various locations and construction sites for a few months at a time. One of those places was DeRidder, Louisiana where Dad worked during the construction of Fort Polk.

We also lived in the Texas Panhandle for a while in a house trailer (before they started calling them "mobile homes"). My mother said we would drive to Tulsa for a weekend and return after two days to find the dust a half inch thick on the floor of the trailer.

We finally settled back in Tulsa and into a semblance of a normal life. My first recollection of my pre-school years was taking an occasional walk with my grandfather. My mother gave me strict orders to hold on to Grandfather's hand when walking and especially when crossing the street. I would dutifully try to grab his hand. He wouldn't let me hold it, explaining that when he walked he liked to swing his arms by his side and holding my hand would inhibit this action. So, I was torn again. I would walk beside Grandfather, swinging my arms like he did and feeling very grown up, but with this overriding guilt feeling knowing that I was not following my mother's instructions.

* * * * *

When we first returned to Tulsa, my grandparents were living in a suite at the Mayo Hotel, Tulsa's finest hotel at the time. My parents and I also moved into the hotel while my grandparents' new home was being built. I was probably the only three-year old living in the Mayo and had the run of the place. It was a safe time and a safe place. There was no such thing as automatic elevators and all the elevator operators knew me and apparently kept close tabs on me as I wandered throughout my very large playhouse.

The Mayo will always have a special place in my heart and it figured in my life rather prominently as I grew older. For example, as a young teenager I went to the movie in Pensacola, Florida, where we sometimes went in the summers to visit my aunt and uncle. The movie "Picnic" was showing. Near the end when Kim Novak asks William Holden, who played a drifter, what his plans were and where he would go, he replied that he had a friend who would give him a job as a bellman at the Mayo Hotel in Tulsa. I was barely able to suppress the urge to jump up and shout: "YES! I used to live there!"

The Mayo's hotel stationery which was in every desk drawer in every

3

room, had a drawing of the hotel's imposing front façade and large revolving door. Underneath the drawing were the words "600 Rooms, 600 Baths."--quite a prestigious deal in those days when only the top hotels had a bath in every room, negating the need to go down the hallway to take a bath. In the fifties, Tulsa Tribune columnist Roger Devlin ("The Rambler") related that a letter had recently arrived at the Mayo from Japan which was addressed simply: "Mayo Hotel, 600 Rooms, 600 Baths". No street, no city, no state. But it made it. (Why is it that nowadays, with 9-digit Zip Codes, automated sorting machines, sophisticated address readers, etc., if one digit is missing, out of place or wrong, the envelope gets kicked back to the sender?)

15 years after I lived at the Mayo, my high school senior banquet and prom was held there in the Crystal Ballroom on the 16th floor, which boasted one of the largest crystal chandeliers in the country. (The Mayo also plays a part in my Elvis Presley story in a later chapter.)

Grandmother Welling   *Grandfather Welling*

Chapter Two
Grandmother and Grandfather

I remember my Grandfather as a well dressed, distinguished, quiet man. It seemed he always wore a business suit, a starched white shirt and a hat. He was a partner in an independent oil company along with several men who were somewhat part of the elite strata of that oil town. They founded the Tulsa Club which was THE place for Tulsa businessmen to meet and greet for lunch or other social gatherings in downtown Tulsa for nearly 60 years, before merging with that upstart Petroleum Club. The senior partner in Grandfather's business endeavors was E.H. Moore, who served one term in the U.S. Senate before giving it up to return to Tulsa. Rumor has it that his dislike of Washington was exceeded only by his dislike of partisan politics. Senator Moore was apparently not one to be involved with anything in which he could not exert a major portion of the control.

My grandfather was well on his way to becoming a pillar of the Tulsa community when, at the age of only 44 he was walking down the street in downtown Tulsa and started to feel ill. He walked into the Bliss Hotel, one of several fine hotels in downtown Tulsa, checked into a room, took off

5

his glasses and placed them on the bedside table, laid down and died of a heart attack. He left a fledgling independent petroleum operation which my grandmother, as a very good businesswoman, took over and ran until her death in 1959.

* * * * *

While my grandfather was a successful businessman, he was far from a millionaire at the time of his death. However, while rummaging through some of my grandmother's belongings, I found a box of his documents when I was about forty, including a couple of copies of his income tax returns for 1936 or 1937. His gross income was reported at about sixty thousand dollars. I remember thinking "Gosh! Grandfather wasn't so rich. He only made sixty thou a year. I make that much!" Then I realized that this was still the depression. In the mid-thirties, the average college graduate was probably making less than two hundred dollars a month—maybe less than three thousand dollars a year. Grandfather was probably making about twenty times the upper middle class average income. In 1980 dollars that would probably have been the equivalent of making about a half million dollars a year or well over a million a year at the turn of this century.

In this box of treasures was a copy of "The New Tribune and The Conception Courier", my grandfather's hometown newspaper from Maryville, Missouri, dated Thursday, January 15, 1942. His picture is on the front page along with an article headlined as follows:

Murray Welling Is Becoming Big Oil Man
In the Oklahoma Field

The caption under his picture reads:

MURRAY WELLING
Former Maryville man acquires interest from E.H. Moore in the
Fitts pool in Oklahoma with 132 producing wells and other
properties. He becomes general manager. The accompanying
picture shows Murray as he appeared when he gave up his place
in the Farmers Trust Company in 1917 to enlist as a soldier
in the first World War.

Coincidentally, the box of memorabilia also contained Grandfather's papers of honorable discharge from the army in 1919.

* * * * *

Not long after his death, my grandmother moved into what I thought at the time was a huge mansion in the Florence Park area of Tulsa. It had two stories, a separate library with adjacent screened-in porch and the greatest little cubby hole room upstairs which my mother used as a sewing room when we lived there. This room, right at the top of the stairs, had a little half door which led into the attic that I could crawl into and use as my "hideout". (Now, as I drive by this house, which is still a lovely home, I see that it is quite a modest sized house—no more than about 2500 square feet.)

Chapter Three
Holland Hall

We lived in my grandmother's Florence Park house for a while and my parents enrolled me in "pre-kindergarten" at a rather exclusive school in Tulsa, called Holland Hall. At that time, Holland Hall was a girls' school but they took boys in pre-k and kindergarten. (It is now a fine, co-educational institution through 12th grade.) In my later years I was always rather surprised that a modest sized city like Tulsa, which was blessed with an outstanding public school system, had so many private schools. In addition to Holland Hall, there was another girls' school, Monte Cassino as well as the prestigious Cascia Hall boys school, which probably was called a "prep school" by many. Unlike Holland Hall, Cascia Hall and Monte Cassino were boarding schools (both were under the auspices of the Catholic Church). There were also several other private schools, mostly Catholic, which were not as exclusive.

It was at Holland Hall that I met my first true love. Ruthie was the cutest little girl you've ever seen. Pudgy little cheeks that were the color of pink rose petals. I would go to her house after school or she would come to mine. We would ride a tricycle for hours, and I do mean "A" tricycle, since there was only one available at each house. (I don't know why my parents never thought of putting my trike in the car when we went to Ruthie's, so we would each have one to ride.) One of us would pedal and the other would stand on the little platform on the back. I liked to stand on the platform since I could lean around every once in a while and kiss Ruthie

8

on one of her rosy cheeks. (This was a harbinger of things to come. A few years later, other vehicles would also play a large role in my love life.)

When we were at my house, my mother would often make scrambled egg sandwiches for us. After trimming off the crust, she would cut them into various shapes and sizes, which we would call: "little, middle and big". No gourmet masterpiece could ever surpass those culinary delights.

My time at Holland Hall also introduced me to another of life's adventures: the school bus. Tulsa Public Schools were, like most communities, organized on a neighborhood basis and had little need for school buses, especially at the elementary level. However, Holland Hall, as a private school, was located about 3 miles from our house and a school bus picked me up every morning. The campus was located on eight acres of prime real estate right in the middle of the silk stocking residential area of Tulsa, surrounded by sumptuous, rambling homes on large, tree-filled lots. (The reason I remember it as being on eight acres is that is what the rather pretentious name of the Holland Hall yearbook was—"Eight Acres". I still have a copy of the 1946 edition.)

My most prominent memory of those bus rides revolves around a bunch of us boys who would scramble to sit on the very back seat across the rear of the bus. Then we would beg the bus driver to go fast when we turned down the road leading to the school. It was a blacktop road which had a big bump running across it a couple of blocks from school. If the bus hit the bump at just the right speed, the rear end of the bus would bounce so much that those of us sitting on that back bench could hit the ceiling with squeals of delight. More fun than any amusement park ride, and a lot cheaper.

The family names of those attending Holland Hall in those days read like a Who's Who of Tulsa society. The girls had such names as Trish and Trinka and, of course, the twins, Muggsy and Melissa. Many of the boys had numbers behind their names, like The Third or The Fourth. While most of them were really nice kids, when I graduated from high school I was really glad I was a product of the public school system in a middle class neighborhood.

A Crosley Sedan, presumed executioner of the horny toad

Chapter Four
The Horny Toad Funeral

My first real group of playmates was in the neighborhood where my grandmother's two-story house was. I ended up going to high school with some of them and remained friends with them for many years.

One summer when we were all playing outdoors someone discovered that a car had run over a horned toad and smashed him in the street. (What ever happened to horned toads or "horny toads" as we called them? They were common when I was a child. I haven't seen one for decades. Surely they're now on someone's endangered species list.)

Someone got the bright idea that we should bury this little dead horny toad and have a funeral for him. The first thing we had to do was get a casket. Someone went home and got a paper box which held kitchen matches—about four inches long. Then, the next problem was who was going to pick him up and put him in the box? No volunteers. So we sort of scraped him with the side of the box until he plopped inside. We then took a soup spoon and dug a little grave under a tree on the corner and dropped the box inside.

After covering the box, someone said that we should say something. So as we all stood around the buried horny toad in a circle for this makeshift, but still strangely tender, graveside service, one of the older kids said something like: "Oh Lord. We're burying this horny toad who was run over in the street by a. . ." At which time he was interrupted by his friend who said: ". . .Crosley. Let's say he was run over by a Crosley. I don't like Crosleys". (For the unitiated, the Crosley was one of Detroit's early attempts to make a compact car. Quite ugly. The Crosley Company made a better refrigerator than they did a car.) To this day, the skeleton of a smashed horny toad rests between the tree and the stop sign at the Northeast corner of 19th and Delaware in Tulsa.

* * * * *

My grandmother's house was about fifty yards from a railroad track which was relatively busy. It afforded an interesting diversion for the kids in the neighborhood and we would frequently put things on the track to be smashed by the train's wheels when they passed over. I watched train wheels smash everything from eggs to rocks to pennies. About two hundred yards down from our house, an overpass carried the tracks over 21st Street, a main thoroughfare. We would sometimes walk down the track to 21st Street and watch the cars go through the underpass. Of course, we could not resist the temptation to toss a pebble or two over the railing to hit the vehicles going underneath.

One day, there were several of us playing on the underpass when we started to throw objects off the bridge. One of the older boys chucked a good size rock off the bridge which struck a car's windshield and cracked it. As the car screeched to a stop I turned around and started running down the tracks toward home. I was appalled when I turned around and noticed that no one else was running. I was only four years old but even I knew that someone was going to be in a heap of trouble, and I didn't want it to be me. How these kids could just stand there and wait for the other foot to drop was beyond my comprehension. I ducked behind a bush and watched in a combination of fascination, fear and even horror as this irate motorist clambered up the embankment to the of the underpass and confronted these children who he no doubt saw as fugitives from reform school.

My curiosity got the best of me and like a moth being drawn to the flame, I proceeded back to the scene of the crime. Seemed like a good idea at the time. As I approached the group, I recall saying something banal like "Hey, wait up you guys! Boy! These after-school hikes sure are fun!" I thought this added a really clever touch. Surely this man could not now believe that these innocent little angels, out for a harmless trek, could perpetrate anything as dastardly as this vandalous deed! I was convinced that my performance would be the clincher—the piece de resistance—that would send us safely back home, scot free with parents none the wiser, and I would be the hero of the day to my peers.

Then I watched in disbelief (and somewhat in admiration) as the culprits, who

11

were probably about six years old, looked at their accuser with totally straight faces and denied the act with a high degree of credulity. In a stroke of what I now can only call juvenile genius these guys blamed the whole thing on some "older boys" who ran off "that way" (pointing South, away from our houses—we lived on the North Side of 21st). All the motorist could say, with a huge dose of skepticism, was "Are you sure?" ("Yes") "Are you sure?" ("Yes") My comrades firmly held their ground. The confrontation was at a stalemate. Having no confession in hand and possibly a reasonable doubt, the motorist had no choice but to leave.

We waited until he left the embankment and then proceeded North toward our homes with a large sense of relief. I couldn't believe that their story to the motorist sounded so plausible that I almost believed it and started questioning what I thought I saw. (Maybe there were some older boys who. . .but. . . Naw!) To someone who had had the importance of always telling the truth drummed into his little head on a continual basis, I couldn't believe how good these guys were at lying. I was terrible at it and it would never have even crossed my four year-old mind that you could successfully lie to an adult. They have an automatic lie detector built into their heads—sort of like some magic ray.

*****

It was about this time that this invincibility of adults, including my parents, started to show signs of weakness. The doctor informed my parents that I should have my tonsils out. I had no particular trepidation about this, having had no experience with any medical treatment or hospital stay since birth and therefore no frame of reference. However, the adults seemed to shift into a constant reassuring mode, telling me how it was no big deal and that I might even enjoy it. (Can you believe this?) I could eat all the ice cream and milkshakes I wanted and I would be home in no time.

When the event came, I found myself back at Morningside/Hillcrest, but this time without the aroma of baking bread. It was not summer and the windows were closed. True to their word, after the operation I was offered ice cream, milkshakes, etc. I didn't want ice cream. I didn't want milkshakes. I didn't want fresh bread. I didn't want anything to get near my throat. I felt betrayed. I was in excruciating pain and all I got was people trying to make the pain worse by putting stuff down my throat. Fortunately, that was my last experience as a patient in a hospital for over forty years.

That experience left me without tonsils. But it left me with a major feeling of skepticism regarding anything medical which adults seemed to be trying overly hard to convince you would not hurt. This was later confirmed numerous times whenever I was about to receive a shot or go to the dentist.

Chapter Five
Grandmother's Wonderful House

In my grandmother's library was a square table about the size of a card table with four leather chairs. Sitting in the middle of the inlaid leather top on this table was a very large, contemporary design, cut crystal vase about 18 inches high. It had a very thick wall and must have weighed about as much as I did. One of my favorite things to do was to crawl up on that table and, while on my hands and knees, stick my face over the top of that vase and sing at the top of my lungs. The echo and reverberation created by this phenomenon was better than one could ever hope to get in the most acoustically favorable shower stall. I developed my rather limited vocal prowess using this method which served me well from my radio debut in the first grade to my days singing rock and roll with my band as a teenager. Oh, how I loved that vase! And for more reasons than its contribution to my early singing development. I thought it was about the most beautiful thing in the world. I still have that vase and it is one of my most cherished possessions, revered even more than my golf clubs.

* * * * *

Going out in the back yard of my grandmother's house was a true experience of mixed emotions. First, it was a lovely place surrounded by a high fence covered with honeysuckle. The aroma on a spring day was second only to that experienced above the Rainbo Bread bakery. My

13

mother taught me that if you pick a honeysuckle blossom and then break off the little nodule at the bottom, you can pull the stem out the bottom and as it comes out a little drop of deliciously sweet nectar is squeezed out with it. Now I knew why those bees had such fascination for those beautiful little blossoms. I would spend a lot of time sucking that nectar out of those blossoms, one drop at a time.

As pleasant as this little piece of heaven was, there was always a cloud over it. The dentist who lived next door owned a Chow dog. This was, to a four-year old, the meanest creature God ever placed on this earth. I know he was a beloved pet to this family, including the little girl, Linda, who was my age and who later became a friend in high school and as an adult. But that dog! With its ugly black lips and snarling teeth! As soon as he heard me come out into the back yard he would start barking and snarling. I couldn't see him nor he me. But we knew each other was there and I had visions of his either just bursting through the fence and hedge or somehow leaping over it in a single bound like the Hound of the Baskervilles and totally devouring me, or, at the least, chewing my leg off. So, I was intimidated into avoiding the back yard most of the time.

* * * * *

I remember how lovely this house, the yard and the neighborhood was when it snowed. What a gorgeous time! However, going out to play in it could be the biggest hassle ever encountered by a four-year old. Among the many true scenes in Jean Shepherd's fabulous movie, A Christmas Story, was when Ralphie's little brother was fully outfitted in his snowsuit to walk to school after it had snowed. Then, when he fell in the snow and couldn't get up, this was not just a figment creation of Shepherd's imagination. As he just lay there with arms and legs flailing like an overturned turtle I was taken back to similar occasions when I experienced the same thing. It would take what seemed like hours to get that snow suit on. When a four-year old hears kids outside frolicking in the snow, the time it takes for Mom to get the warm underwear, heavy pants and shirt, sweater, double socks, snow suit, boots, mittens, cap, scarf and other assorted paraphernalia on is second only to the time it takes for Christmas to arrive.

When the door finally opens and you burst outside, what a feeling of triumph! You survey the world in its lovely white coat and the kids gathered in the yard. But you find that no matter how hard you are trying to move your legs you can only propel yourself forward about as fast as a geriatric inchworm with a severe heart condition, shuffling about three inches at a time in a sort of jerky, robotic zombie motion. Running (or even walking) requires the legs to be bent at the knees—an impossibility in this configuration. Then, about the time you finally get to the spot where the kids are starting to build the snowman to beat all snowmen, you are hit with the nearly uncontrollable urge to go to the bathroom. Even at age four, you know that relieving yourself inside that snowsuit would create a condition even more uncomfortable than trying to sleep in a wet bed. So, you'd turn around with great reluctance to start the whole process again. If you fell down, it really was impossible to get back up to a standing position on your own.

I learned a lot about construction of a snowman at that early age. The biggest problem is that no matter how light and fluffy snow appears, it is heavy. Making the first stage of the snowman is fairly easy. You simply start rolling the snow ball until it picks up enough mass to be the size you desire for the lower part of your snowman's body. Of course, this takes careful planning. When the ball gets too big to roll any farther, this will be the snowman's final resting place. It will be impossible at this stage to move it to another location. So, it's best not to start where you want the snowman to stand. Start somewhere at a distance and hope you end up at the desired place.

The biggest problem now comes at stage two. If your stage one ball is three feet across, then the stage two ball needs to be only slightly smaller or the body will be out of proportion. If you are under ten years old, try lifting a packed ball of snow that is two or two and a half feet in diameter up onto a three foot high perch. I don't want to meet the kid who can do this.

I ended up creating several snowmen who bore little resemblance to the Frosty we have all come to know and love who appears on Christmas cards and in various story books and cartoons. These ideal looking snowmen were probably constructed by the U.S. Corps of Engineers. In order to have enough height, several of my creations ended up having a large number of small, abdominal sections, like a giant, upright ant.

* * * * *

But rain, snow or shine, one indoor activity I observed frequently was card playing. This was years before television, of course. I come from a line of card players and this is one of the early activities I remember at my grandmother's house. My grandmother and mother played a lot of bridge and at least once a week my grandmother played poker with several of her friends, most of whom were members of an organization to which she belonged, called the Quota Club, made up of prominent Tulsa businesswomen.

One afternoon in 1945, my mother, grandmother and two other ladies were playing bridge. For some reason, the radio was on. I was in the next room (probably with my face in the crystal vase) when all of a sudden I heard the biggest commotion emanating from the room where the card game was taking place. As I ran into the living room I could see one of the ladies jumping up and down, running around the living room, twirling and throwing her cards in the air like confetti and yelling: "The war's over! The war's over!" They say you will always remember where you were and what you were doing when most of the monumental events in your life take place—the Kennedy assassination, the landing on the moon, etc. Well, I probably would have never remembered this event had it not been for the way in which it was brought to my attention. I was only four years old. I didn't even know there was a war going on!

Chapter Six
Pop and My First Cigar

Few kids growing up have grandparents as opposite as mine. While my paternal grandparents were affluent (but not filthy rich) and relatively urbane, my maternal grandparents were more simple, small town people. My paternal grandparents had one child—my father. My mother was one of 12 children and when I was a young child, my mother's parents lived on a farm in a small town in East Texas. My grandmother had come over from Germany as a little girl. The difference in these two sets of grandparents was no more evident than in what I was taught to call them. My paternal grandparents were "Grandfather" and "Grandmother". My maternal grandparents were "Pop" (or Papa) and "Mama". Grandfather was an accountant and an oilman. Pop was a farmer and the band director at the local high school in Gilmer, Texas. Grandmother would have probably stuffed me in my favorite vase if I had called her "Grandma" or "Granny"!

My mother's family was quite musical which is likely where I got my love of music and what modest degree of musical talent or propensity I have. For the last couple of decades of the nineteenth century and the first couple of decades in the twentieth century, pre-TV and even pre-radio, the American public could thank some of the country's major newspapers for bringing music to them—especially so-called concert music or bands. It was these newspapers who sponsored bands and produced regular concerts, often held in outside bandstands in city parks or town squares, at no charge. America's most famous bandsman and composer of concert and marching music, John Phillip Sousa, was the director of the Washington Post band. This was also part of my family's heritage. My grandfather (Pop) was the director of the Houston Post band about the time of World War I. At the time, the Houston Post was owned by E.K. Gaylord, Sr. who was sort of the William Randolph Hearst of Middle America. The Gaylord family also owned the Oklahoma City Daily Oklahoman as well as other newspapers and broadcast stations. They also founded TV's Nashville Network, and owned The Grand Ole Opry and Opryland in Nashville.

My mother would recall to me being taken by her father up to Mr. Gaylord's office at the Houston Post for meetings when she was about four or five years old and while Pop and Mr. Gaylord would have a meeting, sitting on the divan in his office, she would play under his huge desk, using it like a play house.

I remember very little of Pop, except one thing. On one of my summer visits to my grandparents' in Texas, I had my sixth birthday. Pop put me up on his knee and told me that now that I was six I was grown up and was no longer a baby. He proceeded to give me the biggest cigar I had ever seen, thrust it into my mouth and lit it. I strutted around the house for about ten minutes just puffing on the cigar like I was sixty instead of six, amid shrieks of protest from my mother and the other ladies in the house at the time. I must have looked like those boys in the wild party scene in Walt Disney's Pinnochio. I was sick for three days and nothing I ate tasted right. I never smoked another cigar even though my dad was a chain cigar smoker all his adult life.

Much of my practical education in a lot of areas came from my visits to my grandparents' in Texas. Actually, they didn't live in Gilmer. They lived in a "suburb" of Gilmer—Bettie, Texas. Actually, they lived in a suburb of Bettie—Simpsonville. (More about these visits in a later chapter.)

The first funeral I remember was Pop's—when I was six years old. Actually, I remember the wake held the night before and thought it was the most bizarre thing I had ever seen in my young life. There was Pop, laid out in the dining room with Mama sitting in a chair beside him. The coal oil lamps were lit all over the house and I cannot smell kerosene to this day without being taken back to that evening. There was a steady stream of people coming to the house. Women were crying. All the men were standing around in the front yard. My uncle was telling how he was at Pop's bedside when he died and what it was like. I just wanted to find a bed in some quiet place and go to sleep.

PART TWO
Chickasha, Oklahoma

2nd Grade in Chickasha, holding precious Junior G-Man Badge

Chapter Seven

The Banner Bowl

Chickasha is the County Seat of Grady County in Southern Oklahoma. Population about 16,000 and holding. Home of the Chickasha Fighting Chicks—not exactly my idea of a team name which strikes fear in the hearts of your opponents. A nice little town with nothing particularly prominent to distinguish it from numerous other county seat towns in Oklahoma and Texas. It was the location of the Oklahoma College for Women (OCW) that later changed its name to Oklahoma College of Liberal Arts, when it became a coeducational institution and is now known as the University of Science and Arts in Oklahoma.

We moved into a house on the edge of town (at 1701 Park Avenue—quite a posh sounding address for a little pre-war two bedroom house with a screened-in front porch.) Park Avenue was a one lane, dirt street at the time and when it rained it became two muddy ruts. I guess in somebody's mind, this was an "Avenue".

One of my father's interests was bowling. So he convinced my grandmother that she should invest in a bowling alley (which is what they were called before the public relations pundits mounted campaigns in the last half of the century to attempt to turn them into Bowling Lanes or Bowling Centers or Family Recreation Centers). So she purchased the Banner Bowl on Kansas Avenue in Chickasha—an eight lane house that my dad took over to run. Unlike many bowling alleys of that time, Banner Bowl was located at street level with a respectable looking front door and a proper sign. In many of the bigger cities, bowling alleys were often located on the second floor and generally shared their space with numerous pool tables and a bar.

In Chickasha, local recreation and entertainment generally consisted of a choice of three things: movies (and Chickasha had five indoor movie theaters, plus two drive-in theaters), sporting events (high school football games in the fall and local softball league in the spring and summer) and the bowling alley. So, it seemed like a good idea to my dad to feed this need. Much of the social life of a portion of the community seemed to revolve around the bowling alley.

In addition to the eight lanes, Banner Bowl boasted the obligatory pinball machines and a snack bar/café with about 8 stools. My father offered the job of managing the snack bar to his brother-in-law who had just returned from the Navy. So Uncle Al and Aunt Clarice, my mother's sister, pulled up stakes and moved from the Syracuse, New York area to Chickasha where Al would get his start as a restaurateur. What a culture shock that must have been!

It became apparent that Uncle Al's compensation would be tied to the net profit of the snack bar operation. The first hint came in the size of the hamburgers. My dad suggested he make about six hamburgers from a pound of ground beef. This would yield a pretty good product and a nice margin for profit. Uncle Al discovered that if he got the meat very cold and put just a small bit of cereal in it, he could really flatten the patties out and get eleven hamburgers from a pound! These things were so thin you could see light through them and they were about the size of a half dollar coin. But never mind. . .I thought they were delicious. However, Uncle Al cut no slack. Everyone paid. I thought that being the owner's son, this would entitle me to a free hamburger every once in a while. But no way. I had to plunk my fifteen cents down for a hamburger just like everyone else. And chips and a drink were extra. One of the first signs to come down after Uncle Al took over was the one that said: "Two hamburgers for a quarter."

When I was at the bowling alley, feeling especially flush, or could talk my folks out of a quarter, I would sometimes go down the street to the Silver Castle diner to eat. The food was good, but the most memorable thing about the Silver Castle was its juke box. They had those individual selection boxes at each booth where you could flip the song lists like stiff pages behind the round glass cover and select what you wanted to hear for a nickel. What I remember most about that juke box's repertoire was the novelty songs of the mid-forties. Songs like "Shoo Fly Pie" (and Apple Pan Dowdy). I never questioned what Shoo Fly Pie was or if Apple Pan Dowdy would really make your eyes light up and your stomach say Howdy.

21

You could also treat your ears to such tunes as "Across the Alley From the Alamo", "Buttons and Bows" and "Maresy Doats" — another song about which I never questioned the nonsensical lyrics. It was probably twenty years later before I even examined the lyrics to that song to discover the play on words contained therein:

"Maresy Doats and Dosey Doats and Liddlelamsey Divey

Akiddle eediveytoo. Woodenu"

Or translated:

"Mares eat oats and does eat oats and little lambs eat ivy.

A kid'll eat ivy too. Wouldn't you?"

(This little phonetic trick was used successfully in the late sixties by the rock group Sly and the Family Stone with their hit: "I Wanna Thank You Fallettinme Be Mice Elf, Again")

Chapter Eight
Too Little for the Team

I walked to Southwest School most days—probably less than a mile. It was nearly a straight shot if I crossed the OCW campus. The campus had some huge conical shaped evergreen trees with large center trunks. The formation of the branches was such that the lower boughs were attached about three or four feet up the trunk but sagged down toward the ground about six feet out from the trunk. The effect was one of a wonderful little tent where a six-year old could crawl into his own little teepee, hidden from the world, and create all sorts of imaginary scenarios.

It was at Southwest School that I met the second love of my life. Her name was Peggy. I don't know if I fell in love with her or her name. Her last name was "Fudge". No kidding! Peggy Fudge. What a great name! But she would have nothing to do with me. She only had eyes for Jack. He was sort of the top dog of the first and second grade, and I liked him. Everybody did. They made a great looking couple.

* * * * *

I was one of the littlest guys in my class. Always was—all the way through high school. In the first grade I weighed 49 pounds. How do I remember that? Well, once a year the school had a big field day in which our school competed against the other elementary schools in town. There were races of various types and other track and field competitions. And each grade put together a team for the tug of war competition. I was not a fast runner. Couldn't jump higher than my ankles. Could barely throw a ball. And forget catching one! But Tug O' War! Now that was my kind of sport! Just grab the rope, hold on and pull. What could be simpler? So they started picking the team for our grade and said that the minimum weight for our team would be 50 pounds. They brought the scales into our classroom. We lined up and one by one each of us stepped on the scales. 62 pounds? OK you're on the team. 57 pounds? OK you're on. 53 pounds? OK you're on. Then it was my turn. I stepped on the scales as heavily as I could and watched with horror as the teacher slid the little weight onto the 50 pound notch and the bar plopped down, indicating I weighed less than 50 pounds. She tried it again. Still no luck. So then she moved the smaller weight up the scale until the bar balanced and I heard her say: "49 pounds. Sorry. Can't be on the team." I desperately looked around for something heavy I could slip into my pockets to add weight. How many Laddie pencils or crayons does it take to make a pound? I cursed my mother for giving me a haircut the night before. She must have cut at least a pound of hair from my head! I was relegated to the position of bench warmer. A place I would grow accustomed to over the next few years, regardless of the sport.

* * * * *

Across the street from Southwest School was the drug store. One of those wonderful emporiums which stocked all manner of remedial, health and hygiene items, cosmetics, school supplies, comic books and magazines, etc. It had a real soda counter with not one but two soda jerks (to serve the after-school rush). One of the things I would get there was their peanut butter and jelly sandwiches. Now I could have a peanut butter and jelly sandwich at home anytime I wanted. It is not something which you need to consult the latest Betty Crocker cookbook for. I had memorized the recipe before I memorized the alphabet. But this drug store's peanut butter and jelly sandwiches were different. They mixed the peanut butter with the jelly before applying it to the bread! At first I thought this was tantamount to heresy! But then realized that it imparted a totally new flavor to the creation. Brilliant!, I thought, when in reality all they were doing was trying to be more efficient and save time, since each sandwich was made fresh when you ordered it.

24

Chapter Nine
The First Exposure to Raw Sex

Another retail establishment I frequented was the small grocery store about a block from my house. The whole place was no bigger than a double garage inside. But it was a life saver for me whenever Mom ran out of something while fixing dinner. I could get a quart of milk or loaf of bread and be back in no time.

During those first post-war years there was apparently a shortage of chicle, the main ingredient in chewing gum. This created a major hardship for young boys to whom bubble gum was a major way of life. It's not hard to see how grown up boys get hooked on chewing tobacco, smoking cigars or cigarettes or dipping snuff. It's not really the nicotine. It's having something in your mouth coupled with the cool way you can talk when your mouth is full of something. And when you're a boy it's got to be bubble gum—preferably Double Bubble. Tops brand was a distant second but still preferable to conventional chewing gums like Juicy Fruit, Doublemint, Spearmint or that mouth-burner, Dentyne.

Our grocer's allotment of Double Bubble was about one box a month. This was usually gone the first day. However, our grocer knew how much it meant to me and he would save back five pieces as soon as the box came in, in case I didn't get by the store on that first, critical day. Five pieces could last me about two weeks, with careful storage each night. But that still left me about two weeks a month to go cold turkey.

25

*****

My first year in Chickasha was devastating in one regard—transportation. I wanted either a bicycle or a pony. Preferably both. I was on foot the entire school year. I had a good friend, Craig, who had a pony as well as several full sized horses. Was this guy lucky or what?! The best my folks could do was to get me a puppy for Christmas. . . A Collie who soon grew as big as a pony, but I couldn't ride him.

But on that Christmas morning when I got this little Collie puppy I thought he was definitely the cutest thing I had ever seen. I had visions of my carrying him around in my pocket forever. He was only about as big as a grapefruit when he rolled up in a ball to sleep. I immediately named him "Trigger", after the famous horse owned by my favorite cowboy, Roy Rogers. Trigger soon emulated his namesake and grew to be taller than me. We had a small back yard and he would run full speed in circles around the fence, until he wore a groove in the yard along the fence rows. He loved me so much but whenever I went out into the yard, he would come and jump up on me with his paws on my shoulders and knock me down. We never really bonded since I couldn't take him anywhere with me. I couldn't control him. If he took off running, he would probably just drag me along behind him, clinging to the leash—all 49 pounds of me.

*****

One day a new family moved in next door to us. They had a boy my age named Ronnie and a girl about a year younger named Wanda June. When I finally got my bicycle in the second grade, Ronnie and I would ride all over that end of town.

I would spend the night at Ronnie's house on occasion or he would sleep over at my house, or on rare summer nights we would sleep out in the yard. One night I caught a quick glimpse of Wanda June in the bathtub as I walked down the hallway and something stirred. I didn't see anything but her head, but the idea that she was sitting in that tub without any clothes was an exciting thought, and I didn't know why.

The next weekend, Ronnie and I were out riding our bikes and playing around the new house being built across the street. Wanda June was there. Ronnie and I started to build a little fort from the odd pieces of lumber lying around. I told Wanda June she could play with us if she would show us her wee-wee. (Obviously blatant extortion.) Without any hesitation, she said: "Sure!" So we headed toward the opening in the partially framed house where the front door would soon be and I told Ronnie to come on.

26

"Wanda June is going to show us her wee-wee!" I couldn't believe it! Ronnie couldn't care less! "Don't you understand? She's going to show us her WEE-WEE!" All Ronnie was interested in was constructing the fort a little higher. Why should he want to see his sister who he probably bathed with every night when I wasn't sleeping over at his house?

OK. Suit yourself, I thought, and I stepped inside for my first peep show. Little five year old Wanda June pulled up her dress and pulled down her panties and I stared in a mixture of surprise and wonderment. "Is that all there is?", I thought. What was the big deal? Why did they even have girls' and boys' bathrooms separated? The bigger thrill seemed to be in seeing someone's underwear, not what was underneath it. ("Teacher, Teacher, I declare. I see someone's underwear!")

* * * * *

One of my fond memories of those times was on summer afternoons when I had nothing to do. Mom would fix me a sack lunch, usually consisting of a baloney sandwich, Fritos and a Grapette soft drink. I'd ride my bike about three or four blocks from the house where I was literally out in the country. There was a large field with some rolling little hills. By July, the grass was no longer green, but had turned brown—actually a sort of buff color, about the shade of a manila file folder. I would pick one of these little hillocks and commence to have my own private picnic. Then I would lie down in the grass and just stare up at the deep blue summer sky. Occasionally the cloud formations would assume various familiar shapes, depending on your imagination. I hadn't a care or a worry in the world. What a wonderfully free feeling of total security and happiness!

(As an adult, I saw a wonderful Peanuts comic strip by Charles Schultz which would take me back to those times. Linus and Charlie Brown were also laying on a little mound, looking up at the clouds. Paraphrased to the best of my memory: The cerebral Linus says, "Charlie Brown, have you ever noticed how the clouds take on various shapes? For instance that one looks like the profile of Benjamin Disraeli and there's one that looks like the shape of the island of Zanzibar. Over there is one which looks like Lake Erie. What do you see Charlie Brown?" A thought bubble appears above Charlie Brown's head and he thinks: "I was going to say I see a horsey, a bunny and a ghost, but I think I'll just keep quiet.")

Chapter Ten
Saturday at the Rialto Theater, The Debut and Western Day

On most Saturdays I, along with every other kid in Chickasha, would head for the Rialto theater at 10 AM for kids' day at the theater. This usually consisted of some sort of stage show, such as a clown, the local ventriloquist, a balloon magician, etc. followed by giveaways of some sort. Then the lights would lower and we would be treated to several cartoons followed by a serial and a kids' feature movie, which was almost always a "B" Western. By then it would be after noon and we would all be turned out onto the streets of downtown Chickasha to wreak havoc on the town's merchants.

Sometimes we would just head straight for one of the other theaters to catch another cowboy movie. In addition to the Rialto, and the more upscale Washita, there was the Ritz, the Pix and The Midwest.

The serials were the greatest! They were pure fantasy pitting an ongoing battle between some evil mastermind and our hero. Whether it was Lash LaRue, Buck Rogers, Spider Woman, Red Ryder or whatever, the story lines were the same. But Oh! What scrapes they could get into (and out of). Spider Woman was one of my favorites. She was the only bad guy who merited lead billing. All the others were named for the hero. The Spider Woman series featured this criminal mastermind and her gang of villains. The neatest thing they had was a fleet of getaway cars that had these little spray nozzles so that as they were fleeing the police, they could get a large enough lead ahead of the police car to round a bend and activate the nozzles which would spray paint on the car and change its color on the run. (Never mind that paint never

28

got on the windows, the chrome trim or the tires.) They would simply make a quick U-turn and pass the hapless police still going the original direction, sirens blaring, looking for a different color car. (Those fools!) Now that's some powerful screenwriting! Not even James Bond's car could do that!

The concept of the serial was that the hero would spend most of the episode almost catching up to the bad guy and then, at the last minute, would fall victim to some sort of evil deed or dangerous situation with the closing scene showing certain death for the hero. Come back next week to see if our hero escapes. This is, of course, the same formula used on many of the continuing radio programs—the sponsor's way of making sure you don't miss a single exciting episode. The typical scene would usually have the hero unconscious or tied up somewhere such as in a runaway wagon about to go over a cliff or inside a building full of dynamite with the fuse burning furiously. The last scene would show the wagon sailing off the cliff and crashing on the rocks below, or the building blowing up. The first scene next week would, of course, show the hero waking up at the last minute, wriggling free from the rope which was binding him and jumping to safety with not a second to spare.

* * * * *

One of the people who frequented the bowling alley was the guy who hosted the Saturday morning shows at the Rialto. He was a local radio personality named Jimmy Weldon (real name: LaVern Shinn—I'd change my name, too. Even if I wasn't in the public eye.) Jimmy not only had a good radio personality but he could do this great Donald Duck type voice, except that you could understand him a little better than Donald. He had this ventriloquists' dummy made which was a cute duck that he named "Webster Webfoot". Jimmy and Webster would put on a show every Saturday morning as part of the pre-movie extravaganza.

Jimmy bowled in at least one league at Banner Bowl so I would see him quite often. He was as close to a real celebrity as we had in town. However, no matter how much I begged him, he would not do his Webster Webfoot voice without having the duck in hand, so as to not blow the image.

One time he came to our school to emcee a program and he heard me sing a solo. So he asked me to sing on the Saturday morning show at the Rialto. Now this was a pretty big deal! Not only was every kid in town there, but the first half hour of the show was broadcast over the local radio station—"The Voice of the Washita Valley".

I selected for my radio debut a song from the current Walt Disney movie, Song of the South—The Uncle Remus Stories. (This is not a Walt Disney movie

29

you see much of these days, since it is no longer politically correct.) The song was "Zip-a-Dee-Doo-Dah" and in the movie it was one of the first successful mergers of animation with live action. As the live Uncle Remus strolled along singing the song, animated birds fluttered around his head, landed on his shoulder, etc. It was wonderful.

One thing which never crossed my mind was accompaniment. I was six years old. When one sings, music just magically appears on cue. At least that's the way it was in the movies. If Fred Astaire felt like dancing, then the music would automatically start up. I think it was the law or something.

Jimmy arranged for a pianist named Joy May Harlan to accompany me, using the published music. We never rehearsed. I never checked to see if it was in my key or not. I simply stepped up to the microphone when introduced, waited for the piano intro and commenced singing. The radio station recorded my debut and cut an acetate record. I still have that record. It went amazingly well except for a little bit of a rough spot in the timing in the middle. I sang it exactly like in the movie, which meant I slowed down at the end of the bridge (the second part of the song) and paused slightly before starting the last verse back in tempo. Well, Joy May never slowed down one bit. She kept the original tempo up steadier than a Sousa march. So, I had to cram the last part of the bridge into about two beats in order to be able to start the last verse in synch with the accompaniment. I zipped through those lines without tripping on a single word and finished big. I must confess that I made it through that rather difficult-to-sing song in perfect pitch for every note. Even nailed the high ones without going flat and inserted some cool "licks" on some of the notes. Too bad the Grammies didn't exist then.

The amazing thing was that throughout the song, the audience was quiet. I mean church quiet. At the end of the song, the applause, screaming, yelling and whistling was deafening! No kidding! I have proof—on the record. Well, I'll tell you, I was hooked. From then on performing arts would likely be a big part of my life whenever possible. What an ego boost to a little kid who couldn't even make the Tug O' War team to have all that praise and adoration showered on him.

It wasn't long after my debut that Jimmy Weldon moved to Los Angeles and broke into the semi-big time, achieving a certain degree of stardom never afforded anyone from Chickasha before. He became one of the early television stars with a successful children's show.

* * * * *

The defining media for children growing up in the forties were movies, radio and comic books and I was heavily into all three. My favorite movie stars were put into two definite categories: cowboys and others.

When I was in college we studied a marketing technique called "USP". The premise is that you must differentiate your product from the crowd of competitors. The factor upon which you create this differentiation is called your Unique Selling Proposition. If you don't have a USP, then you should create one or the appearance of one. It is clear that some of the earliest pioneers in the area of creating USP's were the American cowboy movie stars of the forties. If there are dozens of cowboys trying to make it in the movies, then how can you make yourself different? Maybe you wear all black and use a bullwhip as your weapon, disarming the bad guys with a quick flip of the wrist—enter Lash LaRue. Or maybe you wear a mask, ride a white horse, travel with an Indian as your sidekick and leave a silver bullet as your calling card—enter the Lone Ranger. Or maybe you sort of combine these two--wear all black, including knee-high riding boots, but a white hat with a tall crown and ride a white horse—enter Hopalong Cassidy. Or maybe you wear a mask, a flat top hat with fringe and use a sword to carve a "Z" in everything you see, for Zorro of course. Modern marketers of products could take a valuable lesson from these early masters of self promotion.

One of the things about the B Westerns was that cowboys—good or bad rarely got killed. And if anyone did meet his doom, it was not the hero who perpetrated it, except in those famous face-to-face shoot outs/fast draw contests in the saloon or the middle of main street. Most of the heroes never even shot their guns, except in the air, and Hopalong Cassidy probably never even did that. The gun was used to get the "drop" on the bad guy so he could be taken to jail. It never occurred to me that it was somewhat incongruous that the bad guy who would have the drop on Lash LaRue would not pull the trigger before Lash had a chance to pull out his trusty whip, and snap the gun right out of his hand. (Maybe they were arthritic.)

Hopalong Cassidy (William Boyd) was the nice guy who always had a moral message in his stories. He was one of the few who successfully made the transition from B movies to television, funny looking boots and all.

Unfortunately, this immortality mode extended only as far as the cowboys. Indians were a totally different matter. In those movies where it was cowboys against the Indians, the Indians were shot right and left. They were either riding at top speed yelling that high pitched, yodel kind of scream—at which time they were shot right off their horses, or they were sneakily climbing over a rock with tomahawk in hand getting ready to pounce on our hero who, at the last second, would turn around and shoot the sneakin' redskin in mid-air.

Of course, Red Ryder, who was immortalized in the movie "A Christmas

31

Story" was also one of my heroes. He really made his name more in comic books. There were few Red Ryder movies or serials, as I recall. He was a tall guy with a wide brim hat and a chiseled chin who could handle a carbine rifle as easily as most handled a six-shooter.

The second group consisted of the singing cowboys, which included Tex Ritter, Gene Autry and my all time favorite, Roy Rogers. Roy and Gene, especially, tended to create a whole mini-empire. Their horses (Trigger and Champion), their women (especially Dale Evans, Roy's wife) and their sidekicks like Smiley Burnett and Gabby Hayes and others became almost as famous as their leaders. Gene Autry's sidekick, Pat Buttrum was also an integral part of Gene's persona and went on to fame on the Green Acres TV show.

Of course, Roy was the flashiest of all the cowboys—fancy duds, fancy saddles, fancy palomino horse and fancy wife. Fringe was created for Roy and Dale. He was also the best singer of the bunch. However, it was Gene Autry who recorded the second highest selling record of all time: "Rudolph the Red Nose Reindeer". According to record sales and air play, this record was exceeded only by Bing Crosby's version of "White Christmas". Both of these are played incessantly during the Christmas season and are included on nearly all the anthology albums of popular Christmas music.

The other category of cowboy star, besides the singing cowboys and the unique persona stars, included some who had no gimmick, no signature clothing, no celebrity horse or anything. They just made a lot of movies which were pretty entertaining. These included guys like Wild Bill Elliott, Tom Mix (whose nephew went to high school with me), Johnny Mack Brown and a little guy named Bob Steele. Bob Steele was certainly not a star in the same category as Roy Rogers, or even Johnny Mack Brown. Few even knew his name, but there was something about him I liked. Even on the screen he looked short, which meant he was probably about five feet two or three inches. (The movies had a way of making most people look taller—at least average height. Even one of my favorite actors, Alan Ladd, looked pretty good size, even though he was only about five feet five or six inches tall.)

Bob Steele played in quite a few movies, but you might see him playing a bad guy as often as a good guy. In a few films, he was even the lead. However, I was bothered on a few occasions when he would show up in a suit and hat as a henchman in some sort of cops and robbers movie. I wanted to just yell up at the screen: "Bob Steele! Get outta there and get back where you belong—on a horse!"

All these B westerns not only had the same story line, but most had towns and buildings which looked suspiciously similar from movie to movie, identical stage route scenery and identical rock formations which either the good guys or the bad guys could hide behind. This actually gave the movies a nice feel of familiarity.

These cowboys frequented the screens at the Rialto, the Pix, the Majestic and the Ritz. It cost a dime to get into these movie theaters. But, since everyone knew me through the bowling alley, I freely went from the Rialto to the Ritz to the Majestic and back, strolling in at will and always sitting on the front row looking straight up at the big screen. After nearly two solid years of this I found that I couldn't see the blackboard at school that well. After a trip to the eye doctor, I was prescribed glasses for nearsightedness, which I have now worn for over fifty years. My mother was convinced that countless hours on the front row of darkened movie theaters caused my astigmatism. Doctors have refuted this to me, but I'm sure that particular movie-watching habit didn't help.

One theater I couldn't get into free was Chickasha's first run movie theater, the Washita with its large, overhanging marquee that sheltered its ceramic tiled entry area and box office. This is where I was exposed to the other category of movie stars and it was not long before I had my favorites here as well. Number one on my list was Errol Flynn. He was the swashbucklingest swashbuckler who ever buckled a swash. (What is a "swash" anyway? How do these guys buckle them? And why is that significant?) You can have your Douglas Fairbanks Juniors and your Tyrone Powers. Give me Errol Flynn any time, whether he is Robin Hood or Sinbad the Sailor.

Of course, I was also a huge fan of Alan Ladd, Danny Kaye and Abbott and Costello. It was because of a Danny Kaye movie that I fell in love with Virginia Mayo. I can still see her standing in the middle of some castle while the song "Beautiful Dreamer" played on.

My mother subscribed to several of the movie magazines, like Photoplay, Modern Screen and several others. I liked looking through these and noticed an ad for movie star photos. They had a card in the magazine which you could check off the stars you wanted. They listed everyone, including many I had never heard of. I checked them all and in a couple of weeks received a huge envelope with several dozen photos. It's one thing to see your favorite star's photo in a magazine, but to get a real PHOTOGRAPH! This was really special! You're now only one degree of separation from one of your idols. He actually sat in front of the camera and you are seeing exactly what the camera saw. Unbelievable!

Chapter Eleven
Dish Night at the Washita or
Stay Home and Listen to the Radio?

Saturday morning kids' shows were somehow beneath the dignity of the upscale Washita Theater. Instead, they had dish night. In order to increase attendance during the week they would select a night in which they might show a double feature and everyone who showed up would receive a piece of crockery. This meant that if you wanted to collect a full service for eight, consisting of dinner plate, salad plate, dessert plate, cup, saucer and a few serving pieces, the theater could lock you in to attending for about fifteen years (well, nearly a year anyway). Women were known to put off almost anything, from childbirth to a visit from the governor, in order to attend dish night at the Washita. Never mind if the pattern was not the one you might have chosen and never mind that nearly every household in town had the same pattern. Free dishes were free dishes.

The Washita made a tactical error one year, however. Some new manager analyzed the daily receipts and discovered that Wednesday night was the weakest night of the week in terms of attendance and income so he decided to make Wednesday night dish night. There was a very good reason why Wednesday night attendance at the movies was low—it is church night— prayer meeting at some churches, mid-week services at others, and elders/ deacons meeting at others--but church night nonetheless. The result of this conflict was, of course, the potential for a monumental train wreck in the community--a veritable rip down the middle of the fabric of Chickasha's very religious foundation. After a visit from a contingency of the town's preachers, the Washita's manager agreed to change dish night to another night. Would Thursday be alright? Absolutely not! That's choir practice. How about Tuesday night? Reluctantly, the preachers agreed, although many liked to reserve Tuesday night for committee meetings, such as finance committee, building committee, etc.

* * * * *

In those pre-television days, radio provided more than sufficient home entertainment for both individuals and families. One could sit in front of the radio and listen to virtually any type of program with sound effects so convincing that you were there. The mind is a better special effects medium than anything man can invent.

I wasn't into the programs which tended to appeal to the adults, such as Fred Allen, Edgar Bergen and Charlie McCarthy, some of the music programs like Horace Heidt, some guy with his College of Musical Knowledge (I think it was Kaye Kaiser—a boy named Kaye is just as bad as Johnny Cash's boy named Sue in my book), or any of the soap operas or dramas like Stella Dallas, One Man's Family, Portia somebody and some guy named Pepper Young or something or other who had a family.

What I was into, that even my parents liked, were the mysteries. I glued myself to the radio for such shows as Boston Blackie, Gangbusters, Sam Spade and Mr. Keene, Tracer of Lost Persons (or as my dad called him, "Mister Trace, Keener than most persons"). And of course, there was the king of all the mystery shows. . ."Who knows what evil lurks in the hearts of men? THE SHADOW KNOWS!"

And then Inner Sanctum took you behind the creakiest door in the world to be exposed to horrors beyond the imagination.

The impact of some of these radio programs was significant and far reaching. One week around 1950 or so, a show called "The Big Story", which documented true crimes, featured a murder which took place in Tulsa where the victim's body was cut up and buried in the back yard. They did a great job of playing up the sinister and macabre aspects of the crime while everyone sat with their ears glued to their radio speakers in disbelief. How could a monster like this murderer actually live in our midst? Maybe in New York or Chicago or some faceless town in another part of the country. But not in squeaky clean Tulsa! The newspaper covered this bit of national notoriety which had befallen our fair city and, in the article, happened to publish the address of the house where the crime had taken place. The next day, the biggest traffic jam in Tulsa's history was created when everyone wanted to drive by the "Big Story house" just to look at it.

Some of the shows were aimed directly at kids and these were great for several reasons. Many of them were interactive. You mailed in your request for a decoder ring or a special badge showing you were a member of the in group or some sort of secret message contraption. Shows like The Green Hornet, Batman, Junior G-Men, Little Orphan Annie and others were the height of audio adventure and I belonged to all their clubs. In my class picture taken in the second grade, I can be seen standing on the back row of risers, grinning with my two front teeth missing and holding up my Junior G-Man badge for all to see.

Some of these prized articles had an inordinate number of capabilities, functions or tricks. I sent off for a ring from one of the shows which had more gimmicks than a five pound Swiss Army knife. This thing had a dome on top which housed a compass, a small telescope, an ice pick-like device, a swing out magnifying glass and two or three other tools. Then the whole dome would swing back on a hinge to reveal a secret compartment for carrying notes and coded messages for your fellow agents. It also had a little wheel around the base of the dome which you could dial to decode messages received through the radio program—just like Ralphie did in the movie. The difference was that Ralphie's was from Little Orphan Annie, a show which I did not follow. Mine was from The Green Hornet, as I recall.

Of course there were comedies on the radio as well, but it was difficult for a second grade mind to get into the humor of Jack Benny, Fibber McGee and Molly or even Amos and Andy.

* * * * *

The highlight of my radio week was Saturday morning. It was tough to squeeze in the greatest radio shows on the air and kids' day at the movie theater into the same morning of the week. About eight on Saturday morning, Big John and Sparky would come on, with their theme song:

If you go out in the woods today, you're in for a big surprise.

If you go out in the woods today, you'd better go in disguise.

(Ta-da-da-da-da-da-da-da-da, etc.)

. . .Today's the day the Teddy Bears have their pic-nic.

This was immediately followed by the Buster Brown show brought to you by Buster Brown shoes. Their show (and the commercial) would always start out with the dog barking followed by a youthful voice saying: "That's my dog Tighe. He lives in a shoe. I'm Buster Brown. Look for me in there, too."

Then at a strategic point in the show the host would say: "Plunk your magic twanger, Frog-EEE!"

And as all the children in the country sat in rapt attention, we were treated to some magical fantasy via the airwaves.

Usually I would drag the quilt off my bed, affix it to the top of the console radio and stretch it out over the back of a chair, creating a tent. I could then retreat into my make-believe world via the miracle of radio, undisturbed by the mundane commonalities and trivialities of the real world.

For those times when favorite radio shows were not on, and as I grew older, comic books provided the desired avenue of escape.

* * * * *

Once a year, Chickasha turned out in force for Western Day. I'm not sure what the purpose of this was, but it was a very festive event. One year the Western Day parade, which probably went all of about four blocks, had BOTH Gene Autry and Roy Rogers riding in it, after which they made a brief stop at the Washita Theater to sign autographs before leaving town. With Dad running interference for me, I fought the crowds and got autographs from both of them, although this seemed to be more important to my folks than to me. Most second-graders see little value in a signature which they can't even read. It was enough for me just to see them up close.

On one of these Western Days I was in downtown Chickasha just observing the activities and strange events. In the middle of the main intersection, they had constructed a stockade out of two-by-fours. It was about six feet square and had an oversized lock on it. As I was walking by I happened to look inside and was shocked to see that the person locked up in the stockade was my father! Apparently the deal was that the names of a certain number of prominent citizens, businessmen, etc. were put into a hat and one would be drawn out. If your name was drawn, you had to get into the stockade. You could not be released until you were able to convince people to donate money sufficient to get you released—your

37

"bail" as it were. I think the amount was dependent on how much western wear you were sporting. Full cowboy attire (not farmer duds) could get you off with a smaller "fine"—maybe 5 or 10 bucks. Less western attire, more fine—up to about 25 dollars, which went to whatever charity or fund was behind this indignity. It was sort of a back-handed measurement of your popularity in the community. Then again, it was also an indication of how much your "friends" wanted to embarrass you. Well, my dad was not having such an easy job of it. I had visions of my mother bringing breakfast to him the next morning.

I was more than a little humiliated to see my father that day. Not because he was in "jail" but because he looked unbelievably ridiculous in these cowboy boots with his dress slacks tucked inside them and this too-small cowboy hat perched on top of his head. To cap it off, he was even wearing one of those string, bolo ties with a longhorn steer at the neck. If there is anyone who should have never been seen wearing boots and a cowboy hat, it was my father. It was a rule of Western Day that everyone must dress in Western clothing or pay a fine. I would have gladly given several months' allowance to keep my dad from being seen in that ridiculous garb. Even at age seven, I could see that this was completely inappropriate. I didn't know whether to laugh or to make a hasty retreat to the safety of the Rialto theater.

Chapter Twelve
Setting Pins at Age Seven

One thing our time in Chickasha did was to plant a seed in me regarding the sport of bowling. The standard bowling ball is, of course, slightly smaller in size than a basketball and weighs from about 9 to 16 pounds. At age seven, I couldn't even handle the smallest of the conventional balls. So my father got a duckpin bowling ball, which is about the size of a cantaloupe and weighs about 5 or 6 pounds. He had holes drilled in it to fit my fingers and it became my bowling ball. This was in the days before automatic pin setters. (The modern automatic ball return mechanism could not handle anything smaller than a regulation size ball.)

Banner Bowl had pin boys, the best of whom was a guy named Ernie. He could set pins on two lanes at once (as several of the better pin boys could). One day my mother could not find me although she was sure I was at the bowling alley. One of the pin boys said he thought I was back in the pits on alleys one and two with Ernie. Sure enough, I was back there, not just watching Ernie, but actually down in the pit helping to load downed pins into the rack. As soon as we would clear out the dead wood, Ernie would simply lift me up out of the way while the bowler rolled his next ball.

Manual pinsetting is not an occupation which would likely conform to any Federal OSHA guidelines today. It is a dangerous occupation primarily because a significant number of inexperienced bowlers were guilty of "double balling"—that is rolling their first ball and then, instead of waiting for this ball to be returned to pick up the spare, immediately picking up a second ball and rolling it while the pinsetter is still in the pit. I've seen pin boys come out of the pit on a dead run, charging up the alley to kick the butt of some jerk who was double balling. Sometimes they would be armed with a bowling pin in hand, ready to smash the guy's head in. Usually it was Ernie who de-fused these situations.

Toward the end of my second grade school year my dad decided that he'd had enough of running the bowling alley and we moved back to Tulsa.

PART THREE
Pre-Adolescence

Chapter Thirteen

Ice Storms

In 1947, my grandmother bought three recently built, identical duplexes in East Tulsa. It was into one of these that we moved when we moved back to town in April of that year. Ostensibly this was to be a temporary domicile—no more than about six months. We ended up living there eight years. Ours was the northern most unit of the group and was located no more than about thirty or forty yards off of 11th Street which was Highway 66—The Mainstreet of America, immortalized in song, movies and later a successful television series (the highway, not our house).

Each duplex sported a picture window in the dining room which overlooked the playground of Benjamin Franklin Elementary School, across the street. I'm not sure why the builder thought this would make a sufficiently attractive view to warrant a picture window, but it did make the units a little more interesting than others on the block.

In fact, on rare occasions the builder was vindicated and the picture windows served their purpose well, justifying their existence. This opportunity was presented through a phenomenon known as an ice storm, which Tulsa experienced once or twice every winter—some more severe than others. An ice storm is not really what the name implies. It does not really rain down ice. And, oddly enough, ice storms do not occur because it is too cold. Rather, they happen because it is not cold enough. There are two kinds of ice storms but both create the same situation. It's just like one of the disk jockeys said on the radio one morning when everything was ice covered: "Wow. Somebody was out with the giant Zamboni all over town last night!." (For the non-skaters or hockey fans, the Zamboni is the motorized vehicle that re-surfaces an ice rink between skating sessions or hockey periods.)

One type of ice storm is created when it snows for a day or two, followed by rises in daytime temperature just high enough to start the snow melting slightly. Then when night comes again and the temperature drops well below freezing, the melted snow on the surface freezes into a glaze over everything. This glaze becomes a thick layer of ice, not just a thin crust.

The second type of ice storm happens when the precipitation is a light drizzle or freezing rain. It is not cold enough to produce sleet or snow at higher altitudes but the temperature at ground level is freezing. This produces a Zamboni effect. This type of ice storm is especially dangerous since the ice covers everything. It builds up on tree limbs and power lines which break under the weight and strain. Of course motorized travel is virtually impossible until the sanding trucks make their rounds.

The playground at Franklin School consisted of about 2 or 3 acres with a chain link fence on three sides and a five foot retaining wall at one end — perfectly level with no trees and no grass. It had the appearance of a big sunken arena. The school's elevation was about four or five feet higher than the playground. So was our house. After an especially heavy ice storm, the playground would be turned into one huge ice rink. Of course, school would be closed. But on these days, the playground became a wonderful winter playland which would rival Rockefeller Center's ice rink. People from all over the city would show up and skate. It looked like a Currier & Ives painting. The area was large enough that there would be more than one hockey game in progress — one for little kids and beginners and one for more experienced skaters. The leisure skaters would sort of automatically start skating in an unmarked oval pattern on one side of the area, without conflicting with the hockey games or the racing. The only thing missing was organ music.

In some winters it would stay cold enough for several days running that the lake at Braden Park, about five blocks from my house, would freeze over. This was a lovely little park and the "lake" was really just a little pond about 75 yards across at its widest point.

Chapter Fourteen
Get Your Kicks Near Route 66

The layout of my neighborhood is important to several of the stories I will relate. There were two structures between our house and Route 66. Next door to us was an old brick house with a large front porch. A strange family lived there, who I will detail later. After they moved, it was turned into an antique and gift shop by Mrs. Hummel—yes, THE Mrs. Hummel of Hummel Figurine fame, when she was only semi-famous. The Hummel House Antique Shop didn't last very long. I'm not sure if Tulsa had zoning laws in those days or not. If so, she was clearly in violation. But we never complained. It was a nice little shop with only a small sign in the front window. She moved to Oklahoma City and opened a much larger place in a proper commercial building on Highway 66, Northeast of the city, complete with a sit down restaurant.

Next to this house was a retaining wall with a drop off of about four feet down to the parking lot for Brown's Market. Brown's Market backed right up against the retaining wall, so it was an easy climb, even for a little kid, from the top of the wall (which was almost flush with the yard of the Hummel house) to the flat roof of the grocery store. Once on the roof, you were surrounded and hidden by a short wall on three sides, including the front, which faced Eleventh Street. This would figure in several interesting events during my life in this neighborhood.

Kitty-corner across Eleventh Street from Brown's was a little "L" shaped strip center consisting of another small grocery store ("Kravitz Grocery") run by a couple of little Jewish brothers who must have stepped right out of the Bronx. Their store faced Eleventh Street and, across the street, the North side of the

Franklin School playground. It was part packaged grocery store (with a heavy inventory of Kosher products) and part delicatessen. I assumed that "Kosher" must have been one of the largest brands of foods in the country. They had a broader line than Heinz and Nabisco put together. Every other jar, box or package on Kravitz's shelves said "Kosher".

A few steps out Kravitz's front door was the opening to a concrete staircase which led down to a tunnel that went underneath Eleventh Street and emerged on the other side, leading into the Franklin School playground. This little engineering project saved the Tulsa Public School system untold thousands of dollars in school crossing guard costs to help all the students across the Mainstreet of America. The only thing is that in all my years living within about two hundred yards of the entrance of this tunnel and observing it nearly every day, I never saw a single student use the tunnel. Instead of protecting all the little cherubs from the seemingly impossible feat of negotiating the Route 66 racetrack twice a day, what it did was simply facilitate the access to Kravitz's for all the little old ladies who lived south of Eleventh Street. Harry and Izzy loved it. In that regard, it was still probably worth the money. The kids simply dashed across Eleventh Street at will--at the corner, in the middle of the block, at the traffic light or at the filling station. No one was ever hit by a car or truck while I lived there.

This little tunnel's secondary function was to provide a place for the numerous hitchhikers on Hiway 66 to relieve themselves, as the odor would attest to.

Next to Kravitz's was the dry cleaners and then on the corner was the Comfort's Gulf filling station.

Then, running down the other direction from the Gulf station, North on Allegheny Avenue, were two small stores. The one next to the filling station was unoccupied. In fact, in the eight years we lived there, no entrepreneur ever opened a store in that space. The last space was occupied by a succession of enterprises, the most interesting of which was a small pet shop and tropical fish store.

Up the other direction from my house was a line of duplexes. After the three owned by my grandmother, they all were of different vintage or design. Nearly all of them were inhabited by families with children fairly close to my age or slightly older.

The last duplex on the block was owned by a lady who would have also been in violation of zoning ordinances. On one side of the duplex, she operated a beauty shop. She lived on the other side with her two kids, including a boy who was three years older than me. Roy was his name and he was a bit of a bully but an outstanding athlete.

Chapter Fifteen
The Neighborhood Bully and Blasphemy

Once when I was at Roy's house he and a friend decided to offer me a 7Up to drink. This was totally out of character for Roy. Neither he nor his friend could stifle their snickering. I accepted the 7Up, in its customary green glass bottle, which had already been opened for me. My suspicions about something fishy were heightened when I noticed the bottle was not cold. As I raised the bottle toward my lips and their snickering turned to uncontrollable giggles, I caught the unmistakable odor of urine. I immediately threw the bottle to the ground. Roy did a fairly good job of feigning outrage and said he was going to tell his mother. I told him I thought that was a good idea, which stopped him immediately.

I suspect that Roy's mother's attitudes toward me were probably behind his propensity to bully me. She thought I was the cutest, nicest and most polite little boy in the neighborhood, and why couldn't Roy act more like me? (Oh great! Way to go, lady! Why don't you just tell your son to kill me now?)

Roy's bullying finally caught up with him one day, and I observed an amazing event which was close to a religious experience for me. My mother was Catholic but was only an occasional attendee at mass or confession. My dad was somewhat an agnostic, but converted to Catholicism when I was about ten years old. My exposure to church generally came through attendance with friends and their families, which was very infrequent. I started attending more regularly when I was about 11 or 12 because I was trying to earn the God and Country award in the Boy Scouts. I assumed I believed in God and was a Christian. I knew several Bible stories and we said a blessing every night before dinner. My mother would also tuck me into bed with prayers a few times a week. But at age eight, I hadn't formed any sort of real spiritual agenda and wasn't sure about the power, or even the purpose, of prayer.

When my dad was going through his instructions to become a Catholic, he started saying the prayer before meals. It was the standard Catholic blessing ("Bless us O Lord and these thy gifts. . . "). He would dutifully do the sign of the cross both before and after the prayer and you could understand every word, not like my mother's Uncle Jack. (This is a different Uncle Jack than my Uncle Jack. Her Uncle Jack was actually a Great Uncle whose last name was Lee. He was a great nephew of Robert E. Lee. I am a first cousin, four times removed, of Robert E. Lee. However, I don't even own a Confederate flag.) Mom said that when her Uncle Jack would say the blessing and would cross himself, his "crossing" consisted of waving his hand in front of his nose like he was shooing a fly away from his face, and mumbling "Holy, Holy, Holy".

One afternoon, several of the older kids, including the infamous Roy, were playing baseball on the school playground. I was riding my bike on the school grounds as were a few other kids. One of those riding there was a boy I didn't know. He was a sort of Baby Huey looking kid—pudgy and soft looking, wearing glasses, hair parted down the middle and plastered down. He wore funny looking denim pants—not the conventional blue jeans which the rest of us were wearing. They looked starched and ironed with a crease, like dress pants. His shirt was buttoned all the way up to his neck. He was a classic nerd before the word was even coined.

As we were riding, well clear of the ball game in progress, the ball was hit past one of the outfielders and near where we were riding our bikes. The ball was being chased by one of the players. It was Roy. As he got to where we were, he made some wisecrack about us, including a few cuss words, as we called them. Among the vocal missiles which came from his mouth was something like: "Why don't you get out of the God Damn way?"

At that point, the nerdy kid stopped his bike, with the baseball resting very near his foot, looked directly at Roy and said: "Do not use the Lord's name in vain."

I wasn't exactly sure what was meant by this. But I could tell by Roy's reaction that he didn't take it as a reasonable suggestion.

Roy responded with something like: "Move your goddam foot and give me my baseball!"

The kid replied: "I said, don't use the Lord's name in vain."

Roy then said: "Who's gonna stop me?"

Then something happened I couldn't believe. Instead of moving his foot and pedaling his bike as fast as he could to get out of harm's way, this soft, nerdy, momma's boy-looking kid got off his bike, carefully put down the kickstand and turned around. He stepped up to Roy, about ten inches away from him, toe to toe. Roy was about four inches taller than the kid and probably two years older. My heart was in my throat and my eyes were as big as saucers.

I thought that this was probably the most foolhardy, stupid kid I'd ever seen. He was getting ready to get pulverized. Didn't he realize that this was the legendary ROY???

Roy then said something like: "Who the hell do you think you are, you goddam little twerp!"

The kid then said: "This is the last time I'm going to tell you to quit using the Lord's name in vain."

"God Damn! God Damn! God Damn! How do you like that?" replied Roy.

A shoving match ensued. Glasses were removed. A baseball glove was thrown down. Then it turned into a full fledged fight. The baseball players came running up and gathered around to watch what I felt was sure to be the shortest fight on record. Roy would leave the nerd in a heap like so much Jello, in about thirty seconds.

But the fight was going longer than I (or probably anyone) thought it would. As the two combatants rolled around in the dust I could see that no one was clearly getting the upper hand. Then the tide seemed to turn. Roy and the nerdy kid were back on their feet and it was more of a boxing than a wrestling match. Roy swung with powerful jabs and roundhouses, but wildly. The kid dodged swings and selected his punches strategically. It wasn't long before Roy was on the ropes, so to speak. His face had red blotches—the result of well placed blows. His lip was beginning to swell up. Soon, he started back pedaling and had quit trying to throw any punches. His feet got tangled up and he fell backwards. The pudgy kid immediately jumped on Roy, straddling his chest with the front of Roy's shirt clenched in his fist. Roy was totally out of breath. The kid was not breathing hard at all. He leaned over and calmly said: "Now, for the last time, are you going to stop using the Lord's name in vain?" Silence. He asked it again. Roy looked furtively around at his fellow baseball players all of whom were staring in disbelief. You could just feel Roy's humiliation, which was much worse than the pain of any of the blows.

In a very low voice, Roy murmured: "Yeah". The kid did not further humiliate Roy by making him say it louder. He had his answer and his victory (or the Lord's). He got up, dusted off his pressed denim pants, got on his bike and rode off into the sunset, just like the Lone Ranger. (Who was that masked man?)

"Who is that kid?" I asked. "Does he go to Franklin School?"

One of the guys said he thought the kid lived a couple of blocks on the other side of Eleventh Street. He didn't go to Franklin. He went to a private school run by somebody called the Seven Day Inventors or something like that. Somebody said they thought it was a church. I'd never heard of this church, but it was obvious that one of its members got his power from somewhere. It certainly started my eight-year old brain thinking about some new issues. Whatever this kid had, I wanted some of it.

When I got home I asked my mother who the Seven Day Inventors were. She had no idea, and where had I heard of them? I explained what had happened with Roy and the nerdy kid and she said: "Oh, that's probably the Seventh Day Adventists. They have a church and school about a half mile down Eleventh Street."

Chapter Sixteen
The Spectacular Fire of '48

When we moved into the neighborhood there was still about two months left in the school year. The office at the school said I could simply wait until third grade to start to school if I wanted since my grades and teacher's comments from Chickasha were quite good. However, after a few days of staring out the picture window at the kids on the playground across the street, I decided I wanted to start to school immediately. My parents arranged it.

So, with only a few weeks left in the school year I entered Miss Trusty's second grade class where I met a few friends to carry me through what otherwise might have been a lonely summer. They say that one of the characteristics of second grade boys is that most of them fall in love with their second grade teachers. I was no exception. Miss Trusty was as lovely and sweet a creature as I had ever met. But she was quite old. Probably 23 or 24, at least. Even the fifth and sixth grade boys loved her.

That was one of the few, if not the only, school years which I was sorry to see end. I would have been happy to have it just go right on through the summer and into the next year.

* * * * *

I took the first part of the summer to start exploring the neighborhood on my bicycle, meeting some of the numerous children my age who lived within a couple of blocks of me.

The most memorable event of that summer occurred one weekend when we went to Oklahoma City to visit family. Three of my mother's brothers and one of her sisters lived there, so trips to Oklahoma City became fairly frequent.

On this particular weekend we were driving back on Sunday afternoon. It was a hot summer day and it had not rained for several weeks. The city had imposed restrictions on lawn watering and trash burning. When we were approaching Tulsa on Highway 66 we could see a large column of smoke rising several hundred feet in the air in the distance. As we drove toward our house it became apparent that this smoke originated somewhere in the vicinity of our house. By the time we got to Eleventh and Yale, the main intersection a block from our house, we could see that the smoke was just a few blocks away. The police had Eleventh Street blocked and were diverting all the local traffic (I'm sure there were a large number of irate truck drivers up and down Highway 66 who were delayed several hours in their tight schedules). My dad explained that we lived a block away so the policeman let us through.

As soon as we pulled into the driveway I bypassed going into the house and headed straight for my bicycle to make my way to the source of the excitement. I rode East on Eleventh Street toward the smoke. Six blocks down Eleventh Street was where the railroad tracks crossed. These tracks ran along one side of a large field. On this field were located several large oil storage tanks—the big, cylindrical ones about thirty or forty feet in diameter and just about as high.

Along the other side of the field were the back yards of a line of small houses and duplexes on Erie Avenue. Each of these houses had an incinerator at the back of the yard, next to the field, where people burned their trash (a practice which had been banned during the drought).

When I got about two blocks away from the field, I could see flames shooting in the air and then suddenly heard this huge "FOOMP!" sound. Actually, I felt it as much as heard it. The ground shook. Apparently another of the oil tanks had blown up, shooting flames a hundred feet in the air. The next time I saw anything that looked like that—rolling balls of flame mixed with black smoke--were the pictures of napalm attacks during the Viet Nam war.

As I approached the field, I saw a dozen or more fire trucks with lights flashing and hoses stretched across the street, connected to every hydrant within a couple of blocks. They had even run a hose down Erie for a block and into Braden Park Lake where they were pumping water out of there like crazy. I was horrified! They were going to suck it dry! I could see our lovely little pond, the site of great ice skating in the winter, toy sail boat races in the summer and casting contests for fishermen year 'round, being turned into one big mud pit. Police cars were everywhere. Half of them were trying to control traffic and the ever-growing crowd and the other half were working to keep the fire from approaching the homes on the West side or the truck stop on the East side of the railroad tracks.

By evening, the fire was under control and had burned itself out with no damage to anything other than the oil storage tanks (about three of which were lost). It was a spectacular show for hundreds of people and no one was hurt.

It was the major story in both of the daily papers the next day and the newspapers indicated the fire had likely started when someone was burning trash in one of the incinerators behind the houses on Erie, in violation of the ban, and the sparks caught the dry grass in the field on fire. It spread to the oil tanks within minutes. The Fire Department was mounting a full scale investigation and whoever was found responsible would be dealt with, either with a stiff fine, incarceration or both.

It was about five years later when my best friend at age 13, Jerry, who then lived in the duplex next to ours, confessed that it was his mother who started the famous fire of '48. At the time, they lived in one of the duplexes on Erie which backed onto the field. Jerry said that two or three days after the fire, he and his parents and his little sister, Marcia had been somewhere and were driving home. As they approached their house they noticed a red Fire Chief's car parked in their driveway and two uniformed officers knocking on the front door. I immediately conjured up visions of the officers escorting Jerry's mother to the waiting car—one on each side firmly holding her arms—and thence to jail. This was a picture which simply did not compute. Jerry's mother is a petite, very pretty lady who worked in the children's clothing department at Sears. Everyone knew Vera. She was probably the prettiest and nicest of all my friends' mothers. Imagining her spending even one minute in jail was simply beyond comprehension.

As the family car drew abreast of their house, Jerry said his mother just calmly and quietly turned to his dad and said: "Just keep driving, Dwight." So they went down Eleventh Street and had a piece of watermelon at the watermelon stand before going home. By then, the coast was clear. They never heard another word about it.

Chapter Seventeen
Retribution for Too Much to Drink

On one of our other trips to Oklahoma City that summer we were staying with my aunt and uncle in a new house they had just moved into. It was located on Virginia Drive in Del City, a suburb of Oklahoma City. That summer was scorchingly hot. My mother insisted that I come inside during the hottest part of the day, and take a nap. This house had an attic fan, so Mom and Aunt Helen would push a bed up next to the window where the attic fan was sucking air through the open window at close to hurricane force. But it was refreshing and I could smell the fresh outdoors and usually fell right off to sleep.

One evening while we were there, Aunt Helen and Uncle Johnny had some friends over. I was put to bed rather early. As I lay there I could hear the talking getting louder and louder, including shouting. Not all of the shouting necessarily sounded like anger, although some did. I found it more curious than scary. It seemed to go on for quite a while before I went to sleep.

The next day, a large truck pulled up to the house on Virginia Drive and men started unloading furniture. My aunt and uncle had just moved into the house and could not afford much furniture to start with. However, they suddenly found themselves with a bunch of new living room furniture.

My aunt was at a loss. She thought Johnny must have robbed a bank and was surprising her with this furniture, purchased with his ill-gotten gains. She couldn't reach him on the phone to find out what was going on. She signed for the furniture and the men left in their truck.

Before long, the mystery was solved with a phone call she received. A couple of her neighbors came over to see what the truck had unloaded and I heard my aunt telling them that one of the guests from last night's party had had too much to drink and gotten very "tight" (whatever that meant). He felt he had embarrassed himself and my aunt and uncle in front of their new neighbors (that must have been what all the loud talking was about!). So, to make amends, he decided to buy my aunt and uncle a bunch of new furniture. They couldn't believe it. All I could do was wonder how we might be able to get him to come to the house again, and how "tight" he would have to get to buy me a new pony.

(My aunt denies that this ever took place. However, the incident was indelibly etched on my impressionable 8-year old brain—not the sort of thing I could have made up.)

Chapter Eighteen
The Teacher Cusses and The Bike Has No Brakes

Third grade was spent in Miss Harvey's class at Franklin and was relatively uneventful as I settled into my neighborhood and new set of friends. Miss Harvey was this middle aged, sort of horsey looking lady with black hair, a far cry from Miss Trusty. One day the class was getting a little unruly and Miss Harvey was becoming more and more upset. Finally, she yelled at us to be quiet and that we were all acting like "jackasses". Well! She could not have shocked the class more if she had jumped up on her desk and stripped down naked. We all came to the same immediate conclusion: "Miss Harvey just CUSSED!" This spread through the kids in school like wildfire. "Did you hear what Miss Harvey said???" These were times when no four letter words were ever said in public, at least in polite society. Even movies had standards such as no off-color words or even references. Rhett Butler's "Frankly, Scarlet, I don't give a damn" in "Gone With The Wind" caused a stir for something like twenty years. The Hollywood standards board said that if two people had a scene where they were on a bed, one of them must keep at least one foot on the floor at all times. All married couples pictured in movies slept in twin beds. Apparently no one in movies ever produced children.

* * * * *

Up until age eight, I had miraculously avoided injuries which normally visited active boys. No broken bones, cut feet, etc. However, toward the end of my third grade year several of us were riding bicycles on the school grounds. As a diversion, I had decided to ride an old, girl's bicycle which had belonged to the older sister of one of my friends. This bicycle looked like it had been used to courier messages behind the lines during World War I, except that it was this chalky, faded, tomato red color. (Maybe it had been used by the Red Cross in China or something.) It had been languishing in the back of his garage for years when we discovered it one day and extracted it from a pile of junk just for the heck of it. It was extremely hard to pedal and the brakes did not work at all. I had to stand straight up with all my weight forcing the pedal down in order to get it going because it was geared so high. However, once this dinosaur on wheels got rolling, the momentum could keep you going for miles.

At the South end of the playground, there was a drinking fountain with multiple spouts. It was on an elevated concrete platform, about six inches high with a steel beam at each end holding up a roof. I decided to stop for a drink. Forgetting the fact that I was on this antiquated two wheeler, with brakes that didn't work, I approached the concrete and steel oasis at full speed, applied the brakes and started my turn. Of course, the bike did not slow down one bit. I couldn't negotiate a ninety degree turn at that speed, so I ran directly into the six-inch barrier. The bike stopped abruptly. I flew over the handle bars, over the drinking fountain and struck the steel beam on the other side with my head. The beam met my forehead directly between the eyes, just above the bridge of my nose, breaking my glasses in the process.

The collision knocked the breath out of me and after I recovered my breathing my first thought was that I was fine. I just took a heckuva daredevil spill. Then I saw the blood. Suddenly I thought my head was probably busted in two and my brains were going to spill out all over my new jean jacket. By then, my friends had arrived and hesitantly tried to see what aid they could render. Then one of them saw the blood and he turned white. The other one helped me home and my dad immediately drove me to the clinic. It took three stitches and the scar remains with me to this day.

Chapter Nineteen
City Boy in the Country

That summer, between my third and fourth grade years, my folks sent me to East Texas to spend a couple of weeks with my grandmother and my aunt, uncle and cousins.

These visits were not only fun, they were highly educational for a city boy.

My Uncle Chester and Aunt Jessie Mae had just moved into a house which he built. It was a true East Texas farm house of the forties. No electricity, no running water, but a charming place, nonetheless. They had four children—two boys and two girls. And they all lived in this little house of about 1200 square feet. One of the boys, my cousin Jerry, was about my age. He slept on the back porch in a feather bed which I shared with him when I visited. Feather beds sound really comfortable, don't they? But they have about as much support as one would imagine a pile of feathers would have. So, whatever weighty object is placed on the bed doesn't just sink into the pile of feathers, it first rolls to the middle and THEN sinks. If two weighty objects, such as boys, climb into the bed, they both gravitate to the middle. It makes no difference how big a feather bed is, the middle is still the same size, which is somewhat smaller than the bodies occupying that space. For two weeks, we slept in that bed, bodies fused together in the middle crack created by our weight with acres of mattress on both sides of us which could not be occupied unless you were somehow attached to it by glue or some other means to assist you in defying gravity.

Those nights were not only sleepless, they were extremely short. On a farm, everyone has chores. And these are not like city chores where one might be required to take out the trash three or four times a week. These were REAL chores. One of Jerry's chores was to milk the cows every morning. EVERY morning. This means the cows must first be rounded up and brought into the barn. It also means that milking must be done before dawn. Don't ask me why. I think it's the law or something.

About four o'clock in the morning, Jerry would be rousted out of bed by Aunt Jessie Mae. She said I could stay in bed and sleep if I wanted to. But it was a matter of pride. I was not about to lay there and sleep like some sissified city boy while my cousin wandered around bringing in the cows for milking, no matter how unbelievably tempting it was and no matter how completely exhausted I felt. It mattered not that I was of absolutely no value to Jerry in the carrying out of this chore. I could do little to round up the cows (and this job was done on foot, in total darkness, not on horseback the way most self-respecting cowboys would do it). And no matter how much I tried to get milk out of that dispenser hanging down from the cow's mid-section, I couldn't coax a single drop out. Jerry could get those things to squirt like little fire hoses. I squeezed with one hand, then with two. I tried rolling my fingers down in a cascade motion. Nothing worked. I thought maybe I just didn't have enough strength in my hands—which was, in itself, humiliating enough. Even my cousin Lynn (we called her Linnie Alice at that age), who was a year younger than me and was as petite and cute as she could be, could milk those cows like I couldn't believe.

One of the worst things about getting up to milk the cows was the fact that it was cold. Even in the middle of summer, in the pine covered hills of East Texas, it got cold before the sun came up. While the featherbed had its drawbacks, it was a warm place to sleep. Rolling out at 4 AM and stumbling out to the outhouse, which was about fifty yards from the house, was about as unpleasant a thing as an eight-year old could ever imagine. Of course, the outhouse had no lights, so if there was no moon, hitting the hole in that wooden bench-like seat was a pretty good trick.

* * * * *

In addition to a few dozen head of cattle, my uncle farmed a couple of hundred acres of various crops. One of these was sorghum. On this particular visit, I went with my cousins to cut sorghum and bring it back for delivery to town and subsequent sale. So, four of us piled into this horse drawn wagon for the trip about a mile or so down the road to the field we were going to work. In the wagon was my cousin, Jerry, his older brother Craig, who is about five years older than me, and my Uncle Gene. Gene was the youngest of my mother's siblings and was about six or seven years older than me. He and Craig, while Uncle and Nephew, were peers and were close buddies. Jerry was considered a real pest by the two older boys and I was a virtual non-entity who was destined to just get in the way.

We spent the morning cutting sorghum and throwing it into the wagon. I should say, THEY spent the morning cutting sorghum. I spent the morning sitting on the seat of the wagon, holding the reins of the horses.

When the wagon was full and almost overflowing, they climbed up on the front seat for the trip back home. One of the boys said: "Joe Murray (which everyone in my family called me since my dad's name was also Joe), would you like to ride up high on the pile of sorghum?" Well, that sounded great—perched up on high, riding along like some sort of special guard on the Deadwood Stage. "Sure!", I said. So Gene or Craig grabbed me and lifted me up on top where I straddled a bunch of the sorghum, which had been cut in about four to six foot "poles". As they climbed back up on the seat of the wagon, I thought I heard a sort of sinister, mischievous laughter.

I was wearing only shorts. I had shed my shirt before we even got to the field and I never wore shoes on those visits to East Texas. I would be there for two or three weeks and never have anything on my feet except dirt. I just sat up there and surveyed the country road, the trees and the fields as we traveled home—horses' hooves clomping on the dirt road and the wagon jerking back and forth with every bump in the road.

As we turned into the yard at my grandmother's house (where we were taking the sorghum rather than to my uncle's) I saw my grandmother come out the back door and approach the wagon. Before it even came to a stop, she looked up at me and then toward the boys, with a stern look on her face and said: "What do you boys think you're doing?" The mischievous laughter returned. "You know better than that! I ought to take you behind that barn and whip you—all three of you!" I didn't have the slightest idea what she was talking about or what was happening.

Then she looked at me and said: "You come with me, Joe Murray. We'll get you in a tub right now."

Sorghum is covered with fibers which are similar to glass wool. If your hands are relatively tough, you can handle it with little problem, so long as you wash thoroughly after handling it. However, if your skin is tender, as an eight year old city boy's would be, then the fibers become like

59

tiny needles and imbed themselves in your skin. There is almost nothing you can do about them except itch like crazy until they finally drop out or mysteriously leave of their own accord.

Mama dragged a large wash tub over to the outside pump spout and began pumping the handle up and down to fill the tub from the well. Let me take this opportunity to inform the reader that if one wants a drink of well water, especially from my grandmother's well, there is no need to refrigerate it or pour it over ice to get it cold. It comes from the well about one degree above freezing.

My grandmother jerked off my shorts and plopped me into that tub of water. The shock exceeded anything I had ever experienced including, I'm sure, the shock of passing from the warm womb to a cold hospital delivery room, nearly nine years earlier. She then took a long-handled, stiff bristle brush (the one I had seen her scrub the kitchen floor with) and some sort of foul smelling soap and proceeded to scrub every square inch of my body. She then pumped some more of that liquid ice into a bucket, instructed me to stand up, and poured the contents over my head to rinse me off. I can definitely identify with the winning football coach whose players dump the cooler of ice and water or Gatorade over his head at the end of a big win. She said she hoped this would do the trick. It didn't. I itched constantly for three days. No amount of rubbing would relieve it. It was just that incessant, irritating itch that was worse than if I was wearing scratchy, wool pajamas.

One of the other common crops in East Texas is watermelon. While my uncle did not raise watermelons this particular year, a neighbor did and Gene and Craig would sometimes go down to his field and "requisition" one. The problem is, they had to be eaten while they were hot and the rind disposed of completely lest my grandmother would find out.

There was a creek running through my Uncle's farm and less than a mile down the road, a bridge went over the creek. A little ways off the road, the creek widened out for a bit and formed the perfect swimming hole—right out of Tom Sawyer and Huckleberry Finn. There was even a high embankment on one side with a tree on which a rope had been tied so that you could swing out over the water and drop in. When it got hot in the afternoons, Jerry and I would go down to the swimming hole and go skinny dipping. There were usually other boys swimming there as well, including a few black kids who were sons of some of the sharecroppers who worked some of the fields. It was my first experience with black kids but I thought nothing about it. I really enjoyed playing with them and Jerry knew them quite well.

* * * * *

A few miles down the road was Simpsonville. It was the intersection of two dirt roads and there was a general store, apparently started by Mr. Simpson. This was just like you would see in the movies. A wooden building built on concrete block pillars for a foundation with a big front porch and a few steps going up. On the front porch was a soft drink cooler (a "pop box")—but it wasn't a coin operated vending machine. It was just a big metal box on legs into which Mr. Simpson would put ice and a little water and bottles of pop, including Grapette, RC Cola, Orange Crush, Dad's Old Fashioned Root Beer and Coca Colas in those little 6-ounce bottles. Occasionally you might even find a bottle of Chocolate Soldier. You just helped yourself to whatever brand you wanted, popped off the lid and went inside and gave Mr. Simpson a nickel. If you wanted to take the bottle with you, you also had to give him an additional two cents deposit.

Simpsonville was not within easy walking distance. So, if I wanted to go up there, I had to wait until someone was going with the wagon or on horseback. My favorite thing was when my uncle Gene decided to go. I would beg him to take me every day and he would usually decline. But on those rare occasions when he would take me, it was great. This is because he had the greatest horse you could imagine. It was a gorgeous little filly which he named "Minnie Pearl" after the Grand Ole Opry star comedienne. This horse possessed a combination of gentleness of spirit and feisty exuberance. Gene could get her to rare back on her hind legs with front legs up, pawing the air, just like the Lone Ranger did with Silver. He was a dashing sight on Minnie Pearl. When Gene took me up to the store at Simpsonville, I would sit behind him, arms around his waist, holding on for dear life, while he let Minnie Pearl run full out with the wind blowing all three of our manes (at least I imagined my burr haircut was a mane). I had to hold on tight because Gene usually rode Minnie Pearl bareback. There was no saddle for me to cling to or jam my legs up against.

When we would arrive at Simpsonville and I would get down off Minnie Pearl, I would climb those stairs and go into the store with what I can only describe as a swagger—at least as much swagger as a barefoot eight year old can muster. I pictured myself as a combination of all those cowboys that I worshipped so much. I had just ridden into Dodge City on the greatest horse in ten counties and I was ready to take on any and all bad guys who would dare to even think of doing their evil deeds in my town.

All I needed was to mosey up to the bar in the saloon and have the

61

barkeep pour me a drink. "And while you're at it, pour one for everyone in the house and just leave the bottle. Thanks."

* * * * *

One of the weekends while I was still there, my uncles and their wives from Oklahoma City showed up for a sort of mini-reunion. These were always great times. In the evening, everyone would sit around in the yard and talk and then they would break out the musical instruments. Uncle Tony and Uncle Gene would play guitar. Uncle Chester would get out his harmonica and sometimes one of the kids would use a large pot as a makeshift drum with a wooden spoon as the drum stick.

Uncle Tony had a peculiar style of playing which is forever etched into my brain. It's not that his musical style was peculiar. It was his body english and facial expressions. He played with total concentration like it was the most difficult task imaginable. He would bite on one corner of his bottom lip and stick his tongue out the other corner of his mouth. His brow would become furrowed and he would stare at the neck of the guitar through squinting eyes as if he was trying to will his fingers to go to certain frets and strings. Then his foot would start patting in those size 12 shoes and pretty soon his entire leg would start going up and down as he'd "go to stompin'" He and Gene and Chester and anyone else who wanted to join in would play such classics as "Under the Double Eagle" and "Wildwood Flower" and occasionally a vocal rendition of something like "You're In the Jailhouse Now" or "Wild Side of Life" ("I didn't know God made honky tonk angels. . . ") Gene would usually do the vocals. He was very good and ended up making a career of music until his untimely death in his thirties.

I decided then that I needed to learn to play something quick so I could join in these sessions. It was obvious that the players were having even more fun than the audience.

* * * * *

I loved and admired my Uncle Gene and cousins Craig and Jerry. I wanted to be like them in many ways. But there was one thing I didn't want to emulate: these guys loved to fight. They would get into the biggest brawls and knock-down, drag-out fights one could imagine. Then they would walk off with an arm around the other's shoulder to go get something to drink.

I couldn't understand what motivated this. Fighting with an enemy was easy to comprehend. But fighting with a close relative who you loved? What's the point?

Especially hard to fathom was why Jerry would jump into these frays. He was out-classed in nearly every way. Both Craig and Gene had several years, several pounds and several inches on Jerry. But Jerry would be right in the middle of these brawls. Sometimes he would even start one! It was many years before I learned the word "masochist" and decided that word must have been coined just to have an apt description of my cousin. However, it became a much more even fight in about five years.

What is even more amazing is how the two sisters, Linnie and Nell could put up with these guys. I remember Nell Marita (who is close to Craig's age) yelling at Craig and Jerry continually to keep them in line. She sounded more like their mother, or even a wife, than she did a sister. Even though Linnie was the baby, she could hold her own with them just the same.

Craig carried this love of fighting into a career. He was in the Marines for years and even insisted that they send him back to Viet Nam a second time or he wouldn't re-enlist, in spite of having a wife and family. On his second tour of duty there he caught a bullet in the jaw and had to go through a series of dozens of operations in order to regain use of the jaw. Even then he couldn't stay away from the macho life and became a sheriff in Cheyenne Wyoming. That's right. One of them tin star wearin', gun totin' lawmen. So iffn' you find yourself in Wyoming and mosey into Cheyenne with evil deeds on your mind, I'd advise you to get out by sundown.

* * * * *

I loved those visits to East Texas and even today the family will gravitate to that site for family reunions. Just being there takes me back. Uncle Chester's house still stands and up until his death in his late eighties, he still loved to have the family come down and gather. The house has electricity and indoor plumbing now.

One of the things I remember vividly about visiting my grandmother was the food. There's nothing like farm fresh food—fresh churned butter, fresh baked biscuits and cornbread, etc. But the part of freshness which made the biggest impression on me was when we were going to have a chicken dinner. The expression: "running around like a chicken with his head cut off" is likely only that—just an expression—to most people. But when you actually observe this phenomenon, it assumes a totally different place in your internal lexicon.

When it was time to prepare a chicken dinner, such as Sunday afternoon, the strangest thing would take place. Mama would go out into the yard with a handful of grain. She would throw it down on the ground to attract the chickens who would start pecking at it. She would then spy the one she thought would make a good Sunday dinner and chase it down until she caught it. While chickens are basically domestic creatures, they do not like to be picked up. So the chosen bird would start to run, cackling and flapping its wings.

The first time I saw this I was watching with both awe and humor. Look! Mama's chasing a chicken! I never thought about what might happen next. Mama then did something I can hardly believe to this day. While holding the chicken in the crook of her left arm, she grabbed its head with her right hand and proceeded to swing it round and round, wringing its neck until she was holding only a chicken head in her hand. The headless body of the chicken would drop to the ground, immediately stand up and start running around at top speed in an aimless pattern. I couldn't believe my eyes. It was the most grotesque scene imaginable—something out of some underground horror movie. It was even more surreal because the headless chicken didn't make a sound, since its head was still in my grandmother's hand.

I saw my grandmother perform this stunt many times over the next dozen years and can honestly say I never enjoyed it or even got used to it. (It didn't stop me from eating her delicious fried chicken, though).

After the chicken finally stopped its bizarre dance and keeled over, Mama would enlist someone to sit on a little stool in the yard and while holding the chicken over a bucket, proceed to pluck it by pulling every feather out of its skin by hand. When it was totally nude, Mama would take it, wash it, cut it up and then prepare the most scrumptious chicken dinner in the county.

Chapter Twenty
Getting Accustomed to Rather Strange Neighbors

When I returned to Tulsa I discovered that we had new neighbors on both sides of us. Sharing our duplex, as it were, was a family consisting of a couple with their two young children—Diana who was a couple of years younger than me, and three year old Rory. Also living with them was the grandmother, who they called Mimi.

Rory had the most unusual speech impediment I have ever heard. He substituted the letter "F" for the "T" sound. Thus, "Mommy, I'm tired." Came out "Mommy, I'm fired."

He also dropped any letter which was behind the "T" when he substituted the "F". Therefore, "That's a good trick!" came out "Fat's a good fick!" This made for some interesting conversations and some hilarious comments from Rory. Of course, as soon as my friends and I discovered this peculiarity, we took great pride in having him say "Fire Truck" as often as we could, after which we would roar with laughter. The "Fire" would translate fine. The "Truck" came out as the "F" word, of course. One of the boys brought a toy fire truck from home and would continually hold it up in front of Rory and say: "What is this, Rory?", just waiting for him to answer in his unique style. I'm sure there was a considerable amount of consternation at home, the first time Rory said: "Mommy, please tuck me in bed."

Our side of the duplex was nearly a mirror image of the other side. Both had picture windows and both had the same type of front porch. One afternoon my mother was relaxing in the bathtub when the bathroom door burst open. In rushed Rory who headed directly for the toilet, pulled down his pants and proceeded to take care of his business. When he finished and pulled up his pants, he turned around, saw a strange woman in the bathtub and began to scream at the top of his lungs. He continued to stand there and scream and would not let up. No one else was home, so my mother had to get up (Rory was still screaming), put a towel around herself and try to direct him to the front door.

As soon as she took hold of his arm, he started screaming louder. She finally got him to the front door, opened it, with only the towel wrapped around her and tried to get him to leave, thinking he would then recognize he was in the wrong house and would go into the proper door. He refused to leave. He was convinced that he was home and that some alien had removed his mother and taken her place. His screaming would not stop.

My mother could not stop Rory from screaming and he wouldn't, or couldn't, hear her explanation. She couldn't go back to get clothes on because he wouldn't stop screaming, so she had no choice but to make sure the towel was wrapped around her as best she could, hold the towel with one hand, Rory's arm with the other and take him home. The duplex was laid out such that the steps from the front porches came down parallel to the house instead of straight out from the door. Ours went to the North and Rory's went to the South. This meant that Mom had to go down our steps, turn and walk about fifty feet down the sidewalk, turn and go up the steps next door. Then knock on the door, wait for Rory's mother to answer, explain the situation and then come back home.

She made it to Rory's house just fine, which is a good thing since to most observers she would have looked like a combination of pervert and child molester with a very reluctant victim. But, as luck would have it, on the way back home, even for those brief few seconds, the mailman arrived, Roy and his buddy rode by on their bicycles and a couple of cars came by, both of which honked. By the next day, my mother was famous (or infamous) in the neighborhood.

* * * * *

On the other side of our house, across the driveways, in what would become the Hummel House in a few years, a family moved in which consisted of a man and his four children. No mother was apparent in the family, and I never asked. The four kids all had family nicknames which stuck with them outside the house. The oldest girl. About 17 or 18, was named Wanda or something, but she went by a nickname I can't recall. Then the boy who was about my age was called "Sonny" although his real name was Kenneth.

There was a girl about a year younger than me named Vesta, but they called her "Sissy". The youngest girl was about six and her nickname was "DeDe". She was a very precocious little thing who was knowledgeable well beyond her six years, which apparently stemmed from the liberal lessons in life she received from her older siblings.

Wanda was a very attractive girl, taken to wearing rather tight dresses and high heel shoes. At 18, she looked like she was about 25.

Wanda's boyfriend was somewhat of a celebrity in Tulsa. He was the city's most famous and popular stock car driver. There were stock car races every Saturday night at the fairgrounds raceway and Angelo had been one of the top two or three in point standings for several years.

Angelo had a night job so he and Wanda would do their courting during the day. Several afternoons a week he would bring her home about 2:00 in the afternoon and they would park in front of her house. They would then begin to put on one of the hottest shows in town, smooching up a storm in Angelo's car. This would go on for about an hour.

Remember that directly across the street from their house was the playground for the school. As soon as the lovebirds were spotted, the kids would start to play closer and closer to the chain link fence at that end of the playground. Before long, there would be a couple of dozen boys clinging to the fence just watching the writhing going on in Angelo's car, across the street.

On occasion, when Wanda got out of the car to go in the house, there would be applause from the school grounds. This didn't seem to bother either she or Angelo one little bit.

Sonny and I started out as pretty good friends. We strung a line between his bedroom window and mine, which had to go across both of our driveways and a strip of yard between them, a distance of fifty or sixty feet. We attached tin cans to each end of the string under the belief that this would create a private telephone system. I would press the can to my ear while he spoke his message and he would do the same. It was immediately apparent that either we had been duped into thinking this was a viable communications technology or we were doing it wrong. We could hear better by merely yelling at each other across the driveways.

We then replaced the single line with a double line in a loop and installed pulleys on the window casings. We would attach a note to the string with a clothespin and reel the note from one side to the other. This was fun for about two exchanges of notes. It took what seemed like an hour or more to get the note across. The string would hang up in the pulley and it would start to stretch and sag so that we ended up pulling the note along the ground for about half the distance. This was an early indication that maybe communications was not going to be my best career path.

* * * * *

On Sonny's birthday, his grandmother gave him twenty dollars. He decided to go downtown to spend his loot and asked me to join him. The bus stop was less than a block away, on Eleventh Street, and it was a straight shot downtown. The fare was ten cents. It was also a safe undertaking and parents would think nothing about letting nine or ten year old children go to town on their own, especially during the day.

I decided I had better things to do than ride the bus downtown and watch Sonny spend money. Besides, I didn't have the dime for bus fare and even if I did, there were other things to spend it on. But Sonny really didn't want to go by himself and begged me to go. I still balked. So, he whipped out one of the five dollar bills his grandmother had given him and said it was mine if I would go with him. Five dollars! That was a fortune! In the fourth grade, my weekly allowance was $1.75. This was based on a formula encompassing annual cost of living increases. On my sixth birthday, I was started on a weekly allowance of $1. Then, each succeeding birthday, the allowance was increased by 25 cents per week. So, by age 9 I was getting a whopping $1.75 a week. But to get the equivalent of nearly three weeks' allowance in one fell swoop was a windfall of huge magnitude. I showed no hesitation in taking the five dollar bill and boarding the bus with Sonny.

I showed great restraint in not spending the money on the trip downtown and took it home intact, since Sonny also paid my bus fare. I was afraid my parents would not let me keep it if they knew how I came to have it, so I simply told them I found it on the street. My dad was convinced that I was the luckiest kid he'd ever seen. I went to bed with a certain degree of guilt for lying to my folks. But when I awoke, put on my shorts and felt the treasure in my pocket, the guilt seemed to disappear immediately.

The family lived there for a couple of years but it wasn't long before I decided to not spend too much time with them. Sonny showed all the signs of being much wilder than I'm sure my parents would have approved. This proved to be an accurate assessment when Sonny ended up in prison a dozen years later.

* * * * *

My dad was an inveterate reader of mystery novels. These were the paperback books written by that rather large class of prolific authors such as Mickey Spillane, Erle Stanley Gardner and Dashiell Hammett. He could be found nearly every night in his big, easy chair, unlit cigar in his mouth, wrapped up in the latest escapade of Mike Hammer, Philip Marlowe or Sam Spade.

A block from our house, on the corner of Eleventh and Yale, was a Crown Drug Store with a comprehensive newsstand, including all the magazines, a large selection of paperbacks and a substantial inventory of comic books. When my dad would finish one of his mystery books, he would walk down to the drug store to get a new one. I would go with him every chance I got. My motive was a selfish one. He would buy a mystery book and five cigars (Roi Tan Perfectos). When he would go up to the counter to pay, I would be right behind him with five comic books and my best, angelic, "I'm-such-a-good-boy" look on my face. He would reluctantly say—"All. . .right. We'll get you some comic books. But don't expect this every time we come to the drug store." (But I did, of course. And it always happened.)

There was a secondary fallout of these excursions. I amassed a huge stack of comic books in no time. I would put them in the back of my closet and they would stack up. In about six months, the stack would be about three feet high.

About every six months a couple who had been friends of the family in Chickasha would come through Tulsa and stop to see us. They had two sons—Pat and Mike—who were about my age. They would visit with my folks for a couple of hours and then ask if I had any comic books I had already read that I might like to sell so they could take them back to Pat and Mike. Out would come my stash. We would count them and I would be paid two cents per comic book (which cost ten cents at the drug store). I would usually rake in about three or four dollars in these transactions. Rich again! Of all the business deals I have ever been involved with in my life, I have to say that this series of sales was probably my most successful. Investment in my inventory was zero. Profit margin was 100%. Where did I go wrong after that?

Chapter Twenty One

Introduction to Organizations
and Outside Activities

Fourth grade started out pretty good. My teacher, Miss Thompson, was an attractive red head, but not as attractive as Miss Trusty, of course. However, the class was soon exposed to her darker side. She had a temper which was consistent with the color of her hair.

One day she put the class busy reading something and left the room. She was absent for quite a while, but the class remained dutifully quiet and read as we were instructed. No one wanted to risk incurring the wrath of Miss Thompson should she unexpectedly return while we were engaged in anything other than reading.

While she was gone, an emergency of sorts cropped up. First, it is important to realize that if there was anything you didn't want to do at Franklin school, it was to be caught in the hallway without a pass while class was in session. This meant that you would be taken directly to the principal's office to be interrogated as to why you were not in class and why you did not have an official pass. The principal was a large, angular, sort of Abraham Lincoln type, without the beard. His name was Mr. Hagar (just like the Viking of comic strip fame). He was the original Hagar the Horrible. He spoke in a very loud voice. Our teacher said this was because his wife was very hard of hearing and so he was in the habit of speaking loud to her, which carried over to all conversation. He was imposing and struck fear in the hearts of all the students, Roy included. It was rumored that one kid was caught in the hallway without a pass and taken to Mr. Hagar's office never to be heard from or seen again.

While Miss Thompson was out of the room on this particular day, a kid named Kenneth had to go to the bathroom. He was squirming around and fidgeting. Then he asked the class if they thought it would be alright if he just went down to the bathroom without a pass. The jury's verdict was unanimous: NO WAY! What would be worse—the embarrassment of wet pants or the unknown fate of Hagar's office which might be worse than death?

After a while, poor Kenneth was totally torn between nature's call and the need for self-preservation. Finally, when the teacher had not returned, he went up to the front by her desk, unzipped his pants and proceeded to relieve himself in Miss Thompson's waste basket. The split in class reaction was predictable. The girls were incredulous and shocked. The boys giggled uncontrollably.

A few minutes later, Miss Thompson returned. The class was relatively quiet, with the occasional unstifled giggle coming from one of the boys. Those dark green waste baskets were constructed of fiber material, sort of like cardboard, and were meant to hold dry waste such as paper and pencil shavings, not liquid. Kenneth's deposit had passed right through the basket and spread out in a puddle on the floor. It took only a few minutes for Miss Thompson to notice the puddle and she immediately got upset, or rather, livid. Her first thought was that someone had knocked over the flower vase on her desk, spilling the water on the floor, which meant someone had been messing with her desk in her absence. She picked up the vase and looked inside it, but it was still full.

"What happened here and who's responsible?", she yelled—silence from the class, except for the knees knocking on about half the kids. A few eyes turned toward Kenneth, who just sat there stoically. She was just about to raise her ire to another level when the bell rang indicating the end of class. That classroom was emptied faster than a bottle of ripple in the hands of a thirsty wino.

* * * * *

During the first month of the school year, the PTA hosted a get acquainted night to sign up parents for PTA and to give parents and teachers a chance to meet. They also turned it into a sort of carnival with various fund-raising booths and games. One of the games they had was a Cake Walk. I went over to the school to sign my parents up for the PTA and to take part in the festivities. It should be pointed out that my parents were not much for attending school functions or any of the activities in which I took part, unless I had a prominent role or part. If I was the third snowflake from the left in the Christmas pageant, you could count on my parents not being among those in the audience. However, if I had a solo, they would be on the front row, beaming during my performance and ready to receive any kudos which might be offered as a result. Let me hasten to point out that this was not a major concern or disappointment to me. I rather liked the independence of being on my own on these occasions and attribute much of my ability to cope with a lot of things which I faced as a young adult to the fact that I pretty much handled my own affairs as a child.

The Cake Walk is sort of a combination of Musical Chairs (without the chairs) and Wheel of Fortune. A circle about ten feet in diameter was painted on the floor. The perimeter of the circle had a series of numbers in random order—one to ten or twelve. Each participant stands on a number. When the music starts, everyone starts walking around the circle, moving from number to number. When the music stops, everyone stops and remains on that number. Then, a small wheel is spun until it stops on a number. The person standing on that number wins.

The prize for the winner is a fresh, home-baked cake, donated by various PTA mothers. I paid my fifty cents and stepped on a number. I proceeded around the circle. When the music stopped and the winning number came up, it was mine. I was directed to the table full of delicious looking cakes and picked one. I took it home, since I just lived across the street. But I felt like I was on a roll, and asked my mother for a dollar. I went back across the street and immediately joined the next game. I won again! I couldn't waste the time to take this one home immediately so I joined up again. Another win! So, I picked two more cakes and asked someone to open the door for me as I juggled the two cakes and took them home. My mother was wide eyed and taken aback. Her delight was not as prominent as I would have expected. This was probably due to the fact that she loved to bake and probably was the best cook in town, anyway. (At least in my estimation as well as that of my dad and most people who had been exposed to her culinary prowess.)

I asked for another dollar and went back. As I went out the door, Mom asked me to play some other game since three large cakes were probably enough for our little family for the next couple of weeks. What a ludicrous suggestion! I was hooked! I headed straight to the cake walk again, plunked down my dollar and hopped in the circle again. This time a number other than mine came up. I was deflated. What happened to my streak? Well, the concern was short-lived. I went one more time with my last fifty cents and the magic returned! This time I selected a big double-decker coconut cake. I hate coconut, but my mother loved it. I thought this would appease her sufficiently so that I would not be punished for my failure to obey her instructions. It worked. If I had known about Las Vegas at that age I probably would have begged, borrowed or stolen a way to get there in the belief that I could not lose. I'd break the bank in no time.

* * * * *

My next experience with organizational activities was when I joined the Cub Scouts. I really took to this concept. It provided a creative outlet, new friends and education in areas not taught at school. But I wouldn't really get into this type of activity until I moved up to Boy Scouts at age 11, where I was exposed to a whole variety of experiences, many of which cannot be found in the Boy Scout manual.

About this time, my parents decided that the musical leanings I had experienced through my singing might be better developed if I took music lessons. Once a week, my mother would drive me half way across town to Mrs. Childers' for piano lessons. Armed with John Thompson's "Teaching Littler Fingers to Play", I would go play the one line, simple tunes in the book.

I hated to practice, however. I still progressed fairly rapidly, and by Christmas, she had moved me to the second year, intermediate book, even though I was only about three months into my first year of lessons.

A girl who lived in my neighborhood also took from Mrs. Childers and we would car pool from time to time. She was advancing quickly as well. Mrs. Childers started having us play duets and we were featured in some of the recitals.

The leading radio station in Tulsa was KVOO, "The Voice of Oklahoma". Once a week they had a program called "Stars of Tomorrow" which was hosted by Tulsa's answer to Walter Cronkite, a very popular announcer named Cy Tuma. As one of the leading piano teachers in town, Mrs. Childers was asked to recommend students for the program. My duet partner, Judy, and I played on the program about once a month.

The problem was that Cy Tuma didn't write the patter which was used between performers or to introduce them. Some person in the script writing or production department at the radio station, who had no idea what age the performers were, wrote some of the most banal drivel imaginable. Many times I couldn't even understand what I was being asked or how I was to answer. So, Cy would simply tell me what to say. For example, on one show, I was the only male performer. In addition to me, there was

73

my partner, Judy, plus a female violinist and a female flute player. Before we started our number, Cy introduced Judy and me and then chatted for a minute. He asked me something like: "So, Joe it looks like you are going to have to uphold the masculine aspect of today's program. Do you think you can handle that?" In rehearsal, I didn't have the slightest idea what he said. So Cy just said to answer "Yes". Which I did. I'm sure there were members of the audience who were thinking: "It's a good thing this kid can play piano, because he certainly can't talk."

I was tiring of piano lessons rather quickly. The tunes I was learning on, for the most part, were composed by John Thompson for teaching purposes only. Songs like "The Juggler" or "In a Wigwam". I'd never heard them nor had anyone else, unless they had studied with the same book. I was anxious to play some "real music"—especially popular songs. Thus, under the threat of quitting, Mrs. Childers wrote out some simple chord charts and melody lines, so I could play some songs which someone could recognize.

This appeased me for possibly another year before I quit piano lessons. All my parents' friends kept saying "You'll be sorry when you grow up that you didn't keep with the piano lessons." They were wrong. I was sorry long before I grew up.

One thing which contributed to my feeling of frustration was my parents' record collection. They had a huge collection of 78 RPM record albums. The ones which are about 12 inches in diameter and break easily. In their collection was a significant number of records featuring piano players—everything from Carmen Cavallero, who played with a flourish in a tradition carried on by performers like Liberace, to some of the early jazz greats like Pine Top Smith and Fats Waller--some really great stuff (and I'd give anything to have those records now). I would play these and decide that it would take too long and require way too much practice, to get that good. I wasn't ready to make that commitment.

Chapter Twenty Two
Summer in the City

Toward the end of the school year, they had signup day for little league baseball. Everyone showed up, usually with their fathers in tow. I, of course, was standing in line by myself. I don't think I even told my dad about the signup or that he was supposed to be there. They handed out the forms. I filled mine out, ran across the street to get my mother's signature and the five dollar fee, and went back. I was assigned to the Franklin Eagles.

I had spent months practicing my hand/eye coordination for baseball by throwing a tennis ball against our garage door, which could be partially opened to return a fly ball or a grounder.

It was my luck to be put on a team with some really good players. The bad news is that I was destined to spend a lot of time on the bench. But I was prepared for this, having had the precedent set in the first grade during the Tug O' War. The good news is that I would probably be on a winning team.

Two of the best players were destined to become very good friends of mine. One was a pitcher named Kenny. He was a year older than me and he and I became best friends. The other one was our shortstop, Billy, who enjoyed a great career in baseball, all the way through high school and college and could probably have made it in professional baseball.

Kenny lived two blocks from me and was the youngest in his family. He had a brother who was five years older than us and a sister who was about as old as my parents. This made his parents seem to be quite old, compared with most of my friends' parents. Kenny's dad was a chemist at the Texaco refinery and a very smart man. He set up a pitching range in their back yard. The yard was not very big, so the pitching range had to be set up diagonally across the back yard in order to get the precise sixty feet, six inches from the pitching rubber to home plate. He even built a pitcher's mound of correct height. I was pressed into the job of being the catcher at Kenny's pitching practice, a job which I didn't really mind, except that as Kenny got older his fast ball got faster and faster and my left hand would sometimes be red and throbbing after catching for Kenny for a half hour or so, in spite of the padding in the catcher's mitt.

Sure enough, we had a great team. In addition to Kenny, we had a left handed pitcher named Bill who was outstanding. His full name was William Henry Diffendaffer Burgess the Fourth. No kidding!

We ended up winning our league but we lost the city championship to the Sequoyah Warriors. Sequoyah school was located on the North side of town in somewhat a rough area. At the awards banquet, when they went up as a team to collect their trophy for winning the city championship for 9 and 10 year olds, I could swear several of them had five o'clock shadows.

* * * * *

Other than baseball, the summer days were filled with many other activities. They were rarely lazy, nothing-to-do days. One day a really spooky thing happened.

A new kid had moved into the neighborhood, about a block from my house. Jimmy was my age and we became good friends. His family had moved to Tulsa from Canada and he sort of talked funny sometimes. He would come to my house, knock on the door, and ask my mother if I could come "oot" and play.

He had a dart board which his father put up in the garage. It was a "proper" dartboard, made from horsehair, identical to the kind I observed in English pubs thirty years later. He taught me how to play darts and we taught other of our friends. One of these was my good friend Bobby. One afternoon we were at Jimmy's throwing darts and we were getting bored with the conventional dart game. So we started making up new games and changing the way we threw the darts. We would throw the darts over our shoulders, left handed, side arm or any other different way we could think of. Then we moved further back from the dart board. Soon, we were out the side door of the garage, throwing through the open door toward the dart board—about 25 feet away instead of the regulation 8 feet or so. It was my turn to throw the dart this super-olympic distance, so I stepped out the side door and into the yard and took aim at the distant dart board on the opposite wall of the single car garage.

Bobby was standing in the garage, well out of the path of the darts. In fact, he was so far inside the garage and to the side that I couldn't even see him. So, I let fly with this dart and as it passed from the outside to the inside, through the doorway, the airflow created by the main door at the front of the garage through the side door which I was shooting through, diverted the path of the dart, blowing it off course so much that it literally turned the corner when it got inside the garage.

I was disappointed that I didn't even hit the far wall, much less the dartboard hanging on it. Then I heard this blood-curdling scream. I stepped inside the garage and saw Bobby lying on the garage floor holding his doubled up leg. When I got closer, I saw that the errant dart I had just thrown was imbedded in the side of his knee, behind the kneecap, up to the hilt. It was very apparent since he was wearing shorts.

What should we do now? Jimmy and I stood there horror-struck. Should we tell Jimmy's mother? None of us thought we had done anything wrong, but these are just the kinds of occurrences where someone is going to get in trouble. Maybe it would be Jimmy—after all, it was his dartboard and garage and probably his responsibility to make sure his friends played responsibly. Maybe it would be me—after all, I threw the dart and was not even close to the line where I was supposed to be standing to play the game properly.

Bobby was in pain but was not crying. He looked up at us with a curious look on his face. Then he abruptly reached down and extracted the dart from his knee. We all gasped. Then we couldn't believe our eyes. There was a little hole where the dart had been, but it was not bleeding! How could this be? This dart had been imbedded in his knee at least two inches deep. I didn't know if Bobby was some sort of freak or maybe an alien.

He rubbed his knee a little bit, got up a bit shakily, expecting it to hurt. It didn't hurt. He took a few steps. No apparent damage or repercussions. So, after giving me the expected cussing out, we continued to play and forgot about it.

* * * * *

Next door to Jimmy, in the corner house, lived an older kid named

John. He was about fifteen and had a Model-T Ford pickup truck he had been working on for several months, in anticipation of getting his driver's license when he soon turned sixteen. One day we were playing at Jimmy's and decided to go over to John's to see how the Model T project was coming along. He was in his garage working on it and informed us that he had gotten it running and even taken it around the block a few times in trial runs. We were properly impressed. The part of the project on which he was engaged while we were there struck a chord of fear in me as I realized what he was doing.

In those days, Oklahoma issued new license plates for your car every year. One year the plate would be white with black letters. The next year it was black with white letters. John's Model T had not been running for several years and certainly not since he had acquired it, over a year ago. The vehicle had a 1946 license tag which was black with white letters. But this was 1949 and all cars which were legally tagged had white plates with black letters.

For a fifteen year old kid, paying 25 or 30 dollars for a license tag would have been tough enough, but catching up the arrears and paying it for all the years since 1946 would have been totally out of the question, for someone like John. It probably would have amounted to more than he paid for the entire car. So John had taken the old plate off, painted it white and was painting over all the raised letters with black paint. When we arrived, he was meticulously painting over the 6 in 1946 to make it a 9. I couldn't believe that John was risking what I was sure was a certain jail term by not paying the fee and getting a current license tag. I could just picture some motorcycle cop pulling John over in his Model T, spotting the suspicious looking plate and calling for the paddy wagon to take John to jail—no phone call, no lawyer, no trial, no nothing.

When he finished, I thought the plate looked pretty good, but I could see the alteration if I looked closely enough. He re-mounted the plate and then looked at Jimmy and me and asked us if we would like to take a spin around the block in his prized new chariot. So, now, not only does he have an altered license tag, but he isn't even old enough to have a drivers license yet. I hem-hawed around for a minute, mumbling something like my mother was expecting me home, and made my hasty exit. Jimmy was more foolhardy and hopped into the front seat without hesitation. As I headed toward home, I felt secure in my decision and was sure that I had just dodged a potential bullet. I had no desire to go to jail with my outlaw neighbor. Whew! That was a close one! I was trying to decide which of my other friends would take Jimmy's place as my daytime playmate while he was serving jail time.

* * * * *

Somehow, Jimmy managed to escape the long arm of the law and we continued our regimen of summer activities. A couple of days a week, we would sit on the wall overlooking the parking lot at Brown's Market. When the delivery trucks would show up to make deliveries to the store, we would ask the drivers if they had any decals of their company's emblem (logo). We were enamored with decals. What an unusual and neat device they were. You just soak them in water for a few seconds and then transfer them to the desired surface and you'd have a neat picture which looked like it had been painted on. In our case we wanted to put them on our bicycles—either on the center "tank", which was a common feature on bicycle designs of the forties, or on the fenders. A Coca Cola or Pepsi Cola decal would be prized, as would one from a candy company. We were even ready to settle for one from a less glamorous company.

None of the drivers seemed to carry decals. But one day the truck from the Dolly Madison Bakery company pulled up and the driver got out. Jimmy and I were perched on the wall in our regular observation post, like a couple of Cheshire Cats. As the driver opened the back door of his truck and started to load up the product he would take in to stock the shelves, we yelled at him: "Do you have any Dolly Madison decals with you?" He turned to us and said: "No. Sorry." We showed our disappointment and were resigned to coming up empty again. Then, just before he closed the door to his truck, he turned to us and said: "No decal, but would you like these?" and he tossed us a full package of cinnamon rolls. Unbelievable. A full package of eight Dolly Madison cinnamon rolls! Free! We voiced our sincere thanks and tore into the package, devouring the contents like a couple of piranhas with a plump water rat.

From then on, we figured out when Bill, the Dolly Madison guy, was due to make deliveries (Mondays, Wednesdays and Fridays about 3:00 to 3:30 in the afternoon) and were dutifully planted on the wall. Bill would throw us a package of cinnamon rolls about once a week. It wasn't long before other friends in the neighborhood found out about this windfall and it was not unusual for us to be joined by 3 or 4 others on the wall, as if it were just a casual coincidence.

* * * * *

On some of the hot summer evenings, my parents and possibly some of the neighbors, would sit in the back yard and visit, sipping a cold drink or a beer. My mother would make some sort of a drink called a "Salty Dog". Sounded horrible to me, but people seemed to really like them. A couple of the men would drink beers. The most popular brands on those occasions seemed to be Hamm's ("From the land of sky-blue waters."), Pabst Blue Ribbon and a brand called Griesideick Brothers. In polite company, the brand was pronounced: "Greeze Dyke". But we found out that the actual pronunciation was supposed to be: "Greasy Dick". (I'm not making this up.) When they started advertising on television in the early fifties, before they went out of business, even the announcer would pronounce it this way. No wonder they didn't survive.

Of course, my friends and I found this to be funnier than Rory's speech impediment and would take every opportunity to refer to the beer by name. We would monitor everyone's drink level, especially the men drinking beer, and when they were running low would say: "Mrs. Marshall, would you like me to go get you another Greasy Dick?" My parents would look rather sternly at me while my friends could hardly keep from rolling on the ground in uncontrollable laughter. All us boys thought it was an inside joke, understood only by us, and that it went right over the heads of the adults.

On many of these nights the fireflies (or lightning bugs, as we called them) would be out in full force. We would go in and get a glass jar, like a Mason jar, and punch holes in the lid with an ice pick. Then we would catch the lightning bugs for an hour and put them in the jar until we had twenty or thirty of them. What ever happened to lightning bugs, which were so ubiquitous fifty years ago? They've gone the route of the horny toads, I guess.

Occasionally when the adults would go in, someone would leave a partial package of cigarettes on the table outside. We would quickly grab onto these and hide them in a special place in the garage. It wouldn't be long before the owner would come back out, looking for the cigarettes and when they were missing would ask if we had seen them. In our most innocent voices we would reply that we had not and maybe they had just taken them inside and misplaced them.

Then, on occasion, when there was nothing to do, we would go into the garage, shut the door and light up a cigarette, puffing away like mad, but not inhaling. When I would go into the house, my mother would say: "Where have you been? You smell like old stale cigarette smoke." I would feign total surprise or incredulity. And the subject would be dropped.

* * * * *

One day that summer, my grandmother had been to our house and saw me and my friends riding our bicycles outside, pretending they were motorcycles by attaching playing cards to the fender strut with clothes pins so they would hit the spokes to make the clacking sound of the "motorcycle". She had a great idea which she put forth to me and suddenly this became an opportunity to really do something significant—not just a stupid little game. She asked my dad to transport me and my bicycle to her house, along with a supply of cards and clothes pins. Grandmother had a large, black, standard-sized Poodle named Bo Bo who had the annoying and dangerous habit of chasing cars and barking at the wheels—motorcycles, too. She had a private obedience trainer coming to her house to train Bo Bo better and to break him of the tire chasing habit. She had me install the cards on the bicycle and then ride back and forth in the street in front of her house while Bo Bo chased me, barking at the simulated "motorcycle" sounds, after which the trainer would scold the dog or apply other training methods or incentives to get him to stop. I felt quite important in this job.

Chapter Twenty Three

The Not-so Spectacular Fire of '49
And the Military Academy

One of the significant things that took place that summer, which would open up a lot of new doors, was when Dad bought his woodworking equipment. I'm not talking about just buying some sort of hand jigsaw and a few tools. He outfitted the garage with a complete woodworking shop—power table saw, band saw, drill press, the whole magilla. I didn't know he knew anything about woodworking, but I was not surprised when he started turning out all sorts of neat things and seemed quite adept at operation of all this sophisticated equipment. My dad was quite good with his hands and was very artistic.

Dad's main hobby was model railroading. He belonged to the Tulsa Model Railroad Engineers, a group of about twenty or thirty model railroad enthusiasts, most of whom were into H-O gauge trains. Each member sort of had his own specialty which they called on in building their club layout—a large undertaking in the basement of one of the member's homes. One guy could take a model box car and age it so that it would look like it had been on the road for years, making it all dirty and grungy, but very authentic. Another was great at landscaping and making the small, artificial bushes, trees, hills, etc. My dad's specialty was bridges and trestles. He built the most elaborate bridges with multiple struts and supports, all out of balsa wood. So they always planned the club layouts with big canyons and ravines where very tall trestles would be required. The problem was that they would get the club layout about half finished and then decide to re-design it, tear out the old one and start over. This necessitated the building of multiple bridges and trestles which never were installed. This didn't seem to bother Dad one bit.

When he acquired all his woodworking equipment he started into projects which were not related to model railroading. The first major project he took on was building a back porch. When you walked out our back door, you came down about four steps to ground level and were immediately standing on the driveway. Dad designed a porch so that you walked directly out of the house onto the elevated porch, and then turned to go down new steps which were parallel to the driveway. It was screened in and had a nice roof on it and became the place where Mom stored things like empty pop bottles, the mop and bucket, etc.

Then he really took on a big project. He decided to build a hobby room to work on his model trains. He talked my grandmother into letting him build it across the back of the garage, inside the existing structure, so long as it was elevated enough that the other tenant in the duplex could get his car in with the hood going under the floor of the hobby room. So, he built the room about six feet wide and the total width of the double garage. He constructed a door at the side of the building with steps going up to it. It ended up being a very nice room, although it was quite narrow.

The room was electrically wired and well lit and he had a window air conditioner installed at one end through a hole cut in the wall. For heat, he installed an electric heater. That was his mistake. It was a little heater which simply sat on the floor and was not built into the wall.

One evening I was in the house and Dad came bursting through the back door, nearly knocking me over and headed for the telephone. I heard him yelling into the phone telling them he had a fire and send the fire department immediately.

Then he ran back outside, hooked up a hose and tried to pull it around to the side door leading up to the hobby room. The hose wouldn't reach.

It seemed like a long time before the fire department arrived. By then, there was a full fledged blaze going in the hobby room. They got it extinguished in about an hour, but not before it had done a lot of damage.

It seems that Dad had been painting some of his models and had spilled a can of paint thinner on the floor. The liquid ran across the floor and reached the heater in seconds, bursting into flames immediately, catching Dad's pant leg on fire and scorching his right eyebrow and some of his hair.

Dad figured he lost about $8,000 to $10,000 worth of train equipment, supplies, etc. in the fire. That was equivalent to more than a year's salary for most men in those days. But he went in, cleaned it all out and rebuilt the room. This time he put a wall-mounted heater in.

The good thing about the hobby room is that it created sort of a little cave inside the garage, underneath the raised floor portion, where we could play. One day it would be a hideout for us and our gang. The next day it would be a clubhouse for an impromptu club meeting. Another day it would be a place where we might hide to light up a cigarette and pretend.

* * * * *

The summer before my fifth grade year, my folks decided they would do some traveling and I would likely encumber them. So, they shipped me off to military academy for the summer session. The session was more an extended summer camp than it was school. We had some classes, but they were not in traditional academic subjects. We studied Indian history and lore, etiquette and other stuff which was not exactly super-fascinating to a ten-year old. All of this took place at Wentworth Military Academy in Lexington, Missouri, which is just east of Kansas City.

At Wentworth, I experienced my first case of homesickness. On about the third night out, it hit me. I cried all night. I couldn't believe I had been abandoned in this prison among people who were bent on making my life miserable. After about 3 more nights like this, I seemed to get over it. The only time it would return would be on those Sunday afternoons when parents would come in for parent visits and to observe all the wonderful things their kiddies were doing. Almost all the boys had parents who visited—but most of the boys were from St. Louis or Kansas City, an easy drive to Lexington. One boy's father would fly in from Chicago in his own plane to visit his son. Those were miserable Sundays for me as I killed the time alone.

However, all in all the Wentworth experience was a good one. I found I excelled pretty well at some of the crafts but was a lousy boxer. I earned several medals in both rifle marksmanship and archery.

Amazingly, fifty years later I can remember the names of several of the boys in our dorm. This is because on a rainy afternoon with nothing to do, several of us took the names of some of the boys and made a little word-game sentence out of them. The boys were named Eggman, Cook, Fry, Bacon and Pease. So the sentence came out "Bacon and Eggs, Cooked and Fried with Peas".

Chapter Twenty Four
The Family Expands and I Take on Some New Interests

My fifth grade teacher was Mrs. McCoy. Of all my elementary school teachers, she is the one about which I remember the least. I can't even recall what she looked like, except that when my little brother was born, in March of the school year, she seemed to be extremely excited and pleased for me. When I came to class and told her I had a new baby brother, she was beside herself. She kept saying: "Isn't that wonderful?" And she'd look at the class and repeat: "Isn't that wonderful, class?" I don't think there was a single member of the class who truly thought that it was "wonderful". "OK. He's got a new brother. Big deal! I've got one or two of those pests running around my house, too."

The more significant thing about that year to me was the fact that a boy moved into the duplex next to ours—actually he was three doors down, on the South side of the duplex. We were 1113. He was in 1119. He and I became best friends and his family became like extended family to me.

Jerry and I had a lot in common. First of all, we were born two days apart in the same hospital. So we were nursery mates during our first week of life.

Jerry and I started into several hobbies together that year. The first was Lincoln Logs. We discovered that he had a large supply as did I. One day we talked his mother into letting us move the dining room table and we proceeded to construct a Lincoln Log ranch out of our combined inventories that would rival the Ponderosa and the King Ranch put together. We had a main ranch house, bunk houses, barns, corrals, etc. We had horses, cowboys, Indians and cows. It took up nearly the whole dining room floor. The whole thing was surrounded by a rail fence. It was a beauty to behold.

Jerry decided that we would take some pictures of our creation and send them in to various magazines, such as Boys Life, or other publications. Some might even think it was an aerial view of a real ranch, it looked so good to us. We were bound to get some money or recognition or something. So Jerry pulled out his trusty Brownie Hawkeye camera and we shot a whole roll of photographs.

We took the roll of film down to the Crown Drug to be developed and in about three days we went down there to meet the delivery man when he arrived with our developed pictures. Sure enough, they were in the bag. We paid for them, and went over to the soda fountain to see our masterpiece. Yep. There it was, just as we built it. However, so was the kitchen door with the linoleum floor, the drapes hanging down by one of the corrals in back, the floor furnace grating over about where the North Forty ought to be and in a couple of shots, Jerry's black Cocker Spaniel, Nicky, looking like some sort of giant Godzilla-like creature ready to pounce on the unsuspecting ranch hands. Plus, neatly lined up hardwood planks which comprised the floor of the dining room, didn't really look like the proper ground upon which a ranch would be located. What we learned from this had nothing to do with Lincoln Logs or model creation. It had everything to do with photography and photo composition.

Frequently when I was at Jerry's house playing with Lincoln Logs or working with our coin collections, evening would be approaching and Jerry's mother would ask me if I would like to stay for dinner. I'd phone my mother who would generally say yes, so I would sit down to dinner with Jerry, his little sister, Marcia and his folks.

The problem is that Jerry's mother, who was quite a good cook, would prepare stuff which I had never seen nor heard of and which I know my mother would never even attempt to set before my dad and me. She would serve such things as calves brains and eggs, beef tongue, liver prepared all sorts of weird ways and chicken parts which were not akin to the breast or leg, the only parts I would consider. I knew it was rude to ask your host what they were serving for dinner when asked to join them. However, that did not stop me in the future. Jerry's mother would ask me if I wanted to stay for dinner. I would ask what she was having and she would respond with this delightful little impish sound which I can only describe as a reluctant laugh. It was a laugh which sounded like she was trying very hard not to laugh. It was very much like the laugh used by Lily Tomlin when she is in her Ernestine the PBX operator character, except more delightful (and without the snorts). I knew then that it was going to be something not found in your everyday meat, bread and potatoes cookbook. I found myself not eating at Jerry's quite as much in the future, although the invitations kept coming.

My Schwinn Black Phantom with little brother on the back.
This bike has a current value around $75,000!

Chapter Twenty Five

Patronizing the Local Merchants

That year, a tropical fish store moved into the space down from Comfort's Gulf filling station and Jerry and I became frequent visitors. We became enamored with the fish, learned quite a bit about them and both started aquariums. We would buy various exotic breeds, add different kinds of plants, etc. It was quite a hobby. . .for a while.

Then, the fish store owner sold out to an older lady who cut back on the tropical fish part of the shop and added other pet supplies. She especially liked cats and birds and always had a couple of cats roaming around the store as well as a bunch of parakeets. I was not into either one, but Jerry bought a parakeet and a cage and took it home to replace his aquarium which he had retired when all the fish died.

The pet shop owner obviously saw the store as somewhat a hobby and diversion. She had very little traffic into the shop, which was fine by her, because she would have her friends over nearly every afternoon and they would sit in the back room and play cards. I think they were playing bridge. There was always four of them.

She installed a little bell over the front door so that when the door was open, it would hit the bell and the little tinkling sound would alert the lady that someone had entered. Right near the front door was a very large bird cage hanging from a stand. In this cage was the owner's pet parrot. This bird was not for sale. He could talk fairly well and whistle a couple of familiar tunes as well as the sailor's girl-call whistle.

Jerry and I would still frequent the shop several days a week, looking at what new fish might be in or checking out the parakeets. However, I noticed that every time we were there, Jerry was spending more and more time at the parrot's cage. He would reach up and tinkle the bell over the door with his hand and then say something to the parrot in a low voice. He would do this over and over. One day I asked Jerry what in the world he was doing. He said he was trying to teach the bird to say something. I asked what. He said it was just a greeting for people who walked in the door—especially the owner's old lady card playing buddies.

One day while he was in the middle of this parrot lesson, I crept over behind him to hear what he was teaching the bird. He reached up, slapped the bell, then turned to the bird and said: "Hello you big ol' fat ass!" Like Pavlov's dog, he wanted the sound of the bell to trigger that reaction from the parrot and hoped that the bird would be especially responsive when the card players arrived.

After the tropical fish phase, Jerry and I took up coin collecting, something which we both continued to one degree or another into our adult lives. But when we first started, we were the terrors of the merchant community around 11th and Yale. In retrospect, I can't believe these retailers were as accommodating to us as they were. First, Jerry and I went to the coin shop and bought all the necessary books to value various coins and know what to look for.

In those days, there were still plenty of collector coins to be found in circulation. A lot of coins from the first half of the twentieth century were common and occasionally you would find one from the 1800's still in circulation—especially certain Indian head pennies and Standing Liberty quarters. Many of them had some considerable value over and above their face value. So, what Jerry and I would do is go to each of the merchants toward the end of the day and ask them if we could go through the coins in their cash registers. Really! And they would let us! We'd go to the Golden Drumstick restaurant on the corner and sit at the counter. The manager would dump all the coins on the counter and we would meticulously go through them. If we found one we wanted to keep, we'd just replace it at face value. Then we'd go to the drug store, the bakery, the dry goods store, the coney island hot dog place, Dean's Phillips 66 filling station, the five and dime and others in the neighborhood. There was also an Oklahoma Tire & Supply Store (OTASCO) but the manager would never let us look through his cash register. I thought there might be something sacred about it since it figured so prominently in the OTASCO radio commercials. At the end of each commercial, there would be the sound of a cash register ringing, followed by their slogan: "(Cha-ching!) Thank you. Here's your change. Remember, you always save at your friendly Oklahoma Tire & Supply Company store."

We would spend hours going through mounds and mounds of coins. Occasionally we would find a real treasure—either a rare coin or a secondary treasure such as an Indian head penny, which they had not minted for over 30 years.

Of course, one of the reasons the coins were so prolific was that credit cards were non-existent. Therefore, almost everyone paid with cash and new supplies of coins were coming in every day.

We really hit the mother load one day, however. Jerry's dad knew the head teller of the First National Bank in downtown Tulsa. We took the bus downtown, went into the bank and straight up to Mr. McClelland. We asked him if we could look through the coins which the bank had taken in, before they were rolled up. He was somewhat reluctant at first, so we had to buy the coins—go through them at a lobby counter, and then trade them for another load. This meant we could only go through a couple of dollars' worth at a time, since that's all the money we usually had, if that much. This meant we were trading him handfuls of coins every five minutes.

He finally tired of this and opened up the iron gate and took us back to the vault area. He had someone bring in a bin full of coins and we would sit there on high stools and look through thousands of coins. I'm sure we were the only "outsiders" ever afforded that privilege before or since.

Because of all this, Jerry and I built up fairly impressive coin collections at an early age. Jerry still had much of his as an adult. Unfortunately, I sold most of my collection while in high school in order to finance a trip to Florida.

* * * * *

One of the things Jerry and I had in common was our bicycles. We both were the fortunate and proud owners of the Cadillac of bicycles, the Schwinn Black Phantom. These were sleek, large bicycles with 26 inch tires, chrome fenders and black and red trim on the tank which was between the rider's legs. This tank housed a battery pack with a horn button on the side. The Black Phantom had a headlight, chrome rims and wide, longhorn steer-style handlebars.

Jerry and I had invested in about every cool accessory you could get on a Black Phantom. We had saddle bags, which fit over the back fender, small carry bag behind the seat, hand grips with red and white plastic streamers, and other little goodies. What we didn't have, because they were not cool, were large baskets in front. I think Jerry's even had rear view mirrors.

We waxed our bicycles, took endless pictures of them and generally held them in the esteem they deserved, as our prize possessions. These bicycles were on par, if not above, the James Bond-type bicycle featured in the movie "PeeWee's Big Adventure."

I exhibited a strong entrepreneurial bent even at an early age—not always as successful as my comic book brokerage activities, unfortunately. Jerry and I tried everything from lemonade stands to yard work. One way I found to provide a slight supplement to my allowance was through my haircut stipend. About every two weeks, my mother would give me 75 cents to go down to the barber shop, one block away and just down from the Crown Drug Store a couple of doors. That was the rate for a kid's haircut then, dictated by the local barbers' union. However, I discovered that if I rode my bike about a half mile to the east, crossing the railroad tracks near the oil storage tanks which were the focus of the famous fire of '48, I was outside the city limits and there was a little barber shop just across the tracks which was non-union. I could get my haircut for fifty cents, pocketing a clear profit of a quarter.

With this windfall gain, I would often finance a visit to the soda fountain at the Crown Drug. This was a typical soda fountain in the traditional mold, with about 12 to 15 swivel stools at the counter. At peak times, the counter sported not one, but two soda jerks. Everything was made from scratch.

One of our favorite drinks to get at the Crown was a "suicide". This consisted of a little of everything in the carbonated drink area. A shot of Coke, a shot of root beer, a shot of Seven Up, a shot of strawberry, a shot of ginger ale and a shot of club soda plus dabs of syrups used in sodas and sundaes—chocolate, cherry, butterscotch, etc. It was a conglomerated mess and didn't really taste that good. But it was sort of a macho drink to order. You were part of the in-crowd if you moseyed up to the bar and ordered a suicide.

Our favorite pastime when at the soda counter was to take the paper wrapped straw we received with our drink, dip the end in syrup and shoot the paper wrapping up to the ceiling by blowing through the straw. We would try to get the wrapper to stick to the ceiling, which was about 15 feet high. Most of the time, we were successful. Even if the wrapper only stuck temporarily, when it fell it would leave a little spot on the ceiling. After a while, the ceiling had more spots than Bobby had freckles.

After an especially busy day or two, there would be several dozen straw wrappers still stuck to the ceiling, hanging down like skinny, white stalactites and blowing in the breeze created by the big ceiling fan over that area.

The manager first tried to stop us from engaging in this nefarious activity by issuing verbal warnings. All this did was make us do it on the sly instead of blatantly in front of him or the soda jerks. This just made the exercise that much more challenging. We would prepare the straw wrapper in our laps, hiding it from view. And then at the first opportunity, we would strike—whipping the blowgun up in a second and firing it at the target. Finally, in desperation, the manager instructed the soda jerks to remove the wrappers and insert the straws in the drinks before giving them to us. But, if he wasn't around, we could sometimes talk the soda jerks into giving us the straws still in the wrappers.

Chapter Twenty Six
Ice Skating and The Age of Television Arrives

Tulsa had a magnificent old building called The Coliseum, owned by a long time promoter in Tulsa named Sam Avey. It was located just on the edge of the downtown area. The Coliseum was where the Tulsa Ice Oilers played hockey and where public ice skating sessions were held. It was also the location of Saturday Night Wrestling, a very popular event, as well as concerts and other events.

My dad first introduced me to skating. He was a pretty good skater, having been one of a group of kids who skated a lot during his high school days, since the Coliseum was only two blocks away from Central High School where Dad went to school. This group was called the Rink Rats. Many of these guys ended up playing hockey for the Tulsa Ice Oilers, but Dad did not. He preferred figure skating to hockey so was more at home on figure skates (with the notches on the front of the blades).

My best friend, Kenny, and I started skating together a lot. His older brother, Bill, and his good friend, Duffy (whose dad was also an Ice Oiler) were frequent skaters as well, so Kenny and I could hitch a ride with them when they went to the Coliseum. Bill had a really neat, black '46 Ford Coupe. The interesting thing about these trips is that Bill and Duffy would ignore or forget the fact that these two little stowaways were in the back seat and they carried on these conversations, usually about girls, which we found both educational and fascinating. They commiserated about the likelihood of being successful with certain girls and gave blow-by-blow accounts of dates and their level of success. Kenny and I would just sit quietly and soak all this up.

Those skating sessions were great fun, and we made friends with a whole range of people who were regulars at the Coliseum. Then a major tragedy occurred.

In early 1950 or 1951 the Coliseum caught fire and burned to the ground. It was a major blaze, to say the least. The unusual thing about the whole occurrence was the fact that KOTV, the first television station in Tulsa, had only been on the air a few months. Their studios were located about two blocks from the Coliseum and there was little between them, except for parking lots. The fire broke out one evening, and KOTV took a camera out the back door of the studio and got as close as they could to the fire. Of course, in those days there was very little in the way of remote broadcasts—there were no satellite uplinks or even video taping. Most programming was either originated in the studio or was filmed. In order to cover remote news or events, KOTV film crews went out in their remote van, which was a converted bread delivery truck. To cover the Coliseum fire, one of the KOTV cameras remained connected to the studio by the longest cable they could find, so that they could beam live pictures. In so doing, they succeeded in being the first station to ever air a live broadcast of a major disaster. It made television history and national news.

Kenny's life and mine were severely impacted by this occurrence, since we were avid skaters and hockey players. Sometimes the ice officials would let us on the ice a little early or let us stay a little later, after the public was off, to practice hockey--stick handling and shooting the puck around a little. This was strictly forbidden during public skating sessions, of course. We would play a little one-on-one or sometimes two-on-two if others joined us.

The other impact of the fire was that the Tulsa Ice Oilers lost their home ice. Amazingly, they continued to play in the league, but their home ice was then located in Memphis. Go figure.

I shifted my skating loyalty and activity to roller skating and started going regularly to the Arena Roller Rink, a fairly new facility only a few blocks from where the Coliseum had been. Kenny tried roller skating for a while, but was only lukewarm about it. However, he kept up some interest when it was discovered that there seemed to be a larger contingency of pretty girls who came to the roller rink than went ice skating. Many of them wore those cute, short skating skirts. Obviously, girls don't like to be cold, and falling on the ice in a short skirt can send a shock through your system.

93

* * * * *

KOTV's entrance onto the Tulsa media scene on November 30, 1949, was greeted with a high degree of skepticism by many. My dad was thoroughly intrigued, however. And we were one of the first families in town to have a television receiver. It was in a blonde, console cabinet which was fairly good sized. However, the screen was about as big as a postage stamp and had a definite greeny yellow caste to it. The brand was a Hoffman.

I'd ask some of friends if they had a TV yet. Most would say something like: "No. My father wants to wait for a couple of months until they have color." The first color shows did not start appearing on NBC for about another ten years, and even then it was usually no more than one or two shows a night.

Actually, KOTV was first on the air on October 15, 1949. But all that was shown was the test pattern, which was an oversized gunsight-looking pattern with the KOTV logo in the center. They showed nothing but test pattern for six weeks before programming started. But those of us with TV's would turn on the test pattern and just stare at it in amazement. The music which played behind the test pattern was a beautiful theme which I can still hear in the back of my mind.

The problem was that as soon as programming started up and word got out that we had a TV, people started coming out of the woodwork. Kids that would hardly speak to me before, suddenly became great "friends", seeking out my company and just dropping by to see me in the evenings, when television was on.

In the early days of Channel 6 (KOTV), they were only on the air about two to four hours a night—no daytime programming for a year or two after they went on the air. About half their programming was directed toward children—not because they were so interested in reaching children, but because this was the easiest and cheapest programming to produce. It required little scripting, no change in sets and no real rehearsals. The format was generally a host, a puppet or two and group of kids in the studio. Various skits were performed or dialogue carried on between the host and the puppets. In many regards they were quite clever and featured the early creative talents of geniuses like Bob Clampett.

Most popular of the shows was, of course, Howdy Doody, featuring Buffalo Bob as the host. (A little know fact is that the marionette Howdy Doody was actually designed and created by the wife of the guy who is credited with founding and developing Palm Springs, California.) The

94

show had a variety of characters, including Clarabelle (a cartoonish cow) and Princess Summerfall Winterspring. All were strung marionettes, except Buffalo Bob, of course.

Hand puppets were used on two very popular shows: Time for Beany and Kukla, Fran and Ollie. Beany was a Bob Clampett creation and featured Cecil the Seasick Sea Serpent, the Captain and other characters. On Kukla, Fran and Ollie, created by Burr Tilstrom, Fran was the human who stood directly in front of the puppet stage, sort of like the old Punch and Judy type shows. Kukla was a little round-headed puppet and Ollie was an alligator puppet. The genius in the design of Ollie was in the fact that when something outrageous, funny or incredible was said by Kukla, Fran or any of the other characters, Ollie would turn and look directly into the camera and you would swear he changed expressions. He said not a word in these takes. The same, inflexible face seemed to portray a whole range of emotions, from disgust to frustration to delight to many others. The same approach in human form was used effectively a few years later by William Bendix in his series, "The Life of Riley". My favorite supporting character on Kukla, Fran and Ollie was Cecil Bill (which they pronounced "Sessle Bill"), who spoke his own language, totally unintelligible by anyone except those on the show. But the vocal expressions in the language were hilarious.

One of the shows attempted to take advantage of the interactivity which some of the radio shows had been successful at doing. The show was Winky Dink. Kids could write into the Winky Dink show and receive in the mail a sheet of clear plastic which would stick to your television screen. Also included were special crayons to use on the plastic, which easily wiped off. Then, at the end of the show, they would flash a series of lines, which seemed to be random lines and shapes, onto the screen, one after another. The viewer would then trace each line or shape in succession. When they were completed, those viewers with the special plastic who could accumulate all the lines ended up with a picture which conveyed the message from Winky Dink. It was like using your secret decoder ring with the radio programs.

The early shows which were not as kid-oriented included westerns such as The Lone Ranger, Hopalong Cassidy and Kit Carson and some musical or variety shows like Ted Mack's Original Amateur Hour, Freddy Martin, Toast of the Town and Fred Waring and The Pennsylvanians. There were also mystery and dramatic shows like Fireside Theater, Playhouse of the Stars, Crime Syndicated, Mr. District Attorney, Boston Blackie and Martin Kane, Private Eye. There was also a show called "Mr. Keene,

95

Tracer of Lost Persons" which my dad referred to as "Mr. Trace, Keener than Most Persons". Game shows and variety shows started to break in during the early years as well which created a new kind of star—the television personality or host, who was not an actor, not a comedian, not a singer—he or she just hosted a TV show. These included Faye Emerson, Arthur Godfrey, Ken Murray, Garry Moore, Jerry Lester and a couple of converted movie stars, Don Ameche and Robert Montgomery. The early game shows included Charades and You Bet Your Life (the show on which Johnny Carson got his start), followed in a few years by What's My Line and I've Got a Secret.

Local TV personalities also developed in the early days. Some were extensions of news and weather announcers, while others were simply pleasant or engaging people with a gift of gab. One of these was a delightful lady named Betty Boyd who says, to this day, that she does not understand why Channel 6 gave her her own TV program. As she says: "I had no experience and I had no talent." Yet, over the next three decades she became known as Tulsa's First Lady of Television.

(In my adult years I had the great pleasure of working with Betty Boyd on community projects and the University of Tulsa Alumni Association, and I am convinced that she could have been elected to any city office she desired. No one would have dared run against her and risk the humiliation of getting no votes A more endearing and delightful person you could not imagine..)

The only religious program on TV by 1951was Frontiers of Faith which was aired for thirty minutes at noon on Sunday. It was followed by the only soap opera, One Man's Family, although the soap operas continued to thrive on radio. Of course, both of these genres dominate several channels in today's lineup of programming.

These programs just cited were all network programming, coming in from CBS. There were a few local programs as well, such as "Lookin' at Cookin'" hosted by home economists from Oklahoma Natural Gas Company, "Woman's Page" and "Drawing for Fun" (later known as "Time for Richut"), hosted by Richard Ruhl ("Richut"), a former Walt Disney animator.

In the first couple of months when KOTV was on the air, only one other kid in school had a TV, to my knowledge. That was my good friend Donna. We would love to go to school and carry on conversations like: "Did you see Beany and Cecil last night?" "Yeah. Wasn't it funny when Cecil hit Beany over the head with that big hamburger?" We would make sure there were plenty of other kids within earshot of these conversations and took delight in the envy on their faces.

Nearly every night our living room was filled with all sorts of people, many of whom we didn't even know. In those days, it was thought that all the lights in the TV watching room should be turned out. So we sat there in the dark with assorted friends, neighbors, delivery people and even our mailman, who suddenly took to delivering our mail at about 7:00 in the evening instead of early afternoon, which had been his practice for years. If I had been smart, I would have charged a nominal admission price and sold popcorn. It probably would have been even a more lucrative undertaking than my sporadic comic book sale.

It wasn't long before my mother really tired of this. My dad had his retreat—he'd go out to the hobby room to work on his trains. He would frequently retire to the hobby room and say: "I'll be in my Sanctum Sanctorum". I looked this up in the dictionary and discovered that it meant "One's own private place." Very apropos.

Chapter Twenty Seven
Tricks, with or without Treats

Halloween in our neighborhood was a lot of fun. Starting at about this age and going through about age 14, Halloween consisted of two phases. The first phase was the traditional house-to-house trick or treating. We would sometimes take some of the little kids in the neighborhood. But we realized that the early part of the evening was for them.

Then the second part of the evening we tended to gather with friends and roam the neighborhood like some sort of wannabe gang. We generally didn't do anything destructive, vandalistic or even mean. The worst we would do would be to toilet paper a house, and that was always a house of a friend. If we ran out of ideas, then we would start trick-or-treating again, as a group.

About a block from my house, a couple of doors down from Jimmy's house, lived an old lady who really got into Halloween. She decorated her house and then she made the most delicious popcorn balls imaginable. But there was a price to pay. When you went to her house to trick or treat, she would greet you at the door. You would hold out your bag for one of those popcorn balls. But instead, she would invite you inside. Once inside, she would inspect your costume and then invite you to sit down in her living room. At this point she would give every child in the living room a cup and saucer and proceed to pour hot chocolate, asking each child if he wanted marshmallows in his or not.

Now the hot chocolate was delicious, but the time it took to sit there and take part in this ersatz tea party was precious. We were usually there a good twenty minutes at which time other kids would arrive and be ushered in. Do you know how many houses you can hit in twenty minutes? I could fill a pillow case half full of all manner of goodies in that amount of time. Finally, when we could see an opportunity to take our leave we would. But you couldn't do it until you got one of those precious popcorn balls, and those came at the end of the visit, when she was good and ready. It signified the fact that the party was over and you were free to go, and we all knew that.

* * * * *

Some of our more notorious tricks were not tied to Halloween. Jerry had a great sense of humor—very impish and somewhat on the mischievous side. He loved practical jokes. The family with Rory and Diana still lived in the other side of our duplex when Jerry's family moved in. He disliked Mimi from that family as much as I did. She was a most disagreeable old lady and seemed to yell at us for no reason when we were playing outdoors.

One day when Jerry and I were rummaging around in his garage, we discovered an old minnow bucket which belonged to the people on the other side of his duplex (in 1117—they shared the garage with 1119, Jerry's). We opened up the lid and were immediately knocked back by the odor. Floating in a couple of inches of water were probably a couple of dozen dead minnows. They had decomposed and fused into a sort of jellied mass. The smell was horrific. I said: "Close that up and leave it alone. Let's get out of here." But Jerry said: "No, wait. I have an idea." Uh oh. I knew this meant trouble for someone which could likely end up being trouble for us.

"Which bedroom window is Mimi's?" he asked. I had been in their house on a few occasions so I said I thought it was the corner one and that her bed was right next to the window. Jerry said: "Meet me here after dinner tonight." So, right after dark, about 8 or 8:30, Jerry and I rendezvoused in the garage. He took the minnow bucket and we crept toward Mimi's window. Jerry went over to a bush and broke off a couple of twigs. We then got up to the window and Jerry opened the bucket. Whoa! The smell was even worse than before. He dipped the stick into the decomposed mass, picked up a glob of it and started smearing it on the sill of Mimi's window. "Help me spread this.", he said. I reluctantly stuck a twig in and globbed some more in place.

When we had exhausted the supply of window sill treatment, Jerry poured the water out in the grass just under the window. We then took the minnow bucket back to the garage, put it back in place and went home. It was still warm enough that everyone slept with their windows open. Jerry assumed that our contribution would not necessarily lead to a totally pleasant night's sleep for Mimi. We never found out, since nothing was ever said or ever discussed about it in our presence.

* * * * *

Halloween in Tulsa was on the cusp of the seasons. Some Halloweens were quite warm and some were miserably cold. But the real winters didn't hit until January. That's when we would get whatever snow might come for the season and those ice storms might come and cripple the city.

Snow never lasted more than a few days, but while it was there it was wonderful. One of the things we would sometimes do was to climb onto the roof of Brown's Market and throw snowballs at the cars and trucks going up and down Eleventh Street. It was a perfect vantage point. Of course, we could only do it when the grocery store was closed. Mister Brown could hear us up on the roof when they were open and would come out and run us off. So, we would go up there at night or on Sundays.

One Sunday afternoon we were up there engaged in our target practice at the vehicles. Being Route 66, there was never a shortage of trucks to fire at. This particular day, the temperature had risen and the snow was melting fast. It was really a pleasant day and the snow had become slushy. Some of our snowballs were more like ice balls. They would really fly and make a loud noise when they hit the side of a lot of the trucks.

Kenny was with us this particular day. He took aim at a truck which was coming up Eleventh Street. The truck driver had his window down, since the temperature was fairly warm. He was smoking a cigar which was down to about a three inch stub. Kenny let fly with one of his fast balls and the missile went straight through the open window, hitting the truck driver right in the cigar.

After his first shock of being hit, the truck driver looked up to his left immediately and spotted us on top of the building. He screeched to a halt and came down out of the cab of the truck on the run. This guy was not just mad, he was boiling. We could see the smashed cigar still clinched in his teeth. He came steaming across Eleventh Street without regard for the traffic. A car had to swerve to keep from hitting him, and went up on the curb.

We jumped down off the roof and took off running. Of course, there was still snow on the ground so our trail was not difficult to follow. We ran through the yards toward my house, but I knew we couldn't run into the house. Not only would we be caught, but I'd end up with a confrontation between the victim and my mother and me in the middle. I didn't see how I could win, no matter which way it went.

We back-tracked a little bit, went toward the back of the Hummel House, jumped down a three-foot terrace and into the parking lot for the Tastee Freeze. Unlike Dairy Queen, Tastee Freeze had no inside seating area for the public. They only had walk-up windows. No place to hide there.

Next to the Tastee Freeze was the Laundromat. Kenny worked there part time, so we ducked inside and went behind the counter. He greeted his boss and said he had left something in the back room. So, the three of us went to the back where they stored the laundry detergent, bleach, etc. We picked a good vantage point where we could not be seen but could see the front of the Laundromat. The front of the building was all glass with the door at the corner.

In a few minutes, we saw the truck driver, cigar stub still sticking out of the corner of his mouth, running past the front of the Laundromat. He stopped at the corner, looked up and down the street, then turned around and came inside the Laundromat. Several people were inside, just working and not paying any attention to him. He looked around a bit then walked out.

We waited another ten minutes or so and then went out the side door. We walked to the front of the building and peeked around the corner back up Eleventh Street toward where the truck driver left his rig, still running. By then, he was back at his truck but he had been joined by a police car. He was wildly gesturing, pointing to the roof of Brown's Market and apparently trying to explain why he just stopped his truck in the middle of Eleventh Street and run off.

The policeman looked like he believed the driver but wasn't very happy about it. In a few minutes the truck driver climbed up into the cab and drove off. The police car, on the other hand, turned and went up my street. We suspected he would come around the block and end up at the Laundromat. So, we went back, past the Tastee Freeze and ended up at my house.

When we went into the house, I casually said to my mother: "If the police come to the door, just don't answer it." She said: "WHAT?" "Oh, never mind." I replied.

* * * * *

While living a few yards off of Route 66 presented some interesting opportunities and incidents, it also was a cause of a certain amount of consternation, at least in one case. One year the top news story in the country, creating daily headlines as well as the lead story on radio news, concerned the exploits of a young serial killer named Charles Starkweather and his girl friend, Caryl Fugate. They were on a killing rampage in the Midwest, murdering people they didn't even know, stuffing bodies down wells and all sorts of macabre stuff. They seemed to be working their way Southwest and Route 66 was the obvious avenue for them, since they started somewhere like Illinois or Indiana.

It seemed that just about everyone in Tulsa was terrified. I had visions of these two bloodthirsty killers hitchhiking down Route 66, killing their most recent driver just as they get to Tulsa and picking my house, out of the thousands available, to climb through my bedroom window and murder me in my bed.

It seemed like years before they finally caught up with these two—it was actually no more than a week or two—and there were many nights during this time that I had a hard time falling to sleep.

Chapter Twenty Eight
Entering the Big Time

At the first of this particular school year, my parents decided to take me over to The University of Tulsa to audition for the Tulsa Boy Singers. This was a fairly prominent and prestigious group of about forty boys from all over the city. They rehearsed twice a week—Tuesday afternoons and Saturday mornings— and it was directed by Dr. George Oscar Bowen, head of vocal music at TU.

Out of several hundred auditioners, I was one of the ones chosen to fill the few vacancies in the group, so I started into this regimen of twice-weekly rehearsals. Dr. Bowen was a knowledgeable guy and a good director and knew how to get the most out of a group of young boys with varying vocal timbres and capabilities.

Often when we would show up for rehearsal, if we were early, the rehearsal hall would be locked so we would have impromptu touch football games on the TU campus. These started when one of the guys had a miniature football—about five inches long. So we started tossing it around and running pass patterns. When a small football is thrown, if it is gripped hard, like a full sized football, it often flies in a very erratic fashion, sometimes going end over end or flopping all over the place. However, one of the boys, who showed no interest in playing, happened to pick up the ball when it landed at his feet and he threw it back. The ball flew in a perfect and beautiful spiral. This is probably the first time this guy had ever done anything in the athletic area which approached a favorable outcome. He was undoubtedly the last one ever chosen to be on any team. To say he threw this ball with a limp wrist would be a major understatement. He not only threw like a girl, he threw like a sissy girl with a sprained arm. But his soft touch with the ball, coupled with the limp-wristed release resulted in a beautiful flying ball. So, we had him throw passes to us in a makeshift game. This guy's face just beamed in these games. Suddenly he was a super jock.

My parents were proud of my acceptance into the Boy Singers, so they could be counted on to be at every concert. At the first concert, I was simply one of the forty voices. I was in the soprano section. However, as we were preparing for my first Christmas concert in the group, they auditioned some of us for solos. Dr. Bowen's wife, Dorothy, had written an obligato solo (a counter-melody) to Silent Night. It was beautiful. I was selected to sing this solo. It probably should have been sung by a female as the counter-melody soared above the main part of the carol in a hauntingly lyrical manner. I didn't care. I loved singing that solo and I can remember it, note for note, to this day. Of course, my parents loved it when their baby boy was featured like this. Dr. Bowen included soprano solos in most of the future concerts, and I was designated as the soloist in nearly all these cases. This continued for a couple of years until my voice started to change—the curse of all boys who excel in the soprano range. Only Wayne Newton seems to have successfully pulled off this transition.

Occasionally we would have a concert out of town. In fact, we were a featured group at the national convention of the teachers of vocal music which was held in St. Louis one year. The only other vocal group featured was the world renowned Vienna Boy Choir. Pretty good billing to share, we thought.

On these out of town trips, we generally went by chartered bus. Being a musical group, there was a lot of music on the bus. One of the boys had a ukulele, another had a banjo and one brought a tenor guitar. I was fascinated. I especially liked the ukulele and was delighted when the owner would let me plunk around on it when he wasn't playing it. It fit my small hand just right and I wished I could play it properly.

Imagine my delight and surprise when, upon my return and my relating of my experience with the ukulele, I was informed by my mother that she used to play the ukulele a lot as a younger girl. My mother can play the ukulele?? She might as well have said: "Yes, I used to fly to the moon a lot as a young girl."

Within a week we had purchased a ukulele and my mother had shown me not only the main chords—majors, minors and sevenths in virtually every key—but had taught me the chord progressions on several songs, including "Bye, Bye Blackbird", "Moonlight Bay", "Five Feet Two" and several others. There's no stopping me now, I thought.

Chapter Twenty Nine
"I Can Yo-yo, Can You?"

Every few months a sign would be posted in the five and ten cent stores around the city advertising a date and time when a professional from the Duncan Yo-Yo company would be at that location giving demonstrations, carving names in yo-yos and officiating over contests. I had started working with the yo-yo and had become relatively proficient at it.

I made a note of the date and time when the guy would be at the store in my neighborhood, a TG&Y store. I was there, along with about 20 or 25 kids. We stood there in awe as this little Filipino put yo-yos through their paces, doing all kinds of single yo-yo tricks, then dual yo-yo stunts. He did some amazing things, making the yo-yos do everything but talk.

At the end of the demonstration, he began selling Duncan yo-yos and would carve a little scene on one side along with the buyer's name. The scene was generally a beach with a palm tree and a bird.

After that, he would hold a contest where any who wanted to enter could participate. I entered, along with about ten or twelve others, mostly boys. When the dust cleared, I was the winner. I won a cloth patch which could be sewn on a jacket or sweater. I also won another, new yo-yo and the opportunity to participate in the city championship, competing with all the other winners from around the city from similar contests.

The Duncan Yo-Yo people were big on embroidered patches to go on shirts, sweaters or jackets. You got a patch just for entering the contest. It said "I can yo-yo, can you?". Then the first three finishers in the contest got patches and you got a patch for learning certain tricks. These were sort of like earning merit badges as a scout except that every one of them said Duncan Yo-Yo on it somewhere. The Duncan people obviously had as their goal that every child in America would be wearing a patch advertising their products on every shirt or sweater they owned. I think Calvin Klein, Ralph Lauren and Tommy Hilfiger must have been yo-yo contestants in their youth and were struck by the possibility of having your customers actually advertise your product for you on their clothing.

The city championship was about a week away and was to be held at the Will Rogers Theater, which was the closest theater to my house, and only about a half-mile away. It was on their stage and was held on a Saturday morning. I showed up, went through the contest and won again. I was in a daze. It never struck me that I was the City Champion. It had come so easy. The competition was pretty lame, except for one or two, and I had lucked out in beating them. This time I won a sweater, a larger patch, another yo-yo and the right to participate in the Oklahoma State Championship.

The State Championship was to be held the following Saturday. Coincidentally and luckily, it was also to be held at the Will Rogers Theater, since it had a nice stage. I showed up and the place was packed. There were contestants from all over the state, and each had brought family members, friends, etc.

Being the city yo-yo champion in Tulsa didn't even rate a mention in the newspaper. But it seemed to be pretty big deal to some of the kids from Bug Tussle or Gotebo.

Many of the contestants were standing around down by the stage, warming up. Some of them were good—I mean REALLY good. They were doing loop-the-loops with two yo-yos at once. They were twirling yo-yos around their head. They were catching the yo-yos on the strings and bouncing them. A bunch of stuff which I could not even approach being able to do. I was intimidated, to say the least, before we even got on the stage.

These contests were very simple and straight forward. They were sort of like spelling bees. All contestants started with the simplest of ten tricks. Anyone who failed to execute the first trick was out. Then they went to the second trick, which was a little bit harder. All who failed were out. Then the tricks progressed through the next eight until a total of ten tricks had been executed. The hardest of the group was Rocking the Baby. The other tricks included Around the World, Over the Falls, Walking the Dog and others.

These preliminary tricks were used to weed out the beginners or novices. Then when all ten tricks were completed, those who were left began doing loop-the-loops. This is a trick where the yo-yo is thrown straight out and then brought back, but instead of catching it, you flip your wrist and throw it out front again. This means the yo-yo is in constant motion in a series of ovals—

out and back and out and back, etc. Thus the loops.

In the state contest, there were about twenty contestants. At the end of the first phase, 10-trick segment, about 8 of us remained. The professional asked if we were all ready to start the loop-the-loop segment. This is the opposite of sudden death. The last one standing or continuing to do uninterrupted loop-the-loops is the winner. Let me hasten to add that I was not good at loop-the-loops. Mine tended to be sloppy, wobbly and always on the edge of not making the turn or staying in the loop. I had to work them hard. Some of these good yo-yoers did loop-the-loops almost effortlessly. The yo-yo would fly out straight, make a clean loop and return cleanly only to make the close turn cleanly for the next outward trip. I just knew I was outclassed now.

Everyone nodded indicating we were ready to start. The pro signaled the start and we all began our series of loop-the-loops. True to form, mine were some of the ugliest in the group. However, I kept it going. After about only ten or twelve loop-the-loops, a couple of the guys faltered and lost it. They were out. The other six of us kept going. The audience was counting since all of us were going at the same pace. When we got to about 25, another messed up and he was out.

This left five of us. Before we got to 50, the next guy faltered and he was out. This left only the four of us. The other three were very good. They looked like they could keep this up for days. I was having to struggle with nearly every loop to keep my yo-yo in the air. The other guys were standing up straight with their elbows comfortably at their sides. I was dipping my body and raising my arm with nearly every loop, just trying to coax my yo-yo to keep going.

Then something extraordinary happened. Just like in an auto race, two of the participants came together on the far turn. One of the finalists was left handed. He was standing fairly close to one of the others who was right handed. One of them moved a little too much and their yo-yos came together on an outward loop. The yo-yos crashed together and both fell to the ground. The result was disastrous and both were out.

This left only me and one other contestant. The entire theater was counting—"one-twenty-one, one-twenty-two, one-twenty-three" they would shout. I was having no easier time of it, but I was determined to keep going, no matter how ugly my loops were compared to this guy next to me. We got up to one fifty, then one seventy five. As we were approaching two hundred, something totally unheard of happened. I had never seen this in a contest. As my opponent flicked his wrist to return the yo-yo out on the next loop, the yo-yo went out and then just kept going. It flew out into the audience! His string had broken! There was a tremendous groan from the audience. Everyone

107

knew he was the better player. But, that's the luck of the game. As my dad used to say, "I'd rather be lucky than good anytime."

The bottom line was that I was the State Champion! I won another sweater, an even larger patch, which filled the entire front of the sweater, and best of all, a new bicycle. It was a beautiful, metallic green 4-speed. Bicycles with gears were relatively new on the market. My trusty Schwinn Black Phantom was a fat-tire, 26-inch bicycle with only one speed and coaster brakes. My newly won 4-speed had hand brakes and small format tires. It was beautiful. After the photo session and a quick newspaper interview, I took my new bicycle home to show my mom.

Mom knew I was going to be in a yo-yo contest that day. She thought that if I was lucky I would win another patch. When I rode up to the house and stopped on the driveway I started yelling for Mom. She came out on the back porch and I said: "Well, I won. I'm the State Champion and this is my bicycle to prove it." She refused to believe it. She was sure that they had simply let me ride the bicycle—to borrow it-- but that I hadn't really won it. A few minutes later, a couple of my friends who had been there and seen me win rode up and confirmed that I was, indeed, the winner.

One of the fallouts of this win came a couple of days later when I decided to sell my prized Schwinn Black Phantom. It was like selling a member of the family. "Here... wouldn't you rather buy my baby brother? He's not as useful as my Schwinn!"

My friend David had moved in across the street from Kenny. When I rode my new bicycle over there to show it off, David's mother asked me if I would be interested in selling my Schwinn. She would like to buy it for David. Reluctantly, I agreed. We arrived at a price of twenty five dollars. (They cost about $80, new at that time.) Suddenly all my pangs of reluctance disappeared. Twenty five bucks!

I delivered the bike and she gave me the $25. I took the money down to the drug store and asked them to convert the two tens and a five into twenty five one dollar bills. I stuffed my new wad into my pocket. I never felt as wealthy in my life—before or since.

The next step in the yo-yo contest chain was the nationals. This event was to be held in St. Louis. However, each contestant was responsible for getting there and covering his own expenses while there. My parents didn't exhibit a high degree of interest in supporting this effort and I didn't really press for it. I didn't harbor any great illusions of being able to compete on that level. I had been inordinately lucky to this point. It was not likely that this luck could hold out, so I elected to bypass the national.

Chapter Thirty

Strike Three, You're Out

As the fifth grade school year was drawing to an end, we started preparing for the upcoming baseball season. A very minor change had been instigated in the regulations but it made a huge difference to me. Up until this time, the cutoff date for age to play in each league was October 1. If you were born before October 1, you played with those who were in your grade or possibly one grade ahead of you. My birthday is in August, so I was one of the younger ones on the team. This put me on the team with top players like Kenny and Billy and some of the others who I felt were almost ready for the majors.

When you are in college, a year or two either way doesn't make much difference. A junior is likely to play just as well as a senior in almost any sport. However, during those pre-adolescent developing years, a year can be like a decade. There is a big difference between the ability of a ten-year old and that of an eleven or twelve-year old. That's why the cutoff age between Cub Scouts and Boy Scouts is eleven. I was simply outclassed by most of my peers in coordination and ability.

This particular year, they changed the cutoff day to August 1. That meant I was under the wire by four days to play with guys my own age or slightly younger. Suddenly I had the opportunity to become a big frog in a little pond!

A friend of mine, named Gary, fell into the same age category. He was a catcher. I was a pitcher. So we started practicing together with the goal of dominating the league with our awesome skills. No batter or runner

109

would be immune from our fearsome arsenal of methodologies designed to ensure that they were retired from the inning by any avenue other than crossing home plate. Gary's dad volunteered to coach our team. So while my old teammates proceeded up the ladder, I joined the Franklin Cardinals for my one outstanding season as a baseball player.

Sure enough, Gary and I did well. Instead of striking out against pitchers who were older than me and threw fastballs as fast as my personal idol, Bob ("Rapid Robert") Feller of the Cleveland Indians (whose fastball was clocked at 105 miles per hour!), I was hitting the ball often. My batting average was up around .400. Gary's was even higher. My only nemesis was a pitcher who was a grade behind me and pitched for a team out of Jon Ross school in East Tulsa—the Ross Oilers. His name was David and he was awesome. When we played against them, I could just about count on going zero for four.

The Cardinals did well that season. We won our league, but did not place very high in the city championships. However, I made the All-Star team—something I never envisioned would happen to me. The All-Star game consisted of a game between the best players from all the teams in the city in our age group against the City Championship team. And which team won the championship? You guessed it—the Ross Oilers. This meant I would face David in the all star game. My visions of being the hero at the plate in this game were starting to go up in smoke. Of course I was intimidated. This kid was intimidatingly good.

The date of the All-Star game approached and I started trying to psyche myself up. I was slated to play second base instead of pitch, which was fine with me. I might be brought in as a relief pitcher, if needed. Gary and I decided to forego our pitching practice and practice only on batting. We went to the batting range. I even asked Kenny to pitch to me in batting practice. I felt I was about as well prepared as I could be.

When my first at-bat came in the game, I stepped up to the plate, ready to knock the ball back down David's throat. But when he threw that first, blistering fast ball past me, I caved. My arms turned to jelly. The only way I could swing was wildly. I ended up starting my swings before he had released the ball. I just hoped that he could hit my bat, not that my bat could hit the ball. It didn't work. I struck out in three pitches.

My next time at bat, the same thing happened. Then, when my next turn came up we had a man on third base. Our first opportunity to score a run. The coach called for a squeeze play, which meant he wanted me to bunt. I was elated. Bunting was my strongest talent at the plate. As his first pitch, David delivered one of his patented fast balls which he used to intimidate the batter right off. I squared around to bunt and laid down the prettiest bunt you've ever seen, right down the third base line.

Our runner was prepared, having taken a big lead, and was streaking toward home. David was off the mound in a flash, scooped up my bunt and flicked it to his catcher who tagged our man out at the plate. While it was a big disappointment to the team, I was filled with mixed emotions. I was on base, having successfully hit against the legendary David. Never mind that I got on by a fielder's choice. As far as I was concerned it was a hit.

In later years, David and I crossed paths several times and became friends. I recounted to him that game and told him how satisfying it was to get a hit off him (but didn't remind him that it was a bunt).

* * * * *

At the end of that season, my former team, who had also done well, winning their league, organized a trip to St. Louis to watch the Cardinals play and to have some fun for about three days. My old coach asked me if I would like to join them, and I jumped at the chance.

The St. Louis trip was taken by train and we stayed in a large, old downtown hotel, the Muehlbach. There was a beer by the same name at that time. I assumed the family had been responsible for both, just as the Busch family's name was also all over St. Louis.

While staying at that hotel, I was introduced to the strangest stunt I had ever seen. One day I walked into one of the hotel rooms down the hall where I had seen some of my teammates go in. There, bent over the bed, with his pants pulled down and his bare bottom showing, was this kid named Don, a great catcher. I whispered to a friend: "What's going on?" He replied: "They're lighting farts." "What??!", I said, thinking I didn't hear him correctly. "Watch.", he said.

At that point, one of the kids said to Don: "Are you ready?"

"Yeah!", Don said.

"OK. Fire away!" At which point the kid struck a match and held it very close to Don's rear end.

Don then broke wind, letting loose with a major league fart. As the gas (which is almost pure methane, I later found out) reached the flame of the match, it ignited and spurted rearward like a miniature flame thrower. The room immediately burst into applause, hoots and laughter. I just stood there gaping. I didn't believe what I just saw, but didn't have the nerve to ask him to do it again.

111

* * * * *

In addition to the baseball games, in which we saw many of the greats play, we went to Forest Park Highlands zoo and amusement park for a day and had a great time and then we went on the S.S. Admiral, a large sternwheeler boat which cruised the Mississippi River. On the Admiral was a dance floor on the upper deck with recorded music being played. But also on board was a bevy of the prettiest girls one could imagine. I was impressed that our coach could arrange for this for the team (but of course he had nothing to do with it). The other guys went crazy. There were some really pretty and nice girls on board and it didn't take long for guys like Kenny to partner up with somebody for an evening of great fun. I was very shy in that regard, and tended to hold back, watching everyone have a great time. I spent the evening singling out one girl then another and rehearsing my approach line. I'd spy a likely candidate and stalk her, going over and over my approach until I had it down cold. Then, somebody else would come up and ask her to dance. So I'd pick out another. For some reason, I'd create a totally new approach for each one, which seemed to consume a lot of time. By the time everything had come together--I finally had the best one yet picked out and my monologue perfected and she was standing alone and I had worked up enough nerve to approach her--I felt the boat lurch. We were docking back at the starting point. We had been out for four hours and the cruise was over. Struck out again.

The train rides up to and back from St. Louis were almost as much fun as being there, as far as I was concerned. Several of us would stand on the platform between the cars with our heads hanging out, watching the countryside and smelling the smoke from the engine.

We would go into the dining car and get a snack or something to drink. The food was horrible, but we didn't really care.

* * * * *

When we returned to Tulsa, the little league season was over, of course, but the professionals were still playing, even as school started. I was a big Tulsa Oiler fan and would go to most of the games. They had a section called the Knot Hole Section which consisted of bleachers over the left field fence. It only cost a dime to get in. But I hated sitting there. In the first place, you were quite a ways away from the action. In the second place, you missed the thrill of the crowd and being part of the main body of spectators. The only good thing about being in the Knot Hole Section was that occasionally

112

a home run would be hit into those stands. Or, at the end of the game, the left fielder might throw a ball up to the kids in that section.

My favorite place to sit was above the home team's dugout along the first base line. It was expensive, for my budget. However, my friend Billy's next door neighbor was a ticket taker at the games. We could go to the game and he would let us slide under the turnstile and get in free.

The Oilers' number one fan was named Andy Anderson. Sometime during the last half of the game, depending on when the Oilers might be behind and needed a rally, he would let loose with his yell, which was not only famous, but became the promotional slogan for the team for years. He would wait until just before the Oilers were coming up to bat again. The crowd is generally fairly quiet between innings. All of a sudden you could hear this voice start low and grow louder and louder in volume and higher and higher in pitch. As soon as they caught the sound of it, everyone would stop whatever they were doing. The place became deathly silent except for Andy's yell: "He-y-y-y-y-y-y-y-y-y-y-y-y-y!" (slight pause—probably for a breath) "Let's go-o-o-o-o-o-o-o-o, Tul-sa!" The whole place would erupt with a huge cheer.

He only did it once a night, no matter what. If the Oilers were ahead, he would sometimes do it during the 7th inning stretch or even later, sort of as an appreciation yell for the team rather than a rallying cry.

* * * * *

During those games I have to admit to a huge feeling of jealousy, envy or coveting—whatever you want to call it. One of my friends and classmates was the batboy for the Oilers. This was the greatest job in the world, as far as I was concerned. This meant that James got to wear an Oiler uniform with the number "0" on the back. He got to hang out in the dugout. While we are at bat, he got to be up near the on-deck circle, retrieve bats when the batters got on base, shag balls and all those neat things. Plus, he got to hang around with the players, talk to them, get them to sign his ball glove, get jerseys and balls from them and everything. He even played Pepper with some of them. How does one guy get so lucky? To just be around guys like Eddie Knoblauch, Johnny Temple, James Blackburn, Joe Adcock, Roy McMillan and a bunch of others, some of whom moved up to the Cincinnati Reds from the Tulsa Oilers and became major league stars, would have been worth any price to me. Even future home run king Roger Maris played for the Oilers for a short time before moving on to the Yankees and immortality.

113

* * * * *

When the Oilers were on the road, I listened to the games on the radio. I'd sometimes put the radio under the covers with me in bed and listen to Mack Creager or Hugh Finnerty as they gave the play-by-play of each exciting pitch in those games. I was astounded to learn a few years later that Mack did not travel with the team most of the time. He actually did the broadcast from a studio in Tulsa. As each action was relayed to him by ticker tape, he would convert it to an "eyewitness" account of the action. Whenever the ball was hit, he had a device on his desk which sounded like the bat striking a ball. They had recorded crowd noises which played in the background, along with a volume control whenever something exciting was taking place. It sounded like a live broadcast to me. Mack had considerable talent to pull that off, as far as I was concerned.

Because of the baseball games, I was exposed to my first helping of rhythm and blues. After the games were over, KOME radio (1300 on your AM dial) started the Frank Berry show. Frank Berry was a cousin of the legendary Chuck Berry, who became one of the pioneers of rock and roll and a huge influence on many artists who were to follow him.

Frank, who pronounced his last name "Bare-Ree", played some music and artists which I had never heard or heard of. He always played "my gal Dinah" as he called Dinah Washington. And he would play artists like Muddy Waters and B.B. King, some of the early groups like The Charms, and a bunch more. I was fascinated by this music and loved it. It was a mirror-image of the scene in Steve Martin's "The Jerk". (In that scene, Martin, who says "I was born a poor black child.", was being raised in a black family and considered himself "black". As he was going to bed one night, he was listening to the radio when a very "white" sounding band was playing a "ricky ticky" version of "Crazy Rhythm". As the music progressed, Martin's foot started tapping to the rhythm and pretty soon he was up dancing. "This music really speaks to me!" he said. Well, Frank Berry's music really spoke to me, even though I was not black.) Some of that music was absolutely fabulous. It was rhythmic and soulful (15 years before "soul" music was popular). It was not only well constructed, but very well played.

Chapter Thirty One
The Comet and It's Embarrassing

As sixth grade started we found ourselves in new surroundings. They had brought in several temporary buildings and set them up on the courtyard part of the schoolgrounds, due to the increased enrollment at Franklin Elementary. Our home room met in one of these annexes, which we called the "outhouse". No matter. We were the kings on the hill—the sixth graders. Keep the little babies out of our way.

Another big change came as I moved from Cub Scouts into Boy Scouts. I joined Troop 64 which met at Yale Avenue Presbyterian Church and had a great scoutmaster named Bob Wrench. We formed a new patrol in the troop, called the Cobra Patrol and I was elected Patrol Leader of this little band of newcomers.

Each scout troop has a Senior Patrol Leader. He is sort of the President of the Troop from the ranks of the members. Troop 64 had two Senior Patrol Leaders, Dale and Lyle. Lyle was a good looking, nice guy type. Dale was more of the solid, intellectual type, except that Dale had a motorbike. I had never seen one of these. It was not a motorcycle and not a motor scooter. It was literally a bicycle with a motor on it. It had no kick starter. You simply started pedaling it like a normal bicycle, popped the clutch and the motor would start and take over the work of motivating the vehicle. As I became closer to Dale, he started taking me home on the motorbike. It was great fun. I decided I wanted something that I didn't have to pedal, regardless

115

of how I loved my hard-won 4-speed from the yo-yo contest.

This first year in the Boy Scouts was spent just getting accustomed to the organization and working on earning various levels of rank and merit badges. The camping trips were great, but they were primarily learning exercises. Things really started getting interesting the second year in scouts.

My desire for a motorized vehicle was, of course, rebuffed soundly at home. However, Kenny's brother's friend, Duffy, whose parents were friends of my parents, had a small motor scooter which he was ready to sell. The little scooter had about a one and a half or two horsepower motor. It didn't have a clutch or gears, only a brake and a throttle. When the scooter was at a standstill, idling, it was still in gear, trying to go forward. However, it had such little power, it could easily be held in position with one foot on the ground, until the throttle was advanced.

This little motor scooter (the brand was a Comet) was just my size as far as I was concerned. It had a compartment about one foot square just behind the seat. I really wanted this. This was the equivalent of my Red Ryder B-B gun. Ralphie was continually admonished: "You'll shoot your eye out, kid." Of course, with a motor scooter, you could lose a lot more than your eye. But at age 11, this is not remotely close to being on your list of concerns. Duffy wanted fifty dollars for it. Way beyond my budget. My allowance was only up to $2.25 per week.

Duffy rode the scooter over to our house. I tried to stifle my drooling. My mother conceded that it was "cute" but her reservations about the safety aspects overrode the aesthetics. Dad was somewhat ambivalent.

My first job was to talk my parents into letting me have it. Then I'd worry about how to pay for it. I was begging as much as I could without appearing to be begging. I wasn't making any progress until a stroke of genius came over me like a wave. I blurted out: "It's just like riding a bicycle except you don't have to pedal."

"Well, maybe you're right." Mom said. Hallelujah! I'm going to win, I thought.

Yes! Yes! Yes! Then the realities of economics hit.

Dad said: "How much do you have in your savings, son?" What savings?, I thought. "Not enough" is all I could say. "Well I certainly don't have an extra fifty dollars right now to spend on something like this." Said Dad. Shot down again. I could see this beautiful machine slipping out of my grasp.

Then my mother came to my rescue. Turning to Dad she said: "Well, we've been saving dimes you know. I probably have at least fifty dollars

116

worth." I was still alive!

He shrugged in an approving manner as if to say "OK with me."

Mom went in the house and came out with ten rolls of dimes, held them out to Duffy and asked him if he would take those. He said he would, so the exchange was made. The Comet was mine! Dad took Duffy home in the car and I immediately started up the Comet for my first spin around the neighborhood.

Of course, it was totally illegal for me to ride the Comet on the streets. The law said you could get a license for a street-worthy vehicle with 5 horsepower or less if you were 14 years old. But, the vehicle had to meet certain safety standards regarding brakes, lights, etc. I'm not sure the Comet would have passed any of these. It was probably manufactured to run around inside a large plant, warehouse or industrial yard, and not to go on the street. So, of course it had no license tag.

Therefore, any time I rode the Comet on the street I had to keep a sharp eye out for police. If I spotted one in the distance, I would turn into the nearest driveway and pull around behind a house. I'm sure there was a number of startled people who looked out their windows to see this little motorized kid tooling around their yard. I was never stopped or ticketed in all the time I drove the Comet—about two years.

However, I was in one wreck, and it was a very scary close call. One Monday night after scout meeting, my baseball playing pal, Billy and I decided to go to the Dairy Queen on Eleventh Street before I took him home. After we enjoyed our treat, we were coming back down Eleventh. I was driving very carefully, hugging the curb and going about 20 to 25 MPH. A car in the right hand lane passed us and then abruptly turned right at the next corner, squeezing us between the car and the curb. We tipped over sideways and skidded along the concrete a few feet.

The passengers in the car heard the crash and stopped. A lady opened the passenger side door, looked back and said: "Are you alright?"

I was slightly hurt but not injured. The same for Billy. But my primary concern was to NOT call the police. So, all I could blurt out was: "No. We're OK." As they drove off, I was hoping that the Comet had put a big gash in the side of their car.

The only drawback to the Comet was that it was a pretty ugly color— sort of a cross between hospital green and olive drab. One of Dad's friends had an auto body and paint shop. Dad took it over to his shop and they painted it two-tone, metallic blue and silver. It was beautiful. I was

117

definitely the envy of all my friends.

* * * * *

I was generally a meticulously conscientious boy regarding laws, rules and instructions, the Comet being my only departure from this pattern. This attitude would create a certain degree of anxiety in me from time to time, such as when John was painting his license plate. On one occasion it created a very uncomfortable situation.

There was a strict rule which was put into place at Franklin regarding the bringing of candy and gum to school: NONE. In particular, there were certain types of substances which had become very popular with the kids, and these were singled out as especially undesirable because of their potential to create an unpleasant odor, unsightly blemish on walls, floors or furniture, odor, etc. These included bubble gum, powdered candies, sticky suckers and a new fad consisting of soaking toothpicks in cinnamon oil, which you bought from a pharmacist, and then sucking on the toothpick. A lot of the kids had little bottles of cinnamon oil with toothpicks in them which they carried around. Occasionally one of the bottles would spill or break and the smell was especially potent. Not only that, but if the carrier spilled the pure cinnamon oil on his skin, the area would immediately turn red from the burn.

One of the dry candies which was popular wasn't really a candy. It was called "Lik-M-Aid". It was a flavored sugar which could be eaten directly from the envelope it came in or could be poured into a glass with water and turned into a drink, like Kool-Aid.

The name came from the fact that what you could do is lick your finger, then put the wet finger into the substance and lick the powder off which stuck to your finger. A real hygienic little treat. I finally figured out why Lik-M-Aid tasted different every time you partook. It was dependent upon what had been on your fingers prior to sticking it in the powder.

I had an envelope of the banned Lik-M-Aid in my jacket pocket one day at school. I know—it was a risky thing to do. It was a Friday. The first class after lunch was Mr. McKinney's science class. We sat at tables with free-standing chairs, rather than the one-piece desk/chairs used in some of the classes. I kept my jacket on during class and was shifting my weight around in the uncomfortable chair. About half way through the class I looked down and saw a pile of this pink granulated substance on the floor. It looked suspiciously like Lik-M-Aid. I reached into my jacket pocket and felt that the envelope was empty. I also felt a rather large hole in my pocket where the powder had leaked out and down to the floor.

I looked down again to see how obvious it was. Oh, it was obvious alright. It had been made much worse by the fact that in my shifting around, my chair leg had spread the granules around and ground some of it into a fine powder. It looked like it had permanently dyed the tile on the floor in an area about a foot square. The floor tile was a dark maroon with a faint marbleized pattern. The Lik-M-Aid was cherry flavored and was light pink in color. It stood out like a neon light on the floor.

It was obvious that there is no way I could get it cleaned up while I was sitting in the middle of class. Also, there would be no time between classes. There was only five minutes before the next class arrived.

Even if I had time, how could I clean it up? I had no rags or a mop. If I rushed out and got some wet paper towels, it would probably just turn the spot into a mass of red Kool-Aid type mess. What could I do?

This was not a very attractive possibility for me, no matter how unlikely. So, I made a monumental decision, choosing what I perceived to be the lesser of two evils. Instead of going to my next class, I walked out the door like I was going to one of the annexes, and when the coast looked clear, ran like crazy across the street, ducking behind a house. I made my way home through the back yards. I had to climb four chain link fences to accomplish this, but it kept me out of the front yards, all of which were easily visible from the school.

I spent a miserable weekend. I felt that any minute there would be a knock at the door and it would be a representative of the school—either the janitor who had to clean up the mess or a representative from Hagar's office. I couldn't even fathom the possibility that Hagar himself would deign to chase down a petty criminal like me.

By Monday morning, I hadn't heard anything, which only increased my feeling that the hammer was certain to fall hard as soon as I got to class. I would be called into Hagar's office where I would be found guilty of violating the ban against illegal substances, defacing school property, being out without a pass, leaving the school grounds without permission, cutting class and probably sabotaging the entire school system. They would make an example of me. I would be nailed to the wall outside the door to the cafeteria for all to jeer at and deride as they went into lunch.

I walked to class by hugging the wall, brushing along the front of lockers. I waited until the last minute, then ducked out to the "outhouse" for home room. I tried to sit as far from the door as possible, but Mr. Dailey moved me to my assigned place. I couldn't concentrate.

By lunch time I hadn't heard a word. No one had sent for me. On the way to the cafeteria, I had to walk by Mr. McKinney's room. It was empty, so I ducked in real quick and went to the scene of the crime. I looked all around my chair on the floor. Not a sign of anything on the floor. No telltale residue or remnant of the evil substance. I breathed a sigh of partial relief.

I went into the cafeteria with a little lighter step, but still didn't feel I was out of the woods yet. I stuck it out the full day and went directly home after school. By dinner time I was starting to feel that I had escaped whatever evil befalls errant juvenile delinquents. After dinner, I went to scout meeting knowing that I was hiding this dark secret which was totally in opposition to about half the points in the Boy Scout Creed ("A Scout is Trustworthy, Loyal, Thrifty, etc.").

* * * * *

One of my more enjoyable classes was art, with Miss Humphrey. One day in class she announced that Dental Health Week was coming in a month or so and the Dental Association was holding a poster contest with the first prize being fifty dollars. Now here's something I might have a shot at! My art skills were better than average. So now all I needed to do was come up with some clever saying, theme or approach as a hook which would secure my win and the prized fifty bucks.

I started thinking hard about my approach and finally came up with what I thought would be a winner. I submitted it to Miss Humphrey who thought it had potential and advised me to go ahead.

I worked hard on the poster, taking over a week to finish it. It pictured the profile of a person eating an apple. The apple was about two inches from his mouth and imbedded in the apple was a set of false teeth which had obviously just been extracted from the puckered mouth of my main subject. Across the top, in large letters, was written: "IT'S EMBARASSING" I thought it was perfect. My subject looked pretty good. Not as good as a photograph, but certainly acceptable. My lettering was well spaced and proportional. Each letter was carefully outlined and shaded.

Miss Humphrey also thought it was great. She thought we had a chance to win. It said everything. If you didn't take care of your teeth, you might lose them. Then you'd be forced to wear false teeth and you couldn't eat your favorite foods. You might be embarrassed and all sorts of bad things might befall you. How could the judges pass this by?

On the day we were to deliver the poster downtown to Central High School for judging against all the other posters from schools all over the city, I went by to pick up the poster from Miss Humphrey's class. My mother was waiting in the car to take me downtown. A couple of the other teachers were in the art room and Miss Humphrey was showing them my poster. I was standing there just soaking up the praise when one of the teachers said: "I don't think that's the way you spell 'embarrassing'" My heart leapt into my throat. The other teacher said: "I think you're right." One of them went across the hall to her room and returned with a dictionary. They looked up the word and sure enough, I had left out an "R". I was crushed. Then I said I was going to take it downtown and enter it anyway. Miss Humphrey wouldn't let me. She said she would still give me a top grade for the effort, but she couldn't let me enter the poster with a misspelled word in the city-wide contest.

The thing that makes it especially ironic is that I was the spelling champion for Franklin School that year. Really! I represented the school at the city spelling bee held at Will Rogers High School. While I didn't place high in the city contest, I was a good speller. The embarrassing fact that I misspelled "embarrassing" was doubly embarrassing because of my standing as a good speller. How embarrassing!

* * * * *

One never knows when an opportunity to learn something new, such as how to spell "embarrassing", will be thrust before him. Another opportunity for growth in social graces came through my sixth grade girl friend, Doris. She was really a pretty girl who lived about three blocks from me. On Saturdays we would walk to the Will Rogers Theater to go to the movies, usually holding hands. We would also ride our bicycles together, sometimes along with my friend Billy and his girlfriend, Sharon.

Doris had an older sister or maybe two. They were just as pretty. One day an older sister seized an opportunity to educate her little sister's oafish boyfriend and teach him some telephone etiquette. It was a simple thing, but something I never forgot.

We decided to have a party for our class. So Doris and I started phoning classmates to invite them to the party. We were calling from her house one afternoon. Doris' sister was in the room as we were making calls. I dialed one of the numbers and when an adult answered I said: "Is Bobby there?" He wasn't, so I hung up. Doris' sister immediately looked at me and said: "Did you just want to find out if he was home or did you want to speak with him?" I indicated I wanted to talk to him, of course. "Then why didn't you ask that? Just asking if he is home is actually quite rude." OK, I thought, I'll use that approach on the next one.

121

"Can I talk to Dean?" Dean wasn't home so I hung up. Doris' sister immediately said something like: "Do you realize what you just asked?" I said: "Yeah. I asked to talk to Dean, like you said."

"But that's not what you wanted to do."

"Yes it is" I objected.

"No." she said. "First, 'Can I talk' means 'Am I able to talk'. Certainly you are able to talk or you wouldn't be using the telephone. Second, asking to 'talk to' someone sounds like you want to lecture them. Third, asking to talk TO the person indicates you don't want them to talk back to you. You want to SPEAK WITH them not just TO them.

So, what should you say?"

I thought carefully for a minute and said: "Should it be 'May I speak with Dean'?"

"Right!" she said. "Doris, there may be hope for this boy, yet."

Chapter Thirty Two
Indian Hills

The summer after graduating from elementary school was full of new experiences and expanded horizons. First, my parents had joined Indian Hills Country Club, a nice, middle-class country club nestled in the hills East of Tulsa. The club had a beautiful golf course where I learned to play the game taught by a dashing looking golf pro named Jack Shields who had the thickest eyebrows I had ever seen. He ended up marrying a Miss Tulsa named Marilyn Breno who had become a local television personality and star in the early years of TV in the city. After a couple of years, they moved to Palm Springs where Jack became golf pro to the stars, such as Jack Benny, Bob Hope and others. They also got him some bit parts in movies.

Jack definitely made a better instructor than my dad. Dad was a good bowler, having been Class B State Champion one year. However, golf was not his game. In the first place, he was left handed, but bought right handed clubs and attempted to play right handed. In the second place, an accident when he was a child (he was hit by a bus) left him with one leg shorter than the other, by about an inch and a half. This caused him to tilt slightly as he addressed the ball, resulting in his pulling nearly every shot to the left. I never understood why he didn't just compensate for this by lining up slightly to the right.

Dad never attributed his lousy golf game to either of these conditions.

He usually blamed the clubs. He was famous for wrapping clubs around trees in fits of rage after a poorly hit shot. He would buy a new set of golf clubs about every three months, thinking that these would be just what was needed. (In addition to golf clubs, Dad used to frequently change two other things—wrist watches and cars, coming up with new ones every few months.)

I spent a lot of time at Indian Hills and took my friends out there every chance I got. I introduced some of them to golf in those outings, including Kenny, Billy, Bobby and Jerry. We would go out, play golf and then spend hours in the swimming pool having some great games of "Shark and Minnow", Water Polo and tag.

Occasionally my parents would get the country club bill and see a high number of charges for me and my guests, so they would crack down and I would have to cut back on taking friends out there. They also didn't want me ordering so much food at the club. So, I came up with a solution. I became friends with the head chef at the club. He was a large, black man named "Hash Brown". We became great friends. I would go up to the kitchen in the middle of the afternoon, when it wasn't busy, and sit around and talk to Hash Brown (or "speak with" him).

One afternoon, he asked me if I was hungry, and I said yes. He said he was about to fix a steak for himself and would I like one. "You bet!" I said. So he fixed us both a juicy steak with fresh cut french fries and hot rolls. My kind of meal.

Hash Brown smoked Lucky Strike cigarettes. So, in the future, before I went upstairs to the kitchen, I'd buy a couple of packs of cigarettes out of the vending machine (at 25 cents each). As soon as I walked into the kitchen, I'd toss him the cigarettes. He'd immediately ask: "Want a steak?"

I ate great that whole summer and it didn't impact my folks' bill one bit.

* * * * *

On the Fourth of July, the country club had a full day of fun activities. First, since it was outside the city limits, there were no restrictions on fireworks. So, all day long, we could shoot off firecrackers in a multitude of interesting places—blowing up cans, rocks and all sorts of dangerous things.

In the afternoon, I noticed this kid standing out in the parking lot with one of the staff members standing with him. He was a fat kid who was quite obnoxious and few of us liked him. As I walked by, I noticed that he was standing sort of funny and the staff member had his arm around him.

The kid was wearing a yellow, see-through shirt which was made out of nylon. This style shirt had just recently come on the scene, and didn't stay in fashion very long.

I asked what had happened. The staff member simply said there had been an accident and they were waiting for his parents to pick him up.

I took a closer look and saw that all that was left of the shirt was the collar, the yoke or top portion and one sleeve. The main body of the shirt as well as one sleeve was missing. I said: "Eddie—what happened?" He related that a small firecracker had gone off in his hand and the sparks had caught his shirt on fire. Actually, the shirt didn't burn, it melted. And very quickly. It just sort of flashed up and, Poof! Two thirds of it was gone, scorching his skin thoroughly. I'm sure it was painful. That made a big impression on me.

Later in the afternoon, there was a long drive contest. The club house at Indian Hills sat high up on a bluff. The first tee was just outside the clubhouse, near a patio and terrace area. The tee box sat about thirty or forty feet higher than the fairway. It was a fun place from which to start a golf game. Even if you hit a mediocre drive, you felt like it was really going a long way. Of course, if you really duffed it and it just rolled down the hill, taking your second shot from that spot could be really embarrassing. (There's that word, again.) It was also a spectacular place to observe a long drive contest.

Indian Hills had several really long ball hitters, including a couple of brothers who had been football stars at TU. Their names just sounded like football players: Sax Judd and his brother, Jack. These guys could hit the ball a mile, as could several others. So, we would all gather out on the patio and watch these guys almost knock the covers off some golf balls.

The problem was that the first green was only 375 yards out. Under normal circumstances, it would take two shots, at least, to reach it. But when these guys really wanted to let loose, and shooting from a tee which was elevated forty feet or so, it was not unusual to see one of them drive past the green, especially if there had been little rain and the ground was hard, yielding extra roll to the ball. It was an impressive sight—more like an exhibition than a contest. The same guys won every year.

As soon as it got dark, everyone gathered on the terrace patio again to watch the spectacular fireworks display, which was made even better by our vantage point.

Me, Doris and Will Rogers Methodist Church

Chapter Thirty Three
Poker and Banty Roosters

That summer was my last year playing little league baseball. Once you start to junior high, the teams are no longer affiliated with the school. They are part of a city-wide league, such as the Pop Warner League or American Legion. Competition becomes fierce and the skill level required is significant. I remained the runt in my class. This, coupled with the fact that most of the boys in my class were older than me, made it difficult for me to compete. However, that last year in the Franklin program was fun, albeit not particularly noteworthy.

On some of the days when we had baseball practice scheduled at the Franklin school grounds it might be raining. We would still show up to wait out the rain. However, if it looked like it wouldn't let up, then several of us would go across the street to my house. We started to have frequent poker games. I had been an observer at several of the poker games my dad would have and had become fairly knowledgeable about the most popular games, so I started teaching them to my friends. I was too naïve to take advantage of this golden opportunity to teach special "rules" to some of my neophyte fellow-players. I should have taught them, for instance, that the value of an ace varies with whose hand it is in. These games were generally penny-ante and usually the big winner in the game would take home about three dollars more than he came with. These games became a hobby with me and remained a significant part of my extra-curricular agenda throughout my school career. They also presented the opportunity for me to get to be better friends with some of the players who were not on my team, such as a great catcher named Steve, who is a year younger than me, and a couple of brothers named Bill and Larry. Bill doesn't know what a friend I actually was to him. I broke up with Doris (or maybe she broke up with me). Several years later, Bill and Doris married. Where would he have been if I had continued to turn on my charm with Doris and kept her under my spell? He might have ended up alone, a broken man, sitting by the railroad tracks sipping his dollar wine.

* * * * *

This was a busy summer, but I got to take two trips. Jerry's grandparents lived in Siloam Springs, Arkansas, about an hour and a half's drive from Tulsa. He would frequently go visit them. This summer, he asked me to go along and stay for a couple of weeks. It was an opportunity not only to spend some time with my best friend, but to experience small town life again.

Since Jerry was a frequent visitor to Siloam, he had become acquainted with quite a few of the kids our age. This made it easier for us.

Jerry's grandparents lived in a big old house on the outskirts of town— but still within walking distance of downtown. They raised a few chickens and had a small smoke-house where Jerry's grandfather would occasionally smoke a side of bacon. But basically they were retired.

It was at this lovely old house that I was once again thrust into the bosom of a feather bed shared with a guy named Jerry. This feather bed was located up on the third floor of the house.

Jerry had a pet Bantam Rooster at his grandparents' house. His name was Herschel. On Sunday afternoons Jerry's parents would drive over from Tulsa and be joined by assorted others who would come to the house for Sunday dinner. All the women would gather in the kitchen to help in meal preparation. The kitchen was one of the largest rooms in the house and had a highly polished linoleum floor which was kept spotless. Jerry loved to wait until most of the women were in the kitchen before he threw Herschel into the middle of the kitchen floor.

The word "pandemonium" was coined for just such a situation. First came the screams. Then someone would try to shoo Herschel toward the door. This only made it worse. He would start trying to run but his claws would only slide and scratch the slick floor while he stayed in one place— clack-clack-scratch-scratch. Then he'd start flapping his wings to get some

127

balance or forward motion. This would make the women only scream louder and try to shoo him more, so he would start squawking in protest— the perfect vicious cycle. The only calm one in this entire scene was Jerry's grandmother. Finally, her serene but firm voice would rise above the din and you could hear her say: "JERRY! You get this rooster out of the house, RIGHT NOW!" Jerry would comply, immediately. But the whole affair provided us with great laughs for quite a while.

Chapter Thirty Four
Florida and Another Train Ride

Before I started to junior high school, my parents and I took one of our trips to Pensacola to visit my aunt and uncle and go to the beach. At least one of the nights while we were in Pensacola on these trips, my Uncle Jeff would have one of his famous fish fries in the back yard. He would build a fire and fry red snapper or sea bass in an iron skillet which was nearly as big as a bathtub. I normally hated seafood of any type but I did love Uncle Jeff's fish!

Sometimes we would have a shrimp boil and my Aunt Marian would put out various ingredients on a table with which each person could mix his own shrimp sauce. For some reason, I was able to hit on just the right combination of ketchup, Worcestershire sauce, horse radish, vinegar, spices, etc. to make a really delicious red sauce and everyone abandoned their own efforts and went for mine. That summer I became the official family shrimp sauce chef, a position which I accepted gladly and with great pride.

* * * * *

129

My Uncle Jeff had a part time job working at the dog track in Pensacola at nights, running the pari-mutuel wagering windows on the club level. So, my folks would go out to the track on most of the nights when Uncle Jeff was working. I was too young to get in.

One night at the track, my dad had a really good session and won quite a bit of money (thanks to Uncle Jeff's tips). So, my folks decided they would take a detour on the way home and spend a few days in New Orleans. They decided, owing to the fact that I had become a seasoned train traveler on the previous St. Louis trip, to send me home on the train alone, in order to give them a few days on their own. I was ecstatic.

For the two days before the trip I could think of nothing else. I would be on my own aboard this moving adventureland for nearly two days.

I spent the first couple of hours on the train looking out the window and watching the panhandle of Florida and South Alabama go by. Then I started exploring. I found the dining car. I was given enough money to see me through the trip, and the fact that I could not only order anything I wanted but as much and as often as I wanted was a new feeling of both power and freedom.

Then something happened which threatened to disrupt my independence, my power, my freedom and the whole plan of the trip. I discovered that the railroad had someone on board whose job it was to monitor and supervise unaccompanied minors. I immediately classified him as the enemy—me against him, a challenge which I was ready to take up. He caught up with me about mid-way through Alabama, asked me a few questions, filled out a form and instructed me to stay put in my assigned seat until dinner time. (Fat chance!)

From that point on, my primary goal was to avoid this barrier to my fun. I spent a lot of my time in the vestibule area between cars, looking out the window and letting the wind hit me in the face.

That evening, he was coming through the cars with his clipboard and a very determined look on his face. I started heading toward the end of the train. I was running out of places to go or to hide. I was in a box canyon. So, I ducked into the men's restroom in the last car. I knew this wouldn't be good enough. No way was he going to skip looking into this obvious hiding place.

Then I looked up and saw that the ceiling had what appeared to be a little trap door. I climbed up on the lavatory and pushed the little door open. It was apparently an access hatch to get to the plumbing that ran through the crawl space above the ceiling, rather than under the floor. I hoisted myself up into this narrow space, shut the door and waited. Not long after, I heard the door to the head open and then shut a couple of seconds later.

I waited a few seconds then jumped down. I snuck a look out into the hallway. The coast looked clear, so I went back to standing between the cars and making my frequent trips to the snack bar. I felt like I had won the battle of wits between me and the railroad establishment. Eat your heart out Cornelius Vanderbilt! (I don't know what the kid-monitor-guy told his boss or said in his report. He probably thought I had jumped off the train when we crossed the Mississippi River.)

The real contradiction in this whole episode is that I would have been the last person to ever buck authority, question regulations, break the rules or rebel against anyone older than me. What a new feeling of freedom this gave me!

Ready to tackle the new adventure of junior high school!

PART FOUR
The Awakening Years

Chapter Thirty Five

Bell Bobcats?

In September of 1952, a new junior high school opened in Tulsa—Alexander Graham Bell. I lived one block inside the Bell district although I actually lived closer to Wilson Junior High. One bad thing about this new restructuring was that one of my best friends, Kenny, and I ended up going to the two different schools. Since he was one year older and had already been one year to Wilson, he was allowed to continue rather than starting to the new school.

My other best friend, Jerry, also went to Wilson, even though we lived virtually next door to each other. His folks requested it, feeling it was more convenient for them.

So I sort of started off on this new adventure without some of my primary support group.

The year started off with the election of a Student Council. I was elected from my home room to be the Student Council representative for our class. Then they selected a couple of members from each grade to be on a special committee to select all the key components of the school's identification package—the team name, the school colors, etc. I was one of the 7-B's on this committee. (The upper classmen called all the seventh graders "7-B's"—for Seventh Grade Babies.)

What happened on this committee was nothing short of frustration at its zenith. It became apparent that the 7-B's were token members and would have no real voice on the committee. Everything was totally guided by the adult committee members—a couple of faculty members, with a little input from the ninth graders on the committee.

The first thing we picked was the nickname or mascot for the athletic teams. I thought we ought to try to stick with the theme of Bell. But the committee went for an alliteration. I voted against "Bell Bobcats" but it won, anyway. Bobcats? BOBCATS? What the heck is a bobcat anyway? Has anyone ever seen a real bobcat in the flesh (or the fur)? Could the Bobcats hope to intimidate their rivals, the Rebels or the Warriors or the Trojans? I don't think so. A bobcat is nothing more than a third rate tiger— a housecat with an attitude.

Surely we can come up with something better than the "Bobcats", I pleaded. But I couldn't think of anything quick enough which carried out the Bell theme. I don't think the "Bell Dial Tones" or the "Bell Ding-a-lings" or the "Bell Clangers" would cut it. So, we officially became the Bell Bobcats.

The next order of business was to select the school colors. This was even more disastrous in my mind. Some colors look good together. Some do not. It's just that simple. However, some color combinations connote certain things. Who doesn't think of Christmas as red and green? What colors are used at Halloween? Only black and orange.

One of the silly, adolescent, traditions which was started in those days was that if you wore green and yellow together you were advertising the fact that you were a "queer", a "homo", etc. This was especially true if you wore green and yellow on Thursday (don't ask me why). Everyone would take great care not to wear either color on Thursday, for fear that if you wore a green shirt, for instance, and dropped some mustard on it at lunch, you would suddenly be razzed as a queer, "wearing" green and yellow, even though no one would really believe it.

So. . .you guessed it! The color combination which was put forth as the one for the Bell Bobcats would be green and yellow (actually green and gold, but "gold" fabric is really just yellow). The reasoning behind it was that it was the closest combination to the high school which we would all end up attending. Will Rogers High School had blue and gold as its colors. My question was: "Why don't we stick with the blue instead of the gold? Let's pick blue and some other color, like silver or grey or even tan?" (Blue and white had already been taken—they were the colors of Webster High School, across town.) Once again, the 7-B was ignored.

So, here we were, the Bell Bobcats (and the Bell Homo Bobcats at that), waving our green and yellow pom poms. I spent three years at Bell and never purchased a single shirt, sweater or jacket with the Bobcat logo or the green and "gold" motif.

* * * * *

The administration at Bell imposed a rather strange rule, which showed an appalling lack of trust in 12 to 14-year olds (or perhaps it was well placed). School started at 8:45. So they would not unlock the doors to the school until 8:30, which would give you just about enough time to go to your locker, hang up your jacket, grab a book or two and get to your seat in time for the bell. They didn't want a bunch of unsupervised adolescents running wild in the halls for a half hour each morning.

The problem is that most of the kids came to the school by bus. The school buses started arriving as early as 8:00, and by 8:30, nearly all of them were there. This meant that the entire student body was hanging around in front of the school for anything from fifteen to forty five minutes, waiting for the front door to be unlocked. This was OK until it rained or turned cold. Then it became miserable.

However, one good thing to come out of these forced assemblies was a sort of bonding and opportunity for exchange. It was an innocent time. If it had been twenty years later, it would have provided a perfect forum for anything from drug sales to gang formations.

One of those cold mornings I noticed several boys crowded around another, trying to look at something. I wormed my way into the group and could see that they were all looking at a small comic book, about 6 inches wide and 3 inches high. I couldn't see what the fascination was and couldn't get close enough to make it out.

The front doors were unlocked and everyone started going in. I approached the boy with the comic book as he was putting it in his pocket. He was the older brother of Becky, a girl in my class who was a good friend of mine. "Tom. Can I see that?", I asked. He handed it to me and I just about fell over. My first look at pornography! It was what I later learned was commonly referred to as an "Eight Page Bible". These are a series of pornographic cartoons, always eight pages in length. Sort of an illustrated dirty joke. The name of this one was "The Frigidaire Salesman".

I immediately thought that my buddies who were going to Wilson wouldn't believe this. I decided to transact some business immediately. "How much do you want for this?" I asked Tom.

"What'll you give me?" he said. I thrust my hand in my pocket and pulled out all the money I had—my quarter for lunch. In two seconds the porno was mine. I shoved it into my pocket, anxious to get home and show it to Jerry, Kenny and any others who might be hungering for sex education.

135

* * * * *

Every two or three years, Tulsa would be hit by a plague, almost of biblical proportions. One time it would be grasshoppers. The next time it would be crickets. They would be everywhere, by the millions. Everywhere you walked outside, you'd crush dozens of them.

The cricket plague hit Tulsa my first autumn at Bell Junior High. One morning we were all gathered around waiting for school to open—several hundred of us—and the crickets were especially bad. All of a sudden, there was a commotion and people began running for a point near the front door. "What's going on?" I said. As one kid was running by, he yelled: "Garrison's gonna eat a cricket!"

Garrison was a small, somewhat sickly looking, freckled faced kid with coal black hair who bore a striking resemblance to Alfalfa of Little Rascals fame. Everyone knew him simply as "Garrison", his last name. He was standing at the center of an ever increasing crowd of kids. He was about to get his 15 minutes of fame—condensed into a 2-minute frame. Garrison was a kid who was definitely an outsider. He had no apparent friends and had not distinguished himself in any way at Bell—not academically, in sports, in class activities or anywhere.

That fateful morning, someone issued a dare to Garrison to eat a cricket. It escalated to a double dare and then a double DOG dare! Done deal. Just like Jean Shepherd's kid who stuck his tongue to the frozen metal pole in "A Christmas Story", Garrison couldn't back down. The word spread like wildfire. "Garrison's gonna eat a cricket!" Even the girls, who feigned revulsion, couldn't help approaching the focal point of impending action.

People were stacked 20 and 30 deep. Some people climbed on others' shoulders. Someone suggested that Garrison move up to the top of the four or five steps to the front door, like a stage. Nearly everyone could see at this point.

Then someone caught a live cricket, held it in his cupped hands and took it to Garrison. He reached in and grabbed the creature by a leg and held it out, obviously not wanting to even look at it, much less touch it or eat it. It was clearly apparent that what we had here was someone who had impulsively backed himself into a corner. To say he was reluctant was the understatement of the decade.

Garrison looked at the cricket, then at the crowd. He was turning white, which made the contrast with his black hair even more stark. Then the crowd started clapping simultaneously, like they were trying to get a rally going at the ball park. The rhythm of the clapping got faster and faster and louder and louder. Garrison kept looking back and forth between the cricket and the crowd, getting whiter and whiter and gulping hard.

The clapping moved to a feverish pitch and the crowd was yelling: "GO! GO! GO! GO!"

Finally, he could not avoid it any longer. Garrison tilted his head back, opened his mouth wide, like a baby robin in the nest, lifted the cricket above his mouth and dropped it in. He swallowed it quickly and turned back to face the crowd, which had erupted into a big cheer, interspersed with a chorus of "E-e-e-w-w" and "YUCK!", mostly from the girls.

At that moment, the front doors were opened and everyone simply rushed inside the school, leaving Garrison standing there alone, his moment in the spotlight gone. No pats on the back. No "Way to go!" Or "Atta Boy!" No one walking with him (or wanting to). He was just squirrely Garrison again. He could eat a dozen crickets tomorrow morning and no one would even care.

Chapter Thirty Six
Playing in a Real Band

One of the new experiences I was introduced to was a regular band class. I had been taking trumpet lessons since the fifth grade with once a week group-playing before a director who rotated between several elementary schools. Now we had a full-fledged band, meeting every day. The problem is that the trumpet section was about a third of the band and was not only large but contained the finest players in band. Some of them went on to be the outstanding musicians in the Tulsa Philharmonic and became professionals. This meant that unless I was willing to practice the trumpet several hours a day, I could count on sitting about tenth or twelfth chair in the section. I was not willing to commit that time to practice, so I went the way of the piano lessons and baseball, relegated to the bench.

Our band director was fresh out of college—an imposingly large man named Don Linde, who came from a family of excellent musicians. However, he had a bit of a temper and was taken to slamming his baton down on his music stand whenever the band, or a section, performed to a lesser standard than he expected. Frequently this resulted in the plastic or wooden baton snapping in two. So, several of us chipped in and bought him a metal baton—aluminum, about 18 inches long, with a cork ball on the end he could hold on to.

This didn't stop him from slamming the baton down, but it did keep it from breaking. Whenever he would slam it down and bend it, he would simply straighten it out as best he could. But it wasn't long before it looked like he was directing the band with some sort of a snake with rigor mortis.

The cork handle came off after a while, but he continued to use it. Mr. Linde was a big man and during especially spirited pieces he would work up a significant sweat. His brow would bead up and his shirt become soaked.

While directing one of these energetic pieces, a passage came up which featured the low brass section—the tubas, trombones and baritone horns. A baritone horn is sort of a smaller version of a tuba with a rather large bell which sticks up in the air. When the passage arrived for the large horns to come in, Mr. Linde swung the baton up toward the low brass section (who sat about three rows up in the semi-circular room). The centrifugal force of this action overcame his precarious grip on the slick metal baton by a sweaty hand and it went flying like a javelin. The missile arched over the head of the front row flutes, the second row clarinets and saxes and directly toward Robert, playing the baritone horn.

Just like it was fired from a gun, the metal baton-spear flew toward its target and, slicker than a Bob Cousy free throw, went right down the bell of the baritone horn. Robert didn't even know what happened. The trumpet section had no notes to play and were just counting rests, so we saw everything. Between us and the drum section, the laughter was louder than the band's playing.

* * * * *

In order to fund a lot of things needed for a new band in a new school, outside fund raising efforts were necessary. Mr. Linde arranged for the band to sell magazine subscriptions. Armed with catalogs and order forms we all went out to bug our friends, neighbors and family members to buy subscriptions to everything from Better Homes and Gardens to Popular Quilting.

One of the biggest disappointments (or should I say let-downs?) of my young life happened during this campaign. In order to keep sales at a reasonably high level, Mr. Linde and the guy from the magazine company would offer incentives. As the second week started, Mr. Linde announced that the two band members who sold the most subscriptions that week would be treated to all the ice cream they could eat.

My new best friend, who I had teamed up with after starting at Bell, and I entered into a pact. His name was Al and he played bass clarinet. We decided to work especially hard that week and be the two high salesmen. We were really looking forward to going out to eat ice cream with Mr. Linde. The camaraderie would be great and we would

distinguish ourselves from the rest of the band by becoming buddies with the director. We figured this could pay some handsome dividends at some unspecified time in the future.

Sure enough. At the end of the week, Al and I had zoomed out in front. No one was even close to us for the week. On Friday afternoon, after school, Al and I ran down to the band room where Mr. Linde and the magazine guy were tallying up sales for the week. Al and I hung back and waited patiently while they did their figuring and plotted how we were doing against the goal.

After a while, Mr. Linde turned to us and said: "What do you boys want?"

"Well. . ." we sort of hesitated. "I think we were the top salesmen for the week."

Mr. Linde looked at the records and turned around and said: "You're right. Nice job boys. You've got a chance of winning the whole contest."

"But what about our ice cream?" we asked.

"Ice cream?" he said.

"Yeah. We were promised all the ice cream we could eat and we're ready to go."

Mr. Linde and the magazine guy looked at each other with a surprised expression. Then the recollection hit them and he said: "That's right."

At that point Mr. Linde reached into his pocket and took out some change. He whispered something to the magazine guy who did the same thing. Then he took two fifty cent pieces and gave one to Al and one to me, saying: "This should buy you about all the ice cream you can eat, won't it? If you can eat more than a half gallon of ice cream, come back and see me and I'll buy you some more." (Ice cream was 49 cents a half gallon.)

Al and I just stood there, stunned, staring at the coin in each of our hands. We were both thinking the same thing: "It's not about the ice cream, stupid! It's about the recognition. It's about the camaraderie. It's about being part of the inner circle." We stuck the half dollars into our pockets and shuffled out the door while Mr. Linde and the magazine guy went back to their figuring. Neither Al nor I sold a single subscription after that.

Chapter Thirty Seven
A Rude Awakening from a Fallen Idol

Adolescence brings with it a new awareness and a loss of innocence. The bubble has already burst for virtually all the fantasy characters who form a big part of growing up—Santa Claus, the Easter Bunny, the Tooth Fairy, etc. So, as you approach the teen years, you turn to real life heroes. Boys usually focus on sports figures, and in the 1950's, this meant baseball players.

Every autumn in Tulsa, after the close of the baseball season, The Tulsa Tribune sponsored what was known as "The Diamond Dinner", taking advantage of all the great baseball stars from Oklahoma, such as Mickey Mantle, Warren Spahn, Allie Reynolds and several others. These local luminaries would come to Tulsa for a round of golf and a gala dinner to raise money for some worthy cause. They would entice some of their famous friends to come along as well, so it was a star-studded day and evening. Some of the baseball luminaries who came in 1952 besides the Oklahoma ball players were Whitey Ford, George Kell and his brother, Skeeter, and Dimaggio—not Joe, who couldn't make it, but his brother Dom. Some of the Cardinals were also there, including Red Schoendienst.

In 1952, the golf outing was held at Indian Hills Country Club, where my family still had a membership. It was held on a Monday, when the club was closed, and it was off-limits to everyone but the players, the press and support staff.

During those days, there were precious few electric golf carts—at least at our club. There was a fairly large contingency of caddies, most of whom were boys who lived in nearby Catoosa. There was a strict rule that members or children of members could not serve as caddies. However, I started working on our club golf pro, George (who had taken Jack Shields' place) weeks in advance of the tournament to let me be a caddy on this magic day. After all, few, if any, Indian Hills members would be there to see me caddying. "Please! Please! Please! I'll do anything. I'll wash your car every week for a year. I'll dive in the lake on hole #14 and get all the lost golf balls for you to re-sell. Besides, I know the course as well as any of the regular caddies." He finally acquiesced. VICTORY was mine!

I didn't want to press my luck too much after this first victory. So, I waited a week or so and then started to work toward reaching the summit. "Since you are assigning the caddies to the various players, could you please let me caddy for Mickey Mantle? PLEASE! This would be the highlight of my life." I could hardly believe my ears when he said: "Sure. Why not?" Much easier than I thought it would be.

For the two weeks approaching the magic Monday I don't think my feet hit the ground. I could hardly sleep. The days went by slower than those days approaching Christmas. Just think! In ten more days (nine more days) (eight more days) I would be spending four or five hours with Mickey Mantle, the greatest baseball player who ever played the game. You can have your Babe Ruth and your Ty Cobb. You can even have your Joe Dimaggio. Mickey was it, as far as I was concerned. And this was several years before he tied Babe Ruth's home run record. Besides, he was almost a neighbor—he was from Commerce, Oklahoma, not very far from Tulsa.

When the magic Monday arrived, I talked my dad into getting me out to the club just after dawn, hours before the first tee time. Not only did I not want to risk being late, but I was going to protect my place as Mickey Mantle's caddy and make sure none of the older guys aced me out. Then the first rude awakening hit me. I was told by the caddymaster that all caddies that day would be double caddies. That is, each caddy must carry two bags. Well, OK. I sucked it up. I can handle it. Now I had just turned 12 years old and was still the runt of my class. I probably hadn't gained much more weight over the 49 pounds I sported in the first grade. I wasn't much taller than the golf bags I would be carrying. The average caddy at the club was 15 to 20 years old and looked like he had either spent most of his life working out at a gym or tossing hundred-pound hay bales onto trucks.

The golfers started arriving around 9 AM and the golf clubs were brought around to the side of the pro shop. I was informed that I would be caddying for Mickey Mantle and an outfielder named Lou Kretlow, who I had never heard of. I think he played for the Detroit Tigers.

The head caddy got Mickey's and Kretlow's bags together and yelled out my name. I reported for duty, front and center. He pointed to the bags and my eyes nearly popped out of my head. These were two of the biggest golf bags I had ever seen! They were leather, about two feet in diameter, stuffed full of paraphernalia in every pocket. And the clubs! Hadn't these guys ever heard of the 14 club rule? Each bag looked like it had 50 clubs in it, at least. The only bag I have seen since then which even approached these steamer's trunks I was assigned to carry was Rodney Dangerfield's everything-in-a-bag bag, used in the movie "Caddy Shack".

I hoisted one of the bags onto my shoulder and it nearly pulled me over. I steadied myself, but couldn't get the other one up without the first bag slipping off my shoulder. Two of the other caddies helped me by placing the bags on my shoulders simultaneously so I wouldn't be off balance and fall over.

It didn't matter. I was about to caddy for Mickey Mantle! I was ten feet tall!

I shuffled around the corner of the pro shop and out toward the first tee, high on the hill, and stood there waiting to meet my idol. Pretty soon, here he came. He spotted his clubs and walked up to me. "Are YOU my caddy?"

"Yessir!" I said, trying to not let my voice squeak.

"Well I hope you can make it, kid! You'd better keep up with us or I'm not gonna be very happy. If there's anything I hate it's a slow round of golf."

The other golfer, Lou Kretlow, came up and seemed nice enough. But at that point I only had eyes for Mickey Mantle. Kretlow said: "Are you sure you can handle both those bags, son?"

"Oh, yessir!" I replied. "I do it all the time." I couldn't believe I came up with that lie.

We were about the third or fourth foursome to tee off. We were paired with Allie Reynolds, an allstar pitcher from Oklahoma City who also played for the Yankees, and another Detroit Tiger named George Kell, who I think played third base or outfield.

Lou Kretlow was a big Polish guy with forearms as big as tree trunks. He was tall, but not a giant. Probably about six feet two. But he hit the ball further than any human being I had ever seen. He drove the greenside sand trap on the first hole. And his drives for the rest of the day made my former role models, the Judd brothers, look like they were hitting nine irons. Unfortunately, Kretlow was not always accurate, and spent a lot of time in the woods, looking for wayward drives.

I clambered down the hill after our party drove, and started walking with Mickey toward his ball. I don't know what his hurry was, but even if I had been unencumbered with any golf bags I would have had to run to keep up with him. "C'mon kid. You're gonna have to move your ass better than that or we won't finish before dark." We made it to his ball and he said: "Give me my pitching wedge." Which I promptly did.

We had to wait while both Kell and Reynolds hit their shots, since they were away. So, while waiting, I thought I'd take my first opportunity to buddy up with the great man. "How are the Yankees gonna look for next year, Mickey?", I boldly asked.

"'Bout the same as this year." he replied, tersely. Then, as I was about to ask another question in order to get a conversation going, he shushed me and pointed to Allie Reynolds who was across the fairway about to make his shot. Somewhat humiliated, I shut up quickly and decided to confine my conversation to more opportune times.

Mickey hit his shot onto the green and I hurried as fast as I could to get a sand wedge to Kretlow.

The other caddy tended the pin while they putted out, so I dragged myself over to the second tee and grabbed about two minutes of precious rest. "Made it!" I thought. "One down and only 17 to go!".

The second hole was a long par four, paralleling the first fairway but going the opposite direction. The problem was, as you approach the hole, it's back up the hill to the altitude of the first tee box. However, instead of being a steep cliff, it was a gradual slope starting about a hundred yards from the green.

As we were approaching the second green I was about half way up the slope when my motor gave out. This was worse than climbing Mount Everest. Every muscle in my body was throbbing with pain. All the bones in both my legs had abandoned my body. They checked out about fifty yards back, and must have headed for the coast, leaving nothing but two columns of Jello to support my torso and both of the monster golf bags. The other caddy noticed my condition and came to my rescue. He had me give both the putters to him and told me to go on over to the third tee, instead of climbing all the way up to the green. I couldn't even say thanks. My mouth wouldn't move.

I literally dragged the bags over to the third tee and was trying to figure out a way to make my exit. Could I feign sickness? Could I make myself pass out (which was a distinct possibility, whether I wanted to or not)? I decided that sticking my finger down my throat to make me throw up would probably be noticed.

As I waited on the tee box, Kretlow was the first of the group to approach, having left the green ahead of the others. He came up to me and said: "How you doin', Son?" I croaked something that sounded sort of like "OK".

Then he said some of the sweetest words I had ever heard: "Listen. I don't always hit the ball straight, you know. And I don't want to hold Mickey and the others up too much. So, would you mind if I carried my own bag? Then I can head straight to my ball, wherever it is and you can devote your attention to Mickey. But I'd still like to get your input on yardages and how some of the holes play."

Would I mind? WOULD I MIND? I mustered a response sort of like: "Well. . . if you really want to. But I'm happy to carry it if you want." I lied again. He just smiled and took his bag.

Relieved of half my burden, I felt like a pack mule who had just turned into a gazelle. Now I only had about a thousand pounds to carry, not two tons. It wasn't going to be easy from here on out, but I was confident I could make it.

Things were definitely looking up. Now I could devote some time to getting better acquainted with Mickey.

The third hole was a short, par 3, back down the hill we just walked up. The group ahead of us was still on the green, so while we waited, I sidled up to Mickey and said: "Did a lot of your teammates from the Yankees come to Tulsa for the Diamond Dinner this year?"

He turned quickly to me and said something like: "Look, kid. I'm here to play some golf and spend some time with my friends, not to make small talk with some shrimpy-ass kid who shouldn't even be on a golf course in the first place! The first rule of any caddy is to keep quiet and speak only when spoken to or asked a question. The quicker you learn that, the quicker you and I will get along."

The sick feeling returned, but not because of fatigue. I was totally crushed, of course. Those words I just heard came out of the mouth of my idol. Someone I had built up to be not only the greatest ballplayer in the world but the nicest guy. Well, he may have been the greatest ballplayer, but Lou Kretlow was the nicest guy, as far as I was concerned.

That tirade from Mickey was not the last one I heard that day. He rode me pretty hard for the next six holes but I was determined to keep up, keep out of his way and keep quiet. After the ninth hole, at what golfers call

145

"The Turn", we stopped at the clubhouse for a minute to get something to drink. I went into the pro shop and grabbed one of the caddies who was not carrying that day, but was working in the club storage and maintenance area. I asked him if he would like to caddy for Mickey Mantle for the back nine. He, of course, jumped at the chance and I was totally relieved to get rid of both the physical and mental burden. Besides, Mantle probably wouldn't have even tipped me at the end of the round.

I went into the men's locker room and called my dad to come and pick me up. I left without even seeing Mickey Mantle again, but regretted not saying goodbye to Lou Kretlow, George Kell and Allie Reynolds, who were all really nice guys. (In fact, before the first hole, Allie Reynolds signed my autograph book, not just once, but ten times, on ten blank pages. I planned to sell his autograph to some of my baseball playing buddies for a quarter each. Seemed like a good idea at the time.)

I learned quite a lesson that day. The more you build up an idol, the harder it is for them to live up to it. There is a big difference between idolatry and respect.

THIS IS TO
CERTIFY THAT

Joe Welling

IS A MEMBER IN GOOD STANDING
OF BOY SCOUT TROOP NO. 64
CITY OF   Tulsa
STATE OF   Okla.
FROM   2-53 TO 2-28-54

THIS CERTIFICATE IS NOT TRANSFERABLE, AND IS
VOID AFTER EXPIRATION DATE. IT MUST BE SHOWN
LOCAL DISTRIBUTOR WHEN PURCHASING UNIFORM.

SCOUTMASTER

SCOUT TIVE

PRESIDENT   CHIEF SCOUT EXECUTIVE

B 6266221

Chapter Thirty Eight
Not All Education Comes From School

My second year in the Scouts found the troop without a Senior Patrol Leader. Both Dale and Lyle had "graduated" from scouting. Scoutmaster Wrench liked the idea of having two Senior Patrol Leaders so he selected two new ones to start off the year. I was selected to be one of them and a friend of mine, named Gary, was picked to be the other.

I enjoyed my new position and the prestige it carried with my peers and the younger boys in the troop. I took my position seriously and conscientiously attacked my duties with energy.

Troop 64 went on at least two campouts a year—fall and spring—generally to Camp Garland in Eastern Oklahoma. Then some of the members joined those from other troops and went for a week or two to summer camp, such as Philmont Scout Ranch.

We always learned a lot on these outings, but much of it couldn't be found in the Boy Scout Handbook. For instance on that fall camping trip, someone in the troop informed the rest of us that you could actually smoke grapevine like a cigarette. So we all went on a hunt for grapevine. We

147

found some and cut it into strips about four inches in length. Then we went into our tents and fired up our newly created "cigarettes", sat back and puffed away like we were in some opium den. Those who risked inhaling promptly broke into a severe coughing spell. The rest of us just puffed on the vine and blew the smoke in the air, attempting such tricks as smoke rings. The novelty of the pretense wore off pretty fast, however.

One evening, after dinner, all the men—the scoutmasters and a few of the fathers who came along to assist--were sitting around the campfire, talking. Some of us veteran scouts sent the rookies out on a Snipe Hunt (looking for the fictitious "snipe"—a prized trophy which is difficult to catch and requires one member of the team sitting totally still, holding a burlap bag open while others drive the phantom creature toward the waiting trap). That left the camp fairly quiet, so several of us were sitting around in one of the large tents, talking. The subject naturally turned to sex, as it was bound to do with boys right in the middle of puberty. Theories abounded. Tall stories would be bandied about, which no one believed. Then, the focus was directed toward the subject of orgasms and masturbation. Did you do it? Could you shoot any juice? And so on.

It became apparent that nearly all of the boys in the circle had never had an orgasm or ejaculated, except the other Senior Patrol Leader, Gary, who was physically more mature than most of us and said he did it all the time. Half the guys looked at Gary with awe. The other half said they didn't believe it.

One of the boys said: "Oh, yeah?! Then prove it! Let's see you do it right now!"

"What'll you give me if I do?", Gary asked.

All hands went into pockets immediately. We came up with about 75 cents in five seconds. That was enough for Gary. (Actually, he'd have probably done it for free, just to show off his manly prowess.)

While one of the boys stood lookout at the tent flap, Gary proceeded to perform this little act in front of an audience. In a short period of time, he produced a wad of semen while jaws dropped all around the circle.

I'm sure that every boy in that tent was thinking the same thing: "Wow! It really works! I'm gonna try that the first chance I get!" Too bad they don't offer a Merit Badge in Masturbation, I thought.

So much for accurate and formal sex education. This type of education— "hands on", so to speak--is much more common or frequent than all the professionally produced films combined.

Chapter Thirty Nine

Anne

Every adolescent boy needs either a female confidant or a mentor or both. I wasn't fortunate enough to have a true mentor. But I was blessed with a great confidant.

It was truly a lucky day when Anne and her family moved in next door in the duplex. Anne was my age, and had a younger sister named Ruth. Anne was petite and cute with a dynamite personality, and we became fast friends almost immediately.

What's more, my parents and hers became social friends, which meant we were thrown together frequently. Instead of becoming boy friend and girl friend, we started sharing concerns, questions and advice about our respective love lives.

Anne's family lived next door for about a year and then they built a home and moved into a new development on the East side. We continued to be close, however, and went to the same school.

For the next three years she educated me in the intricacies of such things as what girls thought about certain things, who liked who and even such monumental mysteries as the difference between Tampax and Kotex (and what are they needed for in the first place?)

She would share with me her feelings about certain boys and I would sometimes act as a go-between or even a match-maker. Then she would give me a detailed account of each date.

It was a big blow to me when Anne and her family moved away from Tulsa after our sophomore year in high school and left quite a void in my life. Our contact deteriorated rapidly and didn't resume until we were adults.

(Anne is now a famous Christian speaker and author who makes appearances all over the world and has written a number of inspirational books.)

Chapter Forty

Can you spit across the street?

Even as we got into junior high school, we would still go to the Saturday morning extravaganzas at the movie theater. Except now there was a new dimension and reason for going. We wanted to see what girls might be there and whether we might make a connection.

While the Will Rogers Theater was closer to my house and had Saturday morning kids' programs, it was a little upscale. We found the action was best at the Royal Theater, which was about a mile and a half away—straight up Highway 66.

To our little group who made these Saturday morning treks, the trip to the movie theater was nearly as fun as actually going inside. There were generally about four or five of us, consisting of myself, Kenny (who frequently spent Friday night with me), Jerry, Billy and possibly one or two others.

On our way we would talk about everything from baseball to girls to ice skating to teachers. I don't know how it started, but we began having contests to see how far we could spit. As we approached a corner, we would stop and stand on the curb. Each of us would take turns spitting and then measure how far the saliva missile would go. Of course, this started graduating to small wagers on the distances.

There were two streets that were especially narrow—barely two lanes wide—and our strategy was to save up for these to see if we could actually spit across the street. About the only way you could accomplish this was if you could manage to manufacture a spit wad that contained some phlegm.

We called this "horking up an agate". This offered three advantages over plain saliva: 1) extra weight, 2) cohesiveness so that the wad would not fragment on its journey and 3) sufficient body so that it could be propelled from the mouth by a combination of muscle contraction and expelling of air through your mouth, formed in a tight "o" with cheeks puffed out, sort of like an air gun. Kenny was a master at this and was the only one of us who regularly accomplished the feat of clearing the street with his missile.

This became a rather prominent goal of all of us and there was no little amount of prestige attached to this prowess. My mother would catch me spitting in the back yard and ask: "What in the world are you doing?"

"What does it look like?", I replied. "I'm practicing spitting, of course.", as if it were the most natural thing in the world.

Some years later, I summed up this activity in a poem:

When I was just a boy of twelve, my worth among my pals,
    Was not how well I played a sport or how I did with gals.
You really had the chance to shine and prove that you were neat,
    If you could stand upon the curb and spit across the street!

We would make it to the Royal Theater by about ten in the morning. I usually had a quarter with me to last the morning. It cost a dime to get in. This left enough for a small sack of popcorn (a nickel), a small Coke (another nickel) and a Holloway, all day sucker (which consumed the last nickel). This sucker was not casually named. It really would last a whole day, if you could stand to have it in your mouth that long. It was a slab of thick, caramel substance with a hint of chocolate. It was on a stick, like a Popsicle. It was almost impossible to bite through. It was tough, chewy, unbelievably sticky when wet, and when worked enough, could be stretched into long strands, like taffy. In retrospect I feel certain this concoction was invented by a Pedodontist. There were probably more dental cavities produced by these sinister little slabs than all the bubble gums combined. However, there was a strong second place in this field. (Read on.)

The Royal Theater's Saturday programs attracted kids from all over the city and the place was always packed. One of the most memorable aspects of those sessions was the odor which emanated from this mass of youthful humanity, about half of whom had their mouths stuffed full of a substance called Banana Beich. The Beich candy company made several types of candy. But the most prominent was this package of yellow, square, sticky and chewy substance made from pure, concentrated banana extract, loads of sugar and a sticky binder. Kids would stock up with a package of these, consisting of four or five square disks, as they went into the theater. Most of the squares came to one of three endings: 1) the first one or two from the package were consumed totally and eventually ended up in tummies. This would generally take about an hour since the squares did not dissolve easily and were nearly impossible to chew. They were simply stuffed into countless jaws throughout the theater where each breath exhaled would unleash a small cloud of banana-saturated gas into the closed atmosphere of the theater. Before long you could slice the air (and it wouldn't require a banana knife to do it). 2) By then, the consumer tended to tire of the candy and the next disk would make it only part of the way to total consumption. The un-eaten portion of this one generally ended up on the floor of the theater in a sticky glob. Countless movement by those in attendance tracked the gooey substance throughout the place. (One must remember that no one just went into the theater, took his seat and remained there throughout the two-hour program. There were constant trips to the concession stand, the bathrooms and to various parts of the theater to see if conversations could be struck up with new female arrivals. The theater was a veritable beehive of activity. Pity the rare attendee who really wanted to see the movie being shown.) 3) The remaining disk in the package would frequently be pressed into action as a flying missile, thrown at random into groups of kids across the theater. Sometimes this would generate a full fledged food fight, but not often. It usually was random acts of hit and hide.

These sessions ended about noon at which time hundreds of kids would pour out of the Royal Theater. Directly across the street from the Royal was a block long strip center with another Crown Drug, laundry, TG&Y, etc. Right in the middle of this block was a small donut shop which featured a creation called a "Spudnut", which was a large glazed donut made from potato flour. They were unbelievably good. The owner of the Spudnut shop was one of the true marketing geniuses of our generation. He would check with the Royal to see the exact time the kids were going to be let loose, at the end of the feature movie. About five minutes before this magic moment, he would fire up all the vats and drop the Spudnuts into the hot grease. The first thing you were hit with as you exited the theater was this aroma of the Spudnuts cooking. It may have hit me harder than the other kids, owing to my early conditioning by the Rainbo Bakery during the first week of my life. However, nearly all of us were drawn to the Spudnut shop. Even the Pied Piper would have been envious as all the kids just poured across Eleventh Street like a huge herd of lemmings. Of course, it was lunch time and most of the kids had subsisted for the past two hours on nothing but Banana Beich's and Holloway suckers.

This whole situation tended to bring out one of my character flaws, and in a most painful way. I knew the Spudnuts would be there. I knew they would be irresistible. I knew I would kill for one. Yet, I would spend all my money at the theater. Live for now. Later will take care of itself. I rarely had enough money to go armed with the extra nickel it would take to buy a Spudnut. In fact, by the time Saturday came, most of my allowance had already been spent, so I would have to get an advance on my allowance from my mother. This usually was a quarter—no more.

This put me in the uncomfortable position of having to borrow a nickel from one of my friends. While standing outside the Spudnut shop, with the aroma of the hot Spudnuts crawling into my nostrils and coating my throat like a warm, soothing blanket, I would go from friend to friend. "Can I borrow a nickel, PLEASE!"

I would usually get one of three answers: "I only have one nickel, and I'm using it for my Spudnut", "I don't have any money and I'm hoping someone will loan me a nickel" or "Where's the nickel I loaned you last week? (Or two weeks ago?)"

Chapter Forty One
Wall Street's a Long Way from Eleventh Street

The eighth grade brought with it new types of activities which were not as tied to the neighborhood. More school activities and more extra-curricular.

One of the highlights of this school year was a new math teacher who joined the Bell faculty. He was fresh out of college and his name was Jack Doblebower. He obviously liked the kids and we liked him and he ended up imparting more knowledge about mathematics to most of us than we had ever received in our first seven years of schooling.

Two things about my year in his class are especially memorable. First, he had learned in college that one's brain functions better when it is not too comfortable. Therefore, he tended to keep his classroom a tad on the chilly side. However, when we walked into class with windows open and the temperature down close to absolute zero, we knew we were about to have a pop quiz.

The other notable event that year was a project in which he had the class participate. One day he passed out to each of us a copy of the stock listings from the daily newspaper. Each of us was given an imaginary five thousand dollars and instructed to "invest" this money in various stocks. We were to calculate the number of shares we would buy of each issue, the total amount invested and prepare a schedule of our "holdings", our basis in each stock and the dates.

Then, one day each week we could "sell" stocks, record the sale price and any profit or loss, and shift our investment into other stocks. We would not be graded on how well we did, on a profit and loss basis, but how well we documented our activities.

The project didn't just show a practical use of various types of mathematics, moving averages, dynamics of buying and selling, etc., but taught us as much about economics as most students several years older had experienced.

I also learned quite a bit about my own investment prowess, or lack thereof. One of my friends, named Frank, who is a really intelligent guy, studied some of the stocks, the companies, their history, etc. He "bought" stocks like AT&T (who are they and what in the world do they do?) and US Steel (how dull can you get?).

On the other hand, I bought the fun stocks. Companies like Warner Brothers, Walt Disney, Mars Candies, Pepsi Cola, etc. Stuff I liked. Why shouldn't they do as well as those stuffy old stocks? After all, didn't people like to go to movies and buy candy and drink soda pop?

When my imaginary five thousand dollars started sinking like a rock and Frank's started climbing, I thought I had to do something, fast. It became a contest between him and me—at least in my mind.

I was discussing some of the possible stocks with Frank to find out a little about what he had learned or what he thought looked good. The conversation came around to speculative stocks—a term with which I was not familiar. We were restricted by Mr. Doblebower to dealing only with stocks on the New York Stock Exchange. There were not many speculative stocks there. But as we discussed speculative stocks, something Frank said burned straight through to the gambler section of my brain. "One thing about speculative stocks is that they are very low priced and if they go up just a little bit, you make a lot of money. But if they go down just a little bit you lose a lot of money as well." I heard the first part of this statement loud and clear. The second part just went right over my head. It probably wasn't important anyway.

I searched the NYSE listings and found that the lowest priced stock was a company named Benguet. I thought maybe they were the manufacturer of that stuff your mother rubbed on your chest when you had a cold. But I was told they were a gold mining company in Canada. Great! The gold business. This is cool! How can you lose money in gold?

So I sold about half my stocks and put it all in Benguet, at about seven eighths of a dollar per share. Just think. It only has to go up a quarter and I

155

make all the money back which I had lost to that point. Another quarter up and I'm in the money and looking good. What the heck. Those dull stocks would go up or down a dollar or two every day. A quarter is nothing!

Well, I guess Benguet wasn't finding much gold in those days. It wasn't too long before the stock had slipped down to less than a half dollar per share. I got out of most of it and tried something else, holding just enough so that if it went back up, I'd get a little of my losses back.

By the end of the semester, I think my five thousand was about $1,300. Frank had made enough to hypothetically buy his parents a new Cadillac.

(Prophetic follow-up: Frank became the Senior Vice President and Treasurer of one of the leading publishing companies in the country. He also served a time as Treasurer of the European arm of the world's largest oil company. On the other hand, I continued my winning ways in investment decisions. It was about twelve years after this project in Mr. Doblebower's class that I told a stock broker friend of mine that I was not about to put an extra thousand dollars I had into a ridiculous new stock—a little company in Arkansas that was putting discount stores on the outskirts of small towns. How stupid an idea is this? People go DOWNTOWN to shop in small towns. That's the point! No one is going to buy junk merchandise in cut-rate stores that aren't even located where the action is—especially if they have to serve themselves. Did not seem like a good idea at the time. I'm not sure how much a thousand dollars invested in Wal-Mart stock in 1966 would be worth now. Probably not that much.)*

*Actually, a friend recently told me how he read that 100 shares of Wal Mart stock purchased in 1970 at the then price of $16 would be worth over $11 million in 2002!

Chapter Forty Two

There's not much fair about the fair

In October of each year, the Tulsa State Fair was held. It was several years before I realized that the Fair was more than just a carnival of rides, games and shows—the midway. I saw the horse trailers and smelled the livestock, but it never really sunk in. The only thing my friends and I were interested in was riding the rides, eating the junk food and trying to win something on those games that looked so easy but never seemed to pay off.

In 1953, I had a new girlfriend named Judy. I asked her to go to the fair with me and we were double dating with my best friend, Al and his girl friend. I asked for another advance on my allowance from my mother. She only had a twenty dollar bill, and Al's mother was honking the horn for me to come out. So, my mother reluctantly gave me the twenty dollar bill and admonished me to bring at least ten dollars of it back to her, which I promised her faithfully I would do.

When we arrived at the Fairgrounds, the excitement level was so high it was off the scale. What to do first? Play games? Ride the rides? Which rides?

We selected the giant Ferris Wheel as the maiden voyage. It was the landmark ride, residing at the top of the midway, overlooking the entire layout like the emperor overseeing his domain.

We went up to the ticket booth where I plunked down my twenty dollar bill and asked for two tickets. We then stood in line and waited as each car was stopped at the bottom, the bar lifted from across the seat and we were helped inside the car at which time the bar was lowered and locked.

The wheel continued its halting movement, proceeding a few feet at a time as each car reached the bottom and the current occupants left the ride while the new ones were seated. This exercise was being repeated until the wheel had a complete new set of riders. When our car reached the top of the wheel and was rocking gently back and forth, we could look out over the entire Fairgrounds and, in fact, much of East Tulsa. I could almost see my house from there, which was only about a mile away.

I remember surveying the scene, then looking over at Judy, who was a very pretty girl with long, dark hair that fell to her shoulders in soft, wavy curls. I thought to myself: "It just doesn't get any better than this! This is the perfect age. I wish I could stay this age forever. I know I won't enjoy the Ferris Wheel this much when I get older. I may not even enjoy going to the Fair! (Naw! I'll always enjoy this!)"

Then, it hit me: I DIDN'T GET MY CHANGE FROM THE TICKET SELLER! I had this sickening feeling in the pit of my stomach. I leaned over the side of the car and starting yelling. About that time, the Ferris Wheel started its complete, full speed ride, having discharged its last load of former passengers.

Each time our car would approach the bottom of the circle, I would start yelling for them to stop it and let me off. I didn't get my change! Judy kept asking what was wrong. I had mixed emotions. I didn't want her to know I was such a fool as to forget nineteen dollars worth of change. Yet, I had to let her know why I was acting like such an idiot. I just told her that they miscounted my change and they owed me some money.

The operator of the ride simply ignored me and let the ride keep going round and round. Finally they started letting the passengers off, one car at a time. It seemed like forever until they got to our car. When the bar came up, I ran down the ramp as fast as I could and went up to the ticket booth, crowding in front of the line.

"Remember me?" I said. "I gave you a twenty dollar bill for two tickets and we just rode the ride. You didn't give me my change! I need my change. It's nineteen dollars!"

The ticket seller looked at me like I was from outer space. "I don't know what you're talking about, kid! Get out of the way. These people are in line to buy tickets."

"Please", I pleaded. "I've got to have my money!"

He ignored me and continued selling tickets. I looked around for someone who looked like he was in authority. There was no one. I ran up to the guy who was operating the ride—pulling on this big lever that stood up from the floor.

"Hey!", I said, pointing to the ticket booth. "That guy didn't give me my change for a twenty dollar bill."

"What do you expect me to do about it?" he said.

It became painfully apparent that I had about as much chance of recouping my change as this guy had of regaining the considerable number of teeth missing from his mouth.

All was lost. There was no way I was going to recover the money. My perfect day at the fair had just turned to crap! Worse, my mother was going to kill me. She might not even believe what happened.

I dejectedly walked back down the ramp, approached Al and told him what had happened. He loaned me five dollars, which helped salvage part of the day, anyway. I'd cross the bridge with my mother later.

I should have known that the occurrence at the Ferris Wheel was just an indication that this was not going to be a perfect day.

Al and I decided we wanted to ride the Dive Bomber. This is a ride which is also called The Hammer on some midways. It consists of two bullet-shaped capsules at the end of long arms (about 15 feet in length) that rotate on a vertical axis. As each capsule or car travels toward the top of the arc, the capsule also rotates on its own so that the car is never actually upside down.

The girls decided they did not want to ride this particular ride, which is a pretty scary contraption. But, as we were approaching the ride, we ran into a good friend who said he wanted to ride the Dive Bomber also. So the three of us bought tickets and went up the ramp to board this instrument invented by a former Gestapo operative, I'm sure. As the capsule came around and the passengers got out, the operator grunted: "OK. Next two riders." Al and our friend, Charlie, got into the car. I suddenly realized I was going to either have to ride this thing alone or with a complete stranger. So, I ran up to the car as the operator was closing the door, and said: "Wait! I'm with these two guys. We all want to ride together."

The guy said: "Only two riders per car." Then he looked at me, saw the determination on my face and the fact that I was not about to move from that spot, and said: "Alright! Hurry and get in!"

I clambered up into the car, trying my best to scoot Al and Charlie over. I wasn't all the way in when the operator slammed the little door and pulled the seat belt over to latch. However, since Al and Charlie had not scooted over enough and I was still partly blocking the door, the door did not totally close nor did the seat belt latch completely.

Before I could protest, the ride started and the car began to lift off the pad. As it started to swing upward in its arc, like the head of a large golf club, the car started to rotate on its own axis and the door popped open. I grabbed the seat belt which was now about as useful as grabbing onto a strand of toilet paper. Al and Charlie suddenly looked toward the door in disbelief and in so doing, leaned toward it. That was enough to shove me right out the door, since the car had partially rotated and the door was no longer vertical. As the car rose to a height of about ten or twelve feet, I tumbled completely out of the car, turned a somersault in the air and landed on my feet in a grassy area directly beneath the ride.

When I landed on my feet, my knees gave out and I folded up like a jack-knife. My feet stayed flat on the ground and my chin went down to meet my knees. In so doing, I bit a chunk out of my tongue, which started bleeding profusely.

I just stayed there, hunkered down under the ride as it continued to rotate, somewhat stunned. Then, the guy operating the ride came over to the edge of the platform where he was stationed, leaned over the railing, and said: "Hey, kid! Get out of there! You're not supposed to be in there! Can't you see the railing?"

I started to protest that I just fell out of his lousy torture machine, but decided that even if he could hear me, he probably wouldn't do anything about it.

After losing most of my remaining funds trying to win a teddy bear for Judy on games that were not meant to be beaten, I came away from the fair thinking that maybe it won't be so bad when I get older if I don't go to the fair that often.

Chapter Forty Three
Since when is a hyphen considered a letter?

One of my goals in school had always been to be the city spelling champion. I won my school championship on two occasions, which is equivalent to the semi-finals, and gone to the city finals, only to be defeated by some older student who successfully spelled some bizarre word I had never heard of, like "ectogony" or "brachycephalic".

The eighth grade was my last opportunity. Ninth grade and older were ineligible. I felt I was ready. My time had come. I was confident I would be the spelling champion of Bell Junior High and would go to the city finals at Will Rogers High School. Then on to Oklahoma City and Washington, DC.

The day of the school finals came. The spelling champion from each home room in the seventh and eighth grade gathered in Mrs. Freeman's speech room for the finals. I was in rare form, zipping through the easier words in the early rounds and even handling a couple of tricky ones as the field narrowed.

Then it was down to two of us. Just me and a little kid named Eddie who was a 7-B. We went back and forth, handling tougher and tougher words. Then Eddie was presented with the word: shepherd. He spelled it: S-H-E-P-P-A-R-D.

HA! I thought. I've got him! That's wrong!

The judges asked him to spell it again. He used the same spelling. I waited for the caller to say "Down". But he was silent. Then the judges started conferring quietly among themselves. The presenter returned to his podium and said: "We are going to disqualify this word and give the speller another. Since there is a teacher in this school named Sheppard, we feel it is too confusing and presents an unfair situation."

Confusing? The word is shepherd. The teacher is Sheppard. So what? Mrs. Greene was a teacher, too. But everyone knew you didn't spell the color green with an "e" on the end.

I just stood there in silence as Eddie was given another word. I forget what it was, but it probably wasn't some lexicographer's nightmare. More like "house" or "chair".

Then it was my turn again. The caller presented the word "cooperate". No sweat! I leaned into the microphone and carefully spelled: C-O-O-P-E-R-A-T-E. He asked me to repeat the spelling, which I did. Then, like getting slapped in the face, I heard him say: "Down". I couldn't believe my ears! I knew this word and used it all the time. I was 100% positive that my spelling was correct.

I looked quizzically at one of the judges, who was one of my teachers. She just shrugged and nodded slightly.

Then, as are the rules, the presenter turned to Eddie and repeated: "Cooperate". In order to win, Eddie must correctly spell the word and then one other. I heard Eddie spell: "C-O-'HYPHEN'-O-P-E-R-A-T-E". "Correct" the presenter said.

Hyphen? HYPHEN? That's not a letter! Besides, I was sure that the word had two acceptable alternative spellings: cooperate and co-operate. Shot down by a technicality! (In fact, the current New Comprehensive International Dictionary of the English Language by Funk & Wagnalls doesn't even list "co-operate" with a hyphen as an acceptable alternative spelling. Only "cooperate" is acceptable.) The only acceptable spelling for competition purposes for any word was the spelling used on the official, published list of words from the Tulsa Public Schools. On that list, cooperate was spelled with a hyphen.

Eddie handled the next word with no problem and was declared the school spelling champion. I was crushed. It was a similar feeling to being given the fifty cent piece to buy all the ice cream I could eat.

These were valuable lessons. It was difficult to win in any confrontation with authority. 15 years from then, protesters would call it going up against "the establishment". But I was an obedient student without a rebellious streak, so I simply accepted it.

Chapter Forty Four
Film at eleven

After Christmas break, we came back to school wearing our new sweaters and Christmas togs. One of the girls got a small 8-millimeter movie camera for Christmas and brought it to school to show everyone and take some shots of her friends.

At lunch time, several of us were in the cafeteria having lunch when this girl and several of her friends went out the side door so she could shoot some film of her friends acting up on the playground. I could see them out the window hamming it up before the camera, trying to form a pyramid, doing silly dances, imitating people, etc. while their would-be director panned from one to the other.

After a few minutes, the group came back into the cafeteria giggling and all excited over their first experience at movie stardom. The director was anxious to see how her friends looked on film and what kind of job she did as a cinematographer. As her friends all gathered around her, looking over her shoulder, she opened the side of the camera and pulled the small reel of film out, whereupon she unreeled the first few feet of film and held it up to the light so she could peer at the images she had just recorded there.

My friends and I looked at this exercise in amazement and started laughing uncontrollably. Gazing intently at the film on which there were no images, the poor girl thought she had done something wrong in the way she handled the camera. Maybe she didn't push the right button? Maybe something was covering the lens? None of her friends had a clue and no one could offer any explanation. I think a couple of them were blondes, but not all of them were.

Chapter Forty Five
Almost Ready for Prime Time Players

It didn't take long for someone to figure out that television was not only an entertainment and news medium but held great potential as a vehicle to raise money. Hence, the birth of the Telethon.

The first big Telethon held by Channel 6 was for the March of Dimes. It ran for a couple of days, around the clock. They were desperate for acts to fill up 48 hours of programming and people came from out of the woodwork, playing every type of instrument or performing every type of bizarre act imaginable. Many of them would have been great candidates for David Letterman's "Stupid Human Tricks" forty years later. Every dance studio in town paraded chorus line after chorus line of little girls in tap shoes and ballet tutus. Solo violinists without accompaniment stood before the camera squeaking out sounds which were supposed to resemble the song which had been announced for them. Occasionally there was some excellent, local talent, which they slotted into the prime time spots. However, Modell Phipps playing the musical saw or Fannie Frickert doing her bird calls were relegated to the three or four o'clock time period—AM, not PM.

A group of us in band decided we should form our own group with the goal of appearing on the Telethon before performing for the entire school and then going on to major, national stardom.

What kind of music would we play? Mr. Linde, the school band director, had a few arrangements of Dixieland tunes which he would loan us. So it was decided: we would be a Dixieland band which would eventually move more toward jazz.

164

The band consisted of Bobby on trumpet, Bill on trombone, Al on saxophone, Alan on drums (which consisted of a snare drum and a cymbal on a stand—not a full set) and, since a Dixieland band only had one trumpet or cornet, I was pressed in to play piano. We felt we needed a clarinet, so we recruited my close friend, Jerry, even though he was going to a different school. We did not have a banjo player, but didn't feel we really needed one.

We started rehearsals at Bobby's house and felt we sounded pretty good. So, we phoned Channel 6 and volunteered to appear on the upcoming Telethon. They sent us a form to fill out. Bobby filled it out and promptly returned it. We were subsequently informed that we would go on at about 6:15 in the morning of the second day. OK. Not prime time, but better than the 3 AM slot. We were determined to show them that we were ready for prime time and they would, in all likelihood, ask us back as a headliner after they heard us.

We rehearsed several times and had three or four tunes down pretty good when the day of our debut finally arrived.

Al, Jerry and I arrived at the Channel 6 studios first—about 5 AM. A lady met us and looked on her clipboard. "Let's see.", she said. "OK, here you are. Be-Bop Bob and the Hometown Hepcats at 6:15. Just wait over here in this area and we'll call you a few minutes before you go on."

Al, Jerry and I looked at each other, startled. "Be-Bop Bob and the Hometown Hepcats"??? Who was this? This wasn't the name of the group. In fact, we didn't even have a name, yet. Hadn't even thought about it. It was immediately apparent that since Bobby had filled out the form and returned it, he had decided to name the group. Obviously, he was "Be-Bop Bob", putting himself in as the "front man". But Dixieland bands rarely had a front man. Alright, there was Red Nichols and the Five Pennies. And maybe Louis Armstrong fronted his group, but these were major stars in their own right.

Almost simultaneously, the three of us called out to the lady with the clipboard. "Excuse me!" we yelled. She turned around abruptly. "That's not our correct name."

"Well, that's what was on your entry form.", she said.

"I'm sorry, but that was a mistake." I said.

"Well, OK.", she said. "What is the correct name? How do you want to be introduced?"

I blurted out: "We're the Offbeats!" Al and Jerry jerked around and looked at me with a combination of disbelief and humor. I just shrugged— all I could think of off the top of my head.

165

There was a prominent musicians' magazine called "Downbeat". There was also one of the large dance bands from one of the high schools called "The Downbeats". So I felt that the "Offbeats" would be a whimsical play on this musical term and portray us as a fun-loving, devil-may-care group of young, madcap musicians.

The other guys in the band arrived and we got our instruments out and warmed up. Nothing more was said about the name.

When it came time for us to go on, they placed us on the set while my old radio announcer friend, Cy Tuma, who was now with KOTV, introduced us. "And now, a group of talented youngsters from Bell Junior High. They're going to offer up some hot Dixieland for us. Here they are, The Offbeats!"

Bobby looked over at me with a quizzical yet perturbed look. But we immediately kicked off with that old Dixieland classic, "Muskat Ramble" (which many people erroneously call "Muskrat" Ramble—but the name comes from Muscatel Wine, which many in the South call Muskat, for short).

We really sounded good. No kidding! We zipped right through the song. No major mistakes. Played in key and ended together. Those in the studio applauded energetically, especially for that time of the morning.

We were only scheduled to play one song. But Cy, who appeared impressed, said: "That was great, boys! Can you play another one for us?" So, we followed up with "When The Saints Go Marching In" and, once again, did an acceptable job.

After we received all the accolades at the studio and had visions of a major recording contract, Bobby said—"What's the deal with the 'Offbeats'?"

I replied: "What's the deal with 'Be-Bop Bob and the Hometown Hepcats"?

"It's a great name!" he said. "After all, Dixieland is sort of Be-Bop music and Hometown Hepcats is catchy."

"Are you supposed to be 'Be-Bop Bob'?" I inquired. He nodded. "But who made you the leader?" I asked.

"Well, we practice at my house, don't we?"

Nothing more was said about the name at the time. We seemed to be at an impasse. But I was determined that we would have some sort of democratic selection of a name at the first opportunity.

It soon became apparent that the final name would not be "The Offbeats" after an exchange I had a few days later. We returned to school expecting to be mobbed by fellow students wanting autographs. No one was even aware we had been on TV. Not many were up at 6 AM on a Saturday.

But one guy approached me and said: "Hey. I saw you guys on TV. You sounded pretty good." I beamed with a high degree of pride showing. "So—what was it you call yourselves?" and he started giggling. "The Beat-offs?"

That hit me like a slap in the face. I had never even considered this obvious play on words. I thought The Offbeats was a pretty clever name. But "beat-off" was quite a different matter—it was a common slang term meaning masturbation. Oh, my gosh! The name was killed immediately.

We never selected another name. But it didn't matter. We never played again in public.

Chapter Forty Six

Politics and If-Dog-Rabbit

The first big event of the ninth grade was election of class officers. I decided to go for the gold and run for president.

My campaign manager for the election was my best friend, Al. This was partly because he was a close friend, but mostly because his dad owned a printing company. While the other candidates would be hard at work each night making campaign badges and signs by hand, I'd be taking it easy, having printed millions of everything I needed at Central Printing Company. Al and I would go down to the printing company after school where his dad would let us set cold type for printing campaign badges, signs, flyers, etc. on one of his letterpresses. We printed up hundreds of campaign badges for friends to wear. They were slightly larger than a business card and said "Vote for Welling for Ninth Grade President". We also printed up signs to post around school and flyers to hand out.

What a campaign! Our stuff was everywhere. We got the word out big time. Everyone I talked to promised to vote for me. When the votes were counted after the election, it was something like a three to one landslide. I lost. Either a lot of my friends didn't vote, or they lied to me. The winner was a guy named Mike (remember that name).

Al and I continued our close friendship after the election. We were very close buddies. I still was good friends with Kenny and Jerry, but they went to different schools. Bobby and I were also good friends, but Al and

I seemed to be thrown together more. One of the really interesting things about Al was his family. His mother was a pretty lady with black hair and a fiery temper, having gotten so mad at Al or his brother, Roger, that she was taken to throwing things at them, like the ketchup bottle or even knives as they ran to escape her wrath.

But the real character of the family was his dad. Al's dad drove an old black Ford pickup truck with a spit can in it for his chewing tobacco. While his primary occupation was running the printing company, his real love was raising chickens. They lived in a nice house just outside the city limits. The house sat on a few acres. They had a couple of rows of chicken houses in the back where they raised several hundred chickens.

Al's dad was a colorful kind of crusty guy. The thing I remember most about him was his reply to us whenever he would ask us how we did in some sort of game, and we lost (but there was always a good reason why we lost). Al and I were on the same bowling team in the junior league on Saturday mornings. If Al's dad would pick us up after the league matches, he would ask us how we did. If we lost, we would say something like: "We barely lost. But if James had just picked up that spare in the tenth frame of the last game, we would have beaten them."

Al's dad would simply reply: "If...dog...rabbit, boys."

Or if he asked how the football team did and we had lost, it was something like: "They beat us by a couple of touchdowns, but we got robbed on a couple of referee calls. If we'd just had a referee who wasn't blind, it would have been a different story and we'd have stomped them."

"If...dog...rabbit, boys."

After a couple of years of hearing this from Al's dad, I asked him: "I've heard you say 'if...dog...rabbit' for a long time. What does that mean, anyway?"

"If the dog hadn't stopped to take a leak he'd have caught the rabbit. Losers always have an excuse."

Before we graduated from high school, Al's dad finally did what he had been longing to do. He sold the printing company and bought a chicken ranch with about ten gazillion chickens in Arkansas and moved there. Al had to finish out his senior year in high school living in an apartment by himself in Tulsa (which most of his buddies, including me, thought was really cool).

Al and I put together a team and joined the junior bowling league at Utica Bowl on Saturday mornings. Our dream team consisted of Al and me plus my friend Bobby, and a couple of neighborhood buddies, James and Charlie. However, in the second year, we had to add at least two girls, in order to be within the rules, since it was a mixed league. So I pressed my close friend Anne to join the team and we also got the best girl bowler in the league, named Brenda.

These Saturday morning sessions were weekly highlights. The bowling league play was over by noon. Most of the kids were out the door, immediately. However, Al and I started playing the pinball machines which were against the wall near the front door. It cost a dime to play and you could win games on them. If you hit a good streak, you could rack up dozens of games and play quite a while on your original dime.

But if your game wasn't on, you could end up going through two or three dollars worth of dimes in an hour or two. It didn't seem like much, but I was astounded to find out from one of the guys who worked at Utica Bowl that the owner was putting three kids through college solely on what he made off these pinball machines.

My career in junior bowling was fairly successful. Our team won the league and we competed against winning teams from Wichita, Oklahoma City, Dallas and other cities with a high degree of success. Then, in 1955, as ninth graders, Al and I won the state doubles championship—pictures in the paper, trophies and everything.

I used this experience in junior bowling as a springboard into the adult leagues and then into professional bowling while still a teenager.

The summit of reservoir hill with KVOO Radio towers. From the top, you could see all of Tulsa.

Chapter Forty Seven
Becoming popular in a strange way

Regardless of the blow to my self esteem dealt by the big election loss, I regained some of my standing when all of a sudden a lot of the most prominent guys in the class and most popular people wanted to double date with me. If there was a party of some kind, guys would start approaching me to ask if we could double date and would I arrange it so my dad would drive?

Of course, at age 14, none of us was driving (legally) so we were dependent upon parents (or public transportation) to get us anywhere.

What happened to create this sudden, new interest in my companionship stemmed from something which had taken place after a party one night. I was at the party with my girl friend, Kay—a really cute, sweet girl who was one year younger than me. At the party was my close friend Anne, who had a date with one of the most popular boys in the class, David, who was probably also the outstanding athlete in the class. Anne knew my dad was going to pick me up and take Kay home, so she asked if we could also take David and her home as well. She also informed me that they were double dating with another of the popular athletes, Don, and his girlfriend, Ouida (who had been my eighth grade girlfriend). I said it might be a bit crowded, but it was okay with me.

When Dad arrived to pick Kay and me up, I informed him that we had some others to drop off. No problem, he said. Of course, he knew Anne very well.

Everyone clambered to get into the back seat. Since I was standing next

171

to the car anyway, I ushered Kay into the back seat and joined her. Don and Ouida joined us, leaving David and Anne in the front seat, next to Dad.

As soon as we pulled away from the party, those of us in the back seat began to spark up the back of the car a bit—"making out" or "courting" as some called it. Poor David and Anne just sat self-consciously next to my dad in the front seat, hands folded neatly in their laps.

My dad made a little small talk with Anne, asking about her parents, etc. Then he asked her: "So. Is David, here, your boy friend?"

She sheepishly said: "Yes."

So Dad looked over at David and said. "Do you like Anne?"

David sort of embarrassingly paused, and said: "Yeah."

So Dad said: "Well, why don't you kiss her, then?"

David was taken aback by this, but in light of the action taking place in the back seat, he joined in and started up with Anne, who was not a reluctant participant.

Then Dad said to the entire car: "Does anyone have to be home soon?" (Silence) "OK, then."

He then started driving down Eleventh Street, toward town and we went back to what we were engaged in.

Just North of the downtown Tulsa area is a large hill called "Reservoir Hill". It was the location of several nice mansions which had been built during the twenties and thirties, before the town started expanding toward the South and Southeast. It had always been a favorite parking spot for couples since the view was magnificent and it was very quiet (and safe during those days).

Dad drove up to the top of Reservoir Hill, selected a great vantage point and parked the car. I thought this was a bit weird, and still felt a little up tight about having my dad in the front seat while Kay and I were engaged in a little smooching session in the back seat.

At that point, Dad got out of the car, opened the trunk and got something out. It was a mild, star-filled autumn night, a little on the chilly side. I looked out the window to see him unfolding a lawn chair and placing it in front of the car. He then proceeded to get out a flashlight and the latest paperback mystery novel he was into. He sat there and read his mystery book by flashlight for about an hour, while these six kids steamed up the windows, inside.

Then, he got up, folded up the chair and put it back in the trunk and said: "Well, I guess it's about time to get you kids home."

This night will go down in history among most of my friends at Bell

Junior High School. The story spread like wildfire throughout the school. Envy abounded and suddenly my social calendar was elevated to unheard of heights. Not only that, my dad was requested to chaperone every dance, mixer, sock hop, record party or get together held at that school or private homes for the rest of the year. The kids figured that any parent cool enough to go park on Reservoir Hill would likely be on the liberal side when it came to restricting party activities.

My dad tried to fulfill as many of these calls to action as he could, but it wasn't my mother's kind of thing. Only occasionally would she accompany him. If it was on one of his bowling nights, he'd at least show up early and stay until about 9:00. Then he might come back after bowling, about midnight, and take Kay and me home, along with whoever the lucky triple date companions were for the evening.

Dad became one of the more popular members of our class that year. If they had had a re-call election, he probably would have even beaten Mike out for class president.

* * * * *

Up to this point, like most of my friends, my sex education had come from peers, hearsay or catch as catch can. For some reason, Dad thought he had been remiss in his duties by not having the famous birds and bees conversation with me. So, one day we were driving together to Oklahoma City and while going down the Turner Turnpike, Dad screwed up his courage to approach the subject with me. Obviously, it was sort of late in the game. While I was not exactly experienced, I was pretty much through puberty by then. But he broached the topic with me anyway.

"Son, we've never really had a talk about . . . you know. . . the birds and the bees. You know what I'm talking about."

"Yeah, Dad", I said. "What would you like to know?"

He laughed and we changed the subject immediately. I thought I deftly sidestepped an uncomfortable situation. I didn't really want to hear my dad stumble through trying to explain a bunch of stuff that I already knew. Worse, I didn't want him to know how much or how little I knew, at that age. I figured that when the time came, I would handle it one way or the other.

* * * * *

Athletics are very important in the teenage years, especially among boys. Most of the most popular boys are also the better athletes. Being good at one of the team sports means instant acceptance and credibility. Being good at music or spelling or math means being labeled a geek.

Unfortunately, I had never excelled at any of the team sports and there wasn't much glory in the individual sports—even in being state bowling champion (or yo-yo, if you can call that a "sport") or even in being a fair golfer. Baseball was my most successful endeavor in the team sports field, but even then my success was limited to the year when I could play with boys closer to my age or younger. I was a pitcher who excelled in accuracy, but not speed. You could run from the pitcher's mound to home plate and probably beat my fast ball. But I had a wicked slider pitch.

I loved basketball and had developed a pretty neat spin and jump shot and a reasonable hook shot. This made me fairly competitive in one-on-one games, such as Horse. But I was lousy if there was any defense involved. Besides, I was only about five feet runt inches tall.

I thought I was definitely out when it came to football. Who needs a 120 pound football player who runs about as fast as a second grade girl? And then a door opened up for me, thanks to my friend David (the one who was in the front seat with Anne). David was sort of the top jock in school and was captain of our intramural football team. He was also the quarterback and discovered that I was very accurate at centering the football to him, so he put me in as starting center. This was flag football (no pads, no contact, supposedly) so size was not too big a deal in some positions.

I didn't particularly like playing center, but I did like being on the championship football team and there was a certain amount of prestige attached to being on the starting team.

PART FIVE
Real Life Happy Days

Chapter Forty Eight
High School at last

Starting to Will Rogers High School represented the biggest change in my life to this point. It was a big, imposing, beautiful, art deco style building with huge doors, marble floors, a six foot diameter inlay of Will Rogers' branding iron design, called the "dog iron", in the front hallway floor, a bronze bust of Will, large built-in trophy cases along the walls of the main floors and beautiful chandeliers. The place reeked with atmosphere and tradition.

The first big occurrence of the year was election of the sophomore class officers. Al and I were still best friends, and his dad still had the printing company, so I decided to run for president (again). Why not? After all, I was the state junior doubles bowling champ and former state champion yo-yoer. Many grownup men have run for governor of Oklahoma with fewer credentials than this (and some even won).

We blanketed the school with signs, passed out "Vote for Welling" badges to everyone we could find and I made what I thought was a more than acceptable campaign speech at the sophomore assembly. The election was a landslide. I lost. The winner was a guy named Mike.

* * * * *

Will Rogers High School was an outstanding institution in many ways, due in no small part to the demographic makeup of the student body. It was a middle class school with great diversity, ranging from those of very modest means to the upper middle class. There were no obviously wealthy kids at the school, nor was there abject poverty—at least none that was apparent. Everyone seemed to have just stepped out of one of the television sitcoms—right out of Father Knows Best or Ozzie and Harriet.

That's not to say there weren't some class differentiations or natural social groups. In fact, just as Susie Hinton wrote about in her books—especially in The Outsiders--there were the Soc's (pronounced: "soashes", as in social or socialite) and the Hoods. These represented the two extremes. Most of the student body fell into the mainstream middle ground—kids who were active in one area or another of school, such as band, choir, Future Homemakers of America, working in the office, active in school plays, etc.

The soashes consisted of a lot of the athletes and the popular girls who filled such roles as cheerleaders, beauty queens, etc. The Hoods weren't really hoodlums, they were those who tended to avoid traditional school activities, wore their hair in ducktails rather than flat-tops and sometimes turned the collars up on their shirts. They were more likely to be smokers.

Soashes hung around in the front hall near the bust of Will Rogers in the mornings before school (this was called "Soash Corner"). The hoods tended to hang around in the back part of the school building, near the "Smoke Hole" or the Auto Mechanics shop. I was fortunate. I had good friends in both groups.

In fact, I had one friend who could almost qualify for both groups. This guy was the closest thing to Fonzy on Happy Days that you could imagine. Daryl wore his hair in a well-oiled ducktail and often wore a black leather jacket. He sometimes wore only a tight, white tee-shirt. But if he wore a collared shirt, he usually turned the collar up. He bore a striking resemblance to Elvis Presley with a little bit of James Dean thrown in. All of this would have been sufficient to classify him with the hoods. However, he played in the band, and was a better than average trumpet player. He also was a good athlete. He played shortstop on a baseball team which had won the city championship in junior high school. These qualities were sufficient to keep him from being totally accepted by the hoods. He created his own class of one. (There are those, both classmates and faculty, who would have bet that Daryl would not have amounted to anything. But he ended up serving as the CEO of more than one major nationwide retail chain and now spends a lot of his time showing prize-winning horses in national competitions.)

Dress was very important then, as it has always been. There were few prestige labels in clothes. You could buy Izod shirts with the little alligators, but they tended to be worn by older men. My dad had several. About the only real label which had widespread appeal or prestige was Levi.

Standard uniform for the boys consisted of Levi's with white socks and penny loafers and collared shirt for the soashes and mainstream boys but white tee-shirt for the hoods. Even if you wore a collared shirt, you would have a white tee-shirt showing prominently under it.

Almost all the boys wore letter jackets with leather sleeves, even if you weren't on an athletic team or hadn't won a letter.

One thing you never saw was a tee-shirt with anything written on it. No logos. No slogans. No messages. No pictures. No advertising. No jokes—not even "I'm with stupid."

Try as I might, I could not develop a decent flat top hair style. I went to several barbers and tried all sorts of waxes, creams, etc. to add body to my hair and make it stand up. My hair was baby fine and about all I could muster was a fake flat top. That is, I brushed the front row of hair straight up, coated with wax, and had it flattened straight across. The rest of my hair was a simple crew cut. I couldn't even grow a decent duck tail. When I let it grow and tried to comb it back, it would just fall limply over my ears or stick down and out in back, over my collar, even with Brylcreme or Wildroot on it.

My friend Kenny had the flat top to beat all flat tops. He had coal black, thick and coarse hair. He could get it to grow straight up like some sort of agricultural crop. The barber would trim the entire thing flat, checking his work frequently with a ruler/straight-edge. It was gorgeous and nearly all the guys were envious. You could land an airplane on that surface.

Dress, hairstyles and school gathering points weren't the only things which separated the soashes from the hoods. Each group had its favorite after-school hangout. Instead of the malt shop, like those seen in Happy Days, Grease or Back to the Future, the hangouts were drive-ins, like in American Graffiti. The soashes hung out at Pennington's Drive In while the hoods preferred Cotton's. Actually, the Pennington's frequented by the Rogers crowd was called "Little Pennington's". The original Pennington's was on the far south side of town and was the hangout of our rivals from Central High School and later from Edison, the new high school in town. These institutions figured prominently in a lot of the events which took place in the high school careers of most of us.

There was one group of guys that I fell in with during my sophomore year who fell neither in the soash or hood category. Most of them were seniors and were a group of creative, funny and fun-loving guys a couple of whom were very artistic. I would normally not have even been accepted into this group, since I was but a lowly sophomore. But I had some classes with a couple of them and, for some reason, I was included in some of their antics. One of the ringleaders of this group was a talented guy named Russell Myers. In addition to being a very funny guy, he was the primary cartoonist for the school newspaper. He continued his cartooning through college and into a career and created a comic strip called Broomhilda which has been syndicated in hundreds of newspapers for over thirty years.

Roo (as we called Russell) and a couple of the guys invented this fictitious character named Otis Wonie. I think he must have been inspired by the What-Me-Worry kid of Mad Magazine fame (Aflred E. Neuman), who seemed to be omni-present throughout the magazine, showing up in group pictures of dignitaries, stars or others out of nowhere. Throughout the year, whenever there was a sign-up list for any event, someone would always add the name of Otis Wonie. If there was a group picture taken for anything, one of the guys in the group would give the name Otis Wonie instead of his real name, which would then appear in the caption. If the sign-up required a girl's name, they invented Otis Wonie's sister and added her name, wherever possible. Her name was G. Ophelia Wonie (as in: "Go-feel-your-wonie"). We thought this was a great inside joke

Pretty soon, a big portion of the student body was in on the Otis Wonie joke and sort of accepted him as another member of the class of '56. One of the guys in the group was somehow involved in the planning of year-end activities for the graduating class. I went to the commencement exercises for that class and as I looked down the list of graduating seniors on the official commencement program, there appeared the name of "Otis Wonie". Apparently his poor sister was forced to drop out of school or something, as her name was nowhere to be found. (Rumor was that she found herself "with child" and the father was reputed to be none other than that ubiquitous rascal, Alfred E. Neuman, so she had to drop out of school.)

Chapter Forty Nine
How big is a cue ball anyway?

Within a couple of blocks of Little Penningtons' were located several significant institutions and merchants. In particular there was a great greasy spoon lunch spot called Coney Corner which had some of the best Coney Islands in town. We went there for lunch from school about once week.

Across the street from Coney Corner was a pool hall called "Breezy's". Almost all the guys frequented Breezy's for a game of pool or just to see who was there and what was going on.

One night there were about twenty or thirty of us at Breezy's, shooting pool and just hanging out. In walked a couple of our friends. Several guys asked if they wanted to shoot a game of 8-ball Snooker. But neither of the new arrivals had any money. They tried to borrow some money from others, but hit stone walls. Suddenly one of the guys, who was sort of the class clown, named Benny, got this great idea. He jumped up on the pool table and announced: "We'll bet anyone or everyone in the place that Jimmy, here, can put this cue ball all the way into his mouth." Several guys immediately picked up pool balls and tried to put them in their mouths. None could even come close to doing it, so they said there's no way it could be done. Pretty soon, everyone in the place agreed that it was a physical impossibility.

Benny continued: "OK. Who wants to see Jimmy put this cue ball in his mouth? C'mon. This ought to be worth two bits from each of you. Get it up to two bucks and we'll do it, won't we Jimmy?"

At that point Jimmy looked up and said: "What's this 'we' crap?"

Pretty soon, some of the guys started throwing pocket change onto the pool table. After the first wave of contributions there was less than a dollar on the table. Benny continued to egg the crowd on and the total approached two dollars. "C'mon" Benny said. "Unless we can get at least two bucks, it's no go."

Then Breezy himself, the proprietor, stepped up and threw a dollar on the table. "I gotta see this!" he said.

So there was about $2.75 in the pot and Benny said: "It's show time!"

Jimmy took the cue ball in hand and held it up to the light. We half expected to hear him say: "Alas! Poor Yorick! I knew him well."

Jimmy opened his mouth and began to insert the ball toward his tonsils. It wouldn't go. He turned his head sideways, pulled the ball away and massaged his jaw with his hands. Then he licked the ball all over to make it as slick as possible and went for the next attempt.

On the second attempt, Benny even helped him pull his lower jaw down to its maximum. The opening between Jimmy's teeth, at its maximum, was just a tad narrower than the cue ball. But Jimmy nearly had it. Benny then just reached up and tapped the ball. It popped past Jimmy's teeth and into his mouth

The room burst into applause and Benny picked up the money from the table and put it into his pocket. "OK. Now we're ready to play some pool!" Benny said. "C'mon, Jimmy!"

But Jimmy stared at Benny, his eyes bigger than the pool balls. The cue ball was still in his mouth and it was becoming apparent that he couldn't get it out. He was getting the unmistakable look of panic in his eyes. Then his eyes started watering. Obviously, this was rapidly turning into a serious situation.

Benny stuck his fingers into the corner of Jimmy's mouth and tried to pop the cue ball out, but it wouldn't budge.

Breezy's place was located on Admiral Boulevard in a block which was mostly residential. One of the guys said that a few doors down from Breezy's there was a dentist's office. It was thought that his office was in the front of the house and that the dentist lived there, in the back part of the house. Maybe he would be home. It was about 11 o'clock at night

So, out the front door of Breezy's we all went—about thirty of us, with

Benny and Jimmy leading the parade. About three or four houses down there was a sign in the front yard for the dentist. Funny that most of us had never noticed this sign.

It was a frame house probably built in the twenties or thirties, with a porch all the way across the front. The house was dark. Benny knocked loudly on the door. No reply. Then he knocked louder. We waited a few moments. Then a light came on inside and we could see someone approaching the door. A middle aged man wearing a maroon robe and corduroy house slippers opened the door.

"Are you the dentist?" Benny asked. He nodded. "We've got an emergency here.", and then he explained the situation.

"Well, come on in, then.", the dentist said. So we all started to squeeze toward the front door. "Not all of you! Just you two.", pointing to Jimmy and Benny.

So, the two of them went in. In a few minutes, Benny returned where we were all waiting in the front yard. We asked if the dentist was successful and he replied that the dentist felt confident he could free the cue ball. He would have to give Jimmy a shot of muscle relaxant and some pain killer and then force the jaw open wider. Then he said: "Can someone please loan me two dollars and a quarter? PLEASE. It's a real emergency. The dentist wants five bucks." A couple of the guys came up with the money and gave it to Benny who returned to the operatory to complete the business side of the transaction.

Soon Benny and Jimmy emerged. Jimmy's eyes were red, he couldn't talk and he was clutching the cue ball in his hand. We all applauded. He grinned weakly and headed back toward Breezy's.

The bottom line for this bit of entrepreneurial fundraising by the team of Jimmy and Benny was a net loss of $2.25 plus a lot of pain for Jimmy. After the pain killer wore off, I'm sure Jimmy had several days of pain and soreness.

Chapter Fifty
A Crate Full of English

Teachers at Rogers were a different breed from anything I had encountered in my first ten years of school. Much more professorial. The most unusual we encountered in the sophomore year was Miss Ethel Crate, who taught English from her greenhouse on the fourth floor.

Miss Crate was living proof that there was no mandatory retirement age in the Tulsa Public Schools.

Her classroom was her own private retreat and sanctum. Tarzan would have felt right at home there. Plants lined the window sills, covered her desk, sat on shelves around the chalkboards and rested on plant stands throughout the room. These were not little pansies and begonias but industrial strength, jungle-ready, rain forest specimens. Vines, large leaf (probably carnivorous) wannabe trees and creeping green things of all types occupied more space than the class. The plants, in their normal cycles, took in carbon dioxide and gave off oxygen. But Miss Crate was so faithful in her watering (she even came up on weekends to tend her plants) that the oxygen given off was highly saturated with water, making the room very humid.

Miss Crate was a very professional, serious teacher apparently devoid of any sense of humor—at least none that we could discern. She was intimidating, to say the least. Her relatively short frame was well padded. She was prone to wearing flower print silk dresses whose patterns must have already been rejected by all of the manufacturers of drapery fabric. Her dull, grey hair was always in a neat bun, held at the back of her head by large pins. And, of course, she wore those horrible black "sensible" shoes. The ones everyone called "school teacher shoes". How apropos.

One day one of the boys decided he would play a little practical joke on Miss Crate. He could not have picked a worse subject for the joke nor a worse joke for this subject. He decided to put a Whoopee Cushion in her chair! No kidding! Virtually every other teacher in that school would have likely seen some humor in such a prank, even if some of them might have gotten upset.

The boy who did the dirty deed was a newcomer to Tulsa named Randy. He had just moved there from California. He had "California" written all over him. His hair was partially peroxided and not coiffed in either a flat-top nor duck tail, but sort of wildly wavy. He wore the wildest shirts I have ever seen. No store within a thousand miles of Tulsa, Oklahoma would carry in their stock (not even under the counter) any of the types of shirts like those which comprised Randy's wardrobe. On the day of the big prank, Randy was wearing a lilac colored, blousy shirt with prints of huge spiders all over it. I'm talking spiders which were five or six inches across. It was worn outside his pants and came down to his hips making the image area for the spiders that much larger. It was really gross, by almost anyone's standards. Having never been to California at that time I was sure that everything I had heard about it must be true.

Miss Crate left the room for a few minutes and Randy went up to her desk and slipped the noise maker underneath the pad in her chair.

The class was totally silent, as it always was, even when Miss Crate left the room. No one would dare make a single sound unless answering a direct question posed by Miss Crate. However, as she re-entered the room, you could cut the atmosphere with a knife. The air was charged with a combination of anticipation, fear, nervousness, anxiety and uncertainty. As Miss Crate approached her chair, there was shifting in chairs by a large share of the class. Some were straightening up to get a better look at the reaction. Others were trying to shrink into their chairs, so as to escape.

Miss Crate stood behind her desk and started to sit down. There was an audible, anticipatory gasp from several in the class. Then she abruptly stood back up straight before sitting in order to tell the class to pass the papers we were working on to the front of each row. The class was still holding its collective breath.

Then, she started to sit down for real. A girl named Judy who sat in the chair directly behind me could contain herself no longer and let out a high pitched shriek while Miss Crate's bottom was still a foot or two above the chair. Too late. Miss Crate was already committed to the sitting position. As her ample bottom met the chair pad, the Whoopee Cushion let out its

184

telltale report, like she had sat on a rather large frog.

The group gasp was repeated along with laughter ranging from giggles to guffaws spewing forth.

Miss Crate immediately stood up, walked around her chair a couple of times staring at it and said: "How strange. That chair has never made that noise before."

This just turned up the volume on the laughter even more.

Then she inspected the cushion and discovered the source of the noise. Lifting the device up and holding it like she was holding a dead fish by the tail, she said: "Who is responsible for this?" Silence. "I demand to know who put this in my chair! If the responsible party does not come forward right now, the whole class is going to be severely reprimanded."

At that point, Randy stood, came to the front of the class and almost in tears said: "It was me, Miss Crate. I didn't mean any harm. The class had nothing to do with it."

Miss Crate was at a loss for words, likely upset as much by the class laughter as by the actual prank. She left the room without a word.

In a few minutes, she returned to the room with the Assistant Principal in tow. He asked her to leave the room for a moment. Then he looked at the class and we prepared ourselves for a thorough tongue lashing. He stood in front of her desk with arms folded, leaning up against the desk with his legs casually crossed at the ankle.

"Miss Crate is an unusual person." He began. "You may have noticed that she is a little strange when it comes to certain things", glancing around at the jungle. "We must give people like Miss Crate a little slack when it comes to how we treat them. I would appreciate it if you would be more sensitive towards her. She is basically a lonely person but is a very good teacher. You will get a lot out of her class if you will only give her a chance. I think in view of today's event, you should all read whatever you have in front of you or catch up on homework you may have in this or any other class. Miss Crate will not be returning to class today, since there are only ten minutes left."

He then turned and looked at Randy. "Young man, I'd like to see you in my office after school today." He then glanced down at her desk, picked up the Whoopee Cushion and walked out of the room. (Randy later said that all he got was a mild reprimand and his Whoopee Cushion confiscated.)

* * * * *

One other significant event took place in Miss Crate's class which probably equaled the Whoopee Cushion as one of the most disruptive things she had ever seen in this den of decorum over which she presided. One afternoon, while the class was quietly at work on a writing assignment, a boy named Ralph got up and went to the pencil sharpener which was mounted on the wall between the blackboard and the window. The classroom was on the fourth floor of the building, facing south.

While Ralph was sharpening his pencil, he loitered as long as possible, gazing out the window. Suddenly he let out with a loud: "SON OF A BITCH!"

Someone could have fired a cannon and the room would not have been more shaken. We didn't know whether he hurt himself or what. Ralph started pointing out the window to the southeast. Several of us jumped up and ran to the windows and saw a column of dark gray smoke rising near the horizon.

"A plane just crashed!" Ralph blurted out. Everyone was up and at the windows by this time, including Miss Crate. Then she demanded that everyone take their seats again, that there was nothing any of us could do. Suffice it to say, none of us could concentrate for the rest of the class.

As soon as the bell rang at the end of the class period, several of us ran out of the school, cutting the last class of the day, and looked for anyone who had a car. I stopped one of the guys I knew from band and asked if he was going out to where the plane crashed and if so, would he take us with him

We headed out to the crash site, which was about four miles from the school, but by the time we got there we couldn't get within a half mile. We parked and ran the rest of the way. When we got there, they had a large field already roped off. The field was in the glide path for the airport and a jet trainer had crashed into the field, resulting in a blackened crater about 15 or 20 feet wide. The pilot was killed. The newspaper called him a hero for staying with the plane and heading it into the field, avoiding several residential areas which surrounded the field.

Chapter Fifty One
Sonny

I was really enjoying playing in the band at school, although there were so many trumpets that I didn't make the main band. Most of the sophomore trumpet players played in the sophomore band.

Rogers had a stage band or dance band as they called it. Membership was by audition and was restricted to only three trumpets, like most of the big bands, whose music they played. I didn't make the band my sophomore year, but still wanted to play in some sort of pop music band.

A few of the guys in the Rogers Dance Band, especially a trumpet player named Scott and the best trombonist in town, named Ted, played in a big band called the Sonny Gray Orchestra. Sonny Gray was a piano player who went to Central High School. He had put together the best young musicians in town and they played a lot of dances, for both kids and adults.

Sonny lived in a large house in the Maple Ridge section of Tulsa, which contained several of the early, oil-money mansions of the city. In the basement of this large house, Sonny had a rehearsal room, complete with multi-tiered risers, music stands and a grand piano. The orchestra rehearsed there at least one night a week, and I started going to the rehearsals, hoping for an audition. My parents were acquainted with Sonny's mother, a large, imposing woman named "Babe". She had been widowed several years earlier.

Each rehearsal night, there were always several people in attendance.

Sonny rarely allowed them in the rehearsal room while the band rehearsed. So, we would all sit around in the living room and talk with Babe.

On one of the upper floors of the house was a room which was stacked nearly to the ceiling with rows of Coca Colas—glass bottles in wooden cases. In another room, there was a conglomeration of furniture sort of stacked around, but there was a medium-sized aquarium—maybe twenty gallons or so. Someone asked Sonny about the aquarium one night after rehearsal, and he said there was only one fish in it—his pet Piranha. I didn't know what a Piranha was, but others in the room sort of gasped in awe. He invited everyone to come up and see his prized fish.

We all went up to the aquarium room and Sonny turned on the light over the tank where we could see him better. He was not particularly impressive looking--a rather dull brownish gray with a prominent underbite. Quite ugly, actually. He just sort of stayed in one place.

At this point, Sonny reached over and picked up a jar and unscrewed the lid. The jar contained "blood bait" which fishermen use for certain types of fish. The substance in the jar is about the consistency of bread dough or peanut butter, and can be formed into a ball which can then be affixed to a fish hook.

Sonny took an ordinary, yellow, wooden pencil and dipped it into the jar of blood bait, making sure enough of the substance adhered to the pencil to make a little jacket about an inch long.

He held the pencil over the surface of the water for a few seconds, said "Watch this" and then stuck the end of the pencil down into the water of the tank. WHACK! Faster than a lightning bolt, this creature jumped at the coated pencil end and chopped off about three quarters of an inch before you could blink. You could just imagine this being a finger or other appendage of your body. Just picture what would happen if he had several hundred of his friends with him. We were told that a school of piranha can devour a full grown cow in something like thirty seconds.

I got to sit in with the band a couple of times in rehearsal, if one of the trumpets didn't show or was late. But that was as close as I came to joining the organization. I did sit in with the orchestra on two occasions when I was where they were playing. I didn't impress Sonny enough for him to ask me to join the band, however.

Sonny and I became good friends over the years and played several gigs together, but not in the famous Sonny Gray Orchestra.

Chapter Fifty Two

First Car, A Real Stud-mobile

My dad had made a deal with me when I was about twelve years old. He said that as long as I kept my grades up and if I didn't smoke, he would buy me a car when I turned sixteen.

Well, keeping my grades up was no sweat. I went through junior high school with straight A's. (Actually we got "E"'s for Excellent instead of A's. The Tulsa Public School System did not use the conventional ABC grading scale.) My buddy Al and I had a contest going. The first one to get anything other than an E would lose. The bet was ten dollars. We almost faltered at the eleventh hour. We had both been so busy and active in the ninth grade with various activities and events, that we were frequently pulled out of gym class for meetings, field trips, appearances, etc. Most of the physical education grade is base on the number of days you "suit up".

The last week of school, Coach Riggs called Al and me in and said that we had not met the minimum requirement in suiting-up days to qualify for an E in his class. We started to realize the ramifications of this, as we knew we were likely to get straight E's in the other classes. But Coach Riggs pulled a big surprise on us. He said he looked at our files and knew that our record throughout our career at Bell had been nothing but E's, every semester and every class. He said he didn't want to be the one that spoiled our perfect record, so he was going to give us an E anyway. We thanked him profusely and left his office walking on air.

I continued the record through my sophomore year as well, so I was in good shape when it came to cashing in on Dad's deal.

The other part of the deal with Dad was also no sweat. My experience with smoking, at age six with the cigar from my grandfather, was indelibly etched on my brain. I really had no desire to take up the habit. Plus, this would have been the death knell for dating any of the "nice" girls. No one in my circle smoked nor would any of the girls I knew have tolerated it.

About two months before my sixteenth birthday, Dad came driving up in a slick looking, shiny black, '53 Ford coupe. It was pretty plain looking, but I would soon fix that. It had blackwall tires (a total no-no in the fifties) and little hub-caps. It was a business coupe, with no back seat—just a big rubber mat. We ordered a back seat for it. It was a V-8 with standard transmission and it had a very basic radio—not even push buttons. No power anything—brakes, steering, windows, seats, etc. Heater but no air conditioner. I didn't care. It was luxurious to me.

One problem is that it had this big blotch squarely on the roof. It was almost as if someone had dropped a cup of acid on the top of the car. Something had run down toward the windows and the finish had been permanently marred. Fortunately, you couldn't really tell it unless you were standing next to the car or looking down on the roof somehow.

Dad had bought the car from a friend of his who he met on one of the oil well locations where he had business. The guy worked in the oilfields and lived in the country. He also had a few chickens. Apparently a hen had jumped up on the car one summer day when the temperature was well over 100 degrees. With the black finish, the temperature on top of the roof probably approached a zillion degrees. The poor chicken's feet hit the roof and started to fry. She squawked and out popped an egg which immediately broke. It started to run but also started to cook at about the same time. The result was this permanent stain. No amount of washing or polishing would remove it. The roof would eventually have to be re-painted.

I decided to put a set of "Full Moon" wheel covers on it, rather than spinners. Full Moons were plain, aluminum discs which covered the entire wheel portion, out to the edge of the rim. Then we put the whitewall tires on.

The '53 Ford has a chrome bar which comes across the grill, horizontally. In the middle of this bar is a chrome bullet-type piece, about six inches in diameter at the base and protruding out to a point. This was called a "Dagmar" by many car aficionados, after a well endowed blonde bombshell of the mid-fifties named Dagmar, a regular on a late night TV show called Broadway Open House. She was an import from one of the Scandinavian countries I think—possibly Sweden—and was equipped with a pair of very prominent Dagmars, herself. Some cars had two of these Dagmars, such as Cadillacs, the '57 Chevy and several others, which made them more blatant representations of their namesake. Regardless of the implications, I decided this ornament could easily be removed, lending a bit of customization to the car.

The last thing I decided to do was to have a little bit of pinstriping applied to the car. I decided I could do this myself. I bought a couple of long-bristled striping brushes and some small bottles of white enamel used to paint model airplanes and went after it. What a disaster! I couldn't get the hang of it for anything. I had seen a couple of pros do this at car shows and they made it look so easy.

The most famous of the pinstripers in Tulsa was a guy named Dave Anderson, who signed all his work "King Dave". I took the car over to his house where he applied a couple of nice pinstriping highlights to top off the car. The finished result was a great little machine. I was ready to totally enter the teenage, high school, super stud, cool guy world. Eat your heart out, James Dean.

Chapter Fifty Three
First Job

As summer started in 1956, I was a bit at loose ends. I had given up playing baseball in the summers and had to depend on my parents or others to get out to the country club if I wanted to swim or play golf.

One of my good friends, named Lamar, had gotten a job at a drive-in restaurant called "Brownie's". He worked in the outside order area drawing root beers and loading up trays for the car hops to take out to the customers' cars. It wasn't a full-fledged drive-in, like Pennington's or Cotton's. It was really a root beer stand that served hamburgers.

Tulsa was a pioneer in three types of eating establishments which few cities had—at least in the same format. One was the small establishment which sold nothing but coney island hot dogs. These are the small coneys—almost tiny. The first of these types of establishments was reputed to have started in Cincinnati by a couple of Greek immigrants named Economu. The first one, according to legend, was in about 1921. After a year or so, the brothers sold their highly successful coney place and moved to Dallas where they started another. After a few months there, they sold out and moved to Houston and started another, which is now called James Coney Island, and still exists in several locations in that city.

After a year or so, they sold out again and moved to Tulsa to start up again. This was in 1923. They liked Tulsa so much, they decided to stay. The grandson of one of the founders still owns the place, which has several locations around

Tulsa. He changed the name slightly to "Coney I-Lander". But nothing else changed. Their slogan is: "Since 1923, we haven't changed a bite."

The second type of pioneering effort in the food business somewhat unique to Tulsa is the small hamburger grill in a building about half the size of a small box car. There is a counter with a dozen stools which looks right onto the hamburger grill. They featured the true, old-fashioned hamburger. Small, greasy and delicious. These places were all named for the owner or founder—Van's, Ryan's, Harden's, etc.

The third type of pioneering establishment was the root beer stand, the most prominent one being Weber's. While A&W picked up the concept and started opening places all over the country, Weber's in Tulsa was one of the first. Cars pulled up into the gravel parking lot like spokes protruding from the small orange hut. Car hops took the orders, which consisted of only two items in the early days—root beer or root beer float, small or large. The root beer was made on the spot and served in large, frosty mugs.

Brownie's, where Lamar worked, was a combination of two of these types of establishments—the hamburger stand (it had a counter and booths inside the main building) and the root beer stand, which was sort of tacked on at one end of the building, with a big open window and counter for the car hops to pick up their orders.

Lamar said the boss was going to hire someone else to help work the outside part and would I like the job? At first I had mixed emotions. Then Lamar said: "You get all the root beer you can drink and they have the cutest car hops in town." That did it. When do I start?

I didn't even ask what the job paid, but found out the first day that it paid fifty cents per hour. Not bad! That meant in an 8-hour shift I would make four bucks and probably drink another dollar's worth of root beer. I might also get a free hamburger and fries out of the deal. With one day's pay, I could fill the gas tank on my car and, if I was careful, it might last a week. The rest of my paycheck was pure profit.

Brownie's was located at one corner of a square mile and I lived at the opposite, diagonal corner, about a mile and a half, as the crow flies. I didn't have my drivers' license yet, but talked my parents into letting me drive my new car to work and back, so long as I stuck to the side streets and didn't get onto Eleventh Street or Sheridan, the two main streets which would have been the logical way to get to work.

The summer of '56 was when I really started to feel grown up and independent. My own car. My own job. My own money. My own time schedule. The realities of responsibilities had not even crept into my thoughts at this point. There is no better time in life.

Chapter Fifty Four
First Wreck
–

As an adult businessman, I used to speak annually to a convention of high school students who came together to be taught a little about the free enterprise system and being in business. The event was sponsored by Rotary International and I usually shared the podium on one of the afternoon sessions with one of Oklahoma's Senators, a prominent banker and the owner of a successful advertising agency.

My topic was "What it's like to be in business for yourself." The audience was made up of 16, 17 and 18 year-olds. I always started out by asking: "Do you remember what it was like when you first got your drivers' license and started driving on your own?" Nearly every head in the room would nod.

"Think back to that day. If you were like me, you felt the day would never get here. Worse than Christmas coming when you were six years old. I was at the door of the license bureau at 6 AM, an hour before they opened on my birthday. I wanted to be first in line. Luckily I passed and promptly went out to drive around to as many friends' houses as I could. Do you remember driving all by yourself out on the streets for the first time, legally? Mom or Dad not in the front seat with you? Cars zooming around. You can change lanes whenever you want, turn when you want, go where you want. You're in complete control." (More nods and some laughter.) "This feeling is called 'euphoria'. That's similar to the feeling when you start a new business."

"Do you remember when you had your first wreck or near-wreck?" (Nervous laughter and shuffling in chairs.) "Maybe you hit or nearly hit someone in an intersection—might have been your fault or theirs. Doesn't matter. Then the realization strikes you. 'Hey! It's really kinda scary out here! A guy could get hurt!' Well, that's what it really is like being in business. Euphoria followed by fear followed by more euphoria followed by more fear. No matter how big or how successful your business becomes, there is always that cycle. I guarantee you that the President of General Motors has days filled with euphoria and days filled with fear. You just hope that the peaks of euphoria exceed the valleys of fear in both frequency and intensity."

The euphoria I was feeling, especially pertaining to my car, came to an abrupt halt one night. Well, it actually turned out to be a slight bump in the road more than a total halt. It was a most bizarre occurrence. In the mid-fifties, Oklahoma was still a dry state. No liquor sold legally anywhere. Nothing but 3.2 percent alcohol content beer. So, people who wanted to imbibe or serve wine, cocktails, etc. were taken to patronizing bootleggers. Unlike the movies, the bootleggers were not seedy characters wearing black shirts with white ties and wide brim hats. They were everyday people who had an entrepreneurial bent and would drive a couple of hours to Joplin, Missouri to fill up their cars with several cases of booze. They circulated little business cards to all their friends and acquaintances. Some just said: "Call Johnny. 2-4381". Some had a little advertising message, like "All brands. 24-hour delivery." Then they would sit by the phone and fill orders as they came in, delivering the orders to the houses and being paid in cash. From a business standpoint, it was a very sweet enterprise. As my dad used to say, "Oklahomans will always vote dry as long as they can stagger to the polls."

One night I was going out and my folks said I could take my car. They were having friends in and placed an order with their favorite bootlegger. I yelled goodbye, ran out the back door and hopped in my car. It was a very dark, overcast night—no moon or stars. I crammed it in reverse and started zooming out of the driveway, anxious to get over to Kenny's house. The end of our driveway sloped down toward the street. I hit the slope and at about the time I should have squirted into the street I crashed into something, big time. I don't mean a bush or a mailbox. I mean something like a brick wall. The impact jerked me back and forth and I sat there stunned for a minute. I jumped out of the car and saw that I had just caved in the side of the biggest Chrysler Imperial you could imagine. It was the bootlegger's car. He had parked at the end of the driveway to make his delivery to our house.

At that minute, this guy came running out of our house, having heard the crash. He was followed by my dad. My mom just stood in the doorway. She had no desire to see up close what had happened.

Chrysler cars of the fifties had everything electrical tied into the ignition. If the key wasn't turned on, nothing electrical worked. No horn, no lights, no radio. There was a guy in the Chrysler who had been sitting in the passenger's seat, waiting for his boss or partner or friend to make his delivery. By the time the car's driver and my dad reached the scene, he and I were surveying the damage.

The passenger said: "I saw you coming, but there wasn't nothin' I could do about it. I tried to honk the damn horn, but there weren't no sound. I couldn't do nothin' but brace myself 'cause you was comin' at me like a bat outta hell."

I started apologizing profusely. "It was just so dark I couldn't see you." The Chrysler was a dark gray. My little car did not have the high cost option of backup lights.

"What should we do? We have insurance, don't we Dad? Shall we call the police?"

The bootlegger snapped around and looked at me. "No. I don't think so. I don't believe we need to be involving the police in this." My dad chuckled, which I thought was a strange reaction, under the circumstances.

In a few minutes, the owner said: "It was really just as much my fault as yours. I shouldn't have parked at the end of the driveway. I should have parked here, next to the curb. The car looks like it will still run OK. I'll take it into the shop tomorrow. Just forget about it."

I looked at Dad, who smiled. I decided that there wasn't anything I could say that would make it any better, so I just said "Sorry" again.

After the Chrysler pulled away, Dad and I surveyed the damage to the car. There was surprisingly little. One of the taillights was broken out and the bumper looked like it might be slightly askew. But there wasn't a scratch on the finish that I could see. Dad just said: "Don't worry about it, son. Just be more careful in the future."

Chapter Fifty Five
An Audience with the King

In the summer of 1956, Elvis Presley had taken the country by storm. Most of those in the music industry said they had not seen anything like it since the early days of Sinatra. In July of 1956, Elvis came to Tulsa for a concert in the Fairgrounds Pavilion. I got four tickets and my best friend Al and I planned to double date.

I was about two or three weeks shy of my 16th birthday, but Al had already turned 16 and had his drivers license. So we decided to take my "new" car and Al would drive. Al drove a faded gray '49 Plymouth. Mine was a much cooler date-mobile. The problem was that my car was what was called a "business coupe". It was designed for traveling salesmen and had no backseat, creating a larger cargo area to carry samples, products, etc. Dad had ordered a back seat for it, but it had not arrived yet.

My date for the Elvis concert was a really good looking girl that I had been trying to get a date with for quite a while. Her name was Karen. The fear of any boy in approaching a girl for the first time is rejection. It is the ultimate humility, no matter how diplomatic, sweet or logical the refusal. But the Elvis concert presented the ideal situation. How could Karen turn down a chance to go see Elvis, live? She couldn't, I reasoned. And she didn't.

Karen made it clear that she was hosting a slumber party at her house that night for several girls and her mother wanted her home soon after the concert to be there when the girls started to arrive. OK. Half a date is better than none.

The magic night arrived and Al and I picked up his date, Linda, first and then headed for Karen's house, in my slick little Ford coupe. We got to Karen's and I went to the door to collect her. When we got to the car, I opened the passenger side door, pulled the seatback forward and motioned for her to get in back. She started to step through the door onto the platform in back, which I had done my best to make comfortable, complete with a couple of quilts and pillows. Karen took one look at this quasi-bed scene, stepped back and stood up straight. "No way am I going to ride back there!", she said firmly. I panicked. There's no way we could get all four of us in the front. Besides, it would mean a sure ticket if the police were to catch us.

So, I motioned for Al to get out so we could have a quick conference. "You and Linda will have to ride in back.", I said. "I'll drive."

"But you don't have your license!", Al protested.

"No matter." I said. "I can drive the car and we'll just have to hope I don't get in a wreck."

So Al and Linda shifted to the back "seat" and Linda went quite willingly, for which I was supremely grateful. Karen got into the front seat and we proceeded to the Pavilion.

The concert was fabulous. Elvis was all we had expected and hoped he would be. It was that early, pure Elvis sound with the Jordanaires backing him up and the fantastic, unmistakable guitar work of James Burton and that slapping upright bass. We thrilled to Elvis going through his great repertoire: "Heartbreak Hotel", "I Got A Woman", "I Wanna Play House With You" and many more.

As we walked to the car after the concert there was a festive air which permeated the night. Thousands of people walking toward their cars. Laughter and happy conversation floated on the warm summer evening air. Everyone seemed to feel great. Then someone sang out in his best Elvis voice: "Well. . .I got a woman, way over town, she's good to me. Yeah. Yeah." The guy really had a good voice and sounded a lot like Elvis. The whole crowd within earshot applauded and yelled. We obviously hadn't gotten enough of Elvis at the concert.

I reluctantly drove the girls to Karen's house. Linda was going to the slumber party as well. We dropped them off, wishing the evening didn't have to end so soon.

Then Al and I headed for Pennington's to see who was there and to sort of come down after the concert. We hung around and talked with friends until after midnight and then went home.

The next morning was a Sunday. My dad brought in the Sunday paper from the front porch, opened it up and glanced over the front page.

He yelled at me in the other room: "Didn't you go to that Elvis Presley concert last night with a girl named Karen?" I answered affirmatively. "Well, is this her, by any chance?"

I came into the living room and grabbed the paper out of his hands. There on the front page of the Tulsa World in a picture bigger than Texas was my date, Karen, being kissed on the cheek by Elvis! What's the deal? She was with me until the slumber party started.

I got on the phone to Al who had already seen the picture. He didn't have the answer either. Linda was still at Karen's so he couldn't get in touch with her yet. I wasn't about to call Karen and give her the third degree. Besides I didn't know if I was mad, disappointed, frustrated or what.

Al came by and picked me up about noon and we headed directly to Linda's house to get the full story. Here's the way it went. The whole deal was planned even before we had the date. One of the girls at the party had learned that Elvis would be staying at the Mayo Hotel. She also found out the suite he would be given, so they planned to go down to the Mayo as soon as everyone got to Karen's.

The group of six or eight girls went en masse down to the Mayo and tried to go in, with the goal of going up to his room on the fifth floor. The doorman stopped them. Security was fairly tight. So the girls stood around on the sidewalk under his window for a while trying to decide what to do. They looked up and saw that the French doors were open and the drapes were blowing in the breeze. So, they started to yell. "Elvis! EL-VIS! Come out and wave to us!" In a few minutes, the King himself actually appeared on the balcony. He yelled down: "Hi, Girls! Did you come and hear me sing tonight? How did you like the show?"

"Elvis! Please come down and talk to us for a few minutes."

"OK.", he said. "I'll be right down."

In a few minutes Elvis came walking through the revolving door and out onto the sidewalk. There was a surprisingly small number of people in front of the hotel. Few even knew he was staying there and most would assume there was no way they would be able to see or meet him.

However, there was a reporter and cameraman from the Tulsa World there, who had requested a brief interview with Elvis. So they were there when Elvis made his appearance.

Elvis came down, talked with the girls for a few minutes and signed autographs. Then one of the girls asked for a kiss and he dutifully planted a kiss on the cheek of each of the girls. The photographer was ready and it was Karen who was caught on film.

Well, I couldn't be mad. I just wished she had included us on the adventure. I overlooked the rather sneaky way in which the whole affair was handled.

Chapter Fifty Six
"Some drunk guy is backing down Peoria at 50 MPH!"

After I got my drivers' license, in August, my world opened up totally. I was cruising Little Pennington's, Big Pennington's and Cotton's every night. You didn't do anything there. You just cruised through, to see and be seen. Occasionally you parked, ordered a Coke and stood around talking with friends.

One night at Little Pennington's, a friend of mine name Ronnie was admiring my car and asked if he could ride in it. I suggested he hop in and we would go across town to Big Pennington's to see if there was anything going on there.

We drove over to Big Pennington's where the guys from Central hung out. Pennington's was located on Peoria Avenue in Tulsa, which came to be known as the "Restless Ribbon" because of the steady stream of teenager-filled cars going up and down about a six-block stretch.

As we cruised through Pennington's, I was looking around to see if I could spot anyone I knew. The cupboard was bare. No familiar faces. As we pulled out the side entrance and onto the street which leads into Peoria, I was stopped behind a couple of cars at the stop sign which were waiting to pull out onto Peoria. A car full of guys pulled up behind us. They saw that it was an unfamiliar car, so one of them yelled something at us—called us names or made some socially unacceptable macho remark, meant to intimidate the newcomers.

It worked. A pang of fear shot through me, so I chose to simply ignore the taunters and hoped they would turn a different direction. I elected to turn left, away from the action. Most turned right to cruise into the heart of the Brookside area.

As we pulled one car closer to the stop sign, Ronnie turned to me and said: "I showed them! I gave them the finger!"

"You WHAT??? You idiot!", I said. Of all the stupid, foolhardy things to do, this has got to be at the top of the list. Here's a car full of what I was sure by then could only be classified as thugs, looking for a fight and we're two little sophomores who, together, wouldn't weigh as much as a beefy lineman on the football team. I was approaching panic level. What to do? What to do? My mind raced. Ronnie sensed the mistake he had made and I looked over at him. He was white.

I turned left, onto Peoria and prayed they would turn right. No such luck. They followed right behind me, running the stop sign and making cars screech to keep from plowing into them. I cruised down Peoria, trying to be cool. Past the bowling alley, past the fire station. (Why wasn't that a police station?)

The car full of thugs pulled up beside me and a guy leaned out the window, yelling for me to pull over. "Pull into that parking lot!" They smelled fresh blood and were relishing the opportunity of having a little fun. I continued to try to ignore them.

Then they started swerving toward me, coming within inches of my precious little car. I sped up. They sped up. I slowed down. They slowed down, staying right beside me. They swerved closer, then away, then closer, then away. There's no way I was going to pull over and I didn't see a hope of outrunning or out-maneuvering them. That seemed like a plan for disaster.

So, I did the only thing I thought I could do. At about thirty miles an hour, I slammed the car in reverse and popped the clutch. Seemed like a good idea at the time. The tires squealed in protest and started smoking. The gears ground terribly and the engine growled this horrible sound. I just ignored all this and floored the accelerator. We ground to an abrupt halt with the rear wheels spinning backwards and immediately started going back down Peoria in the opposite direction. My first thought was: "If you are going backwards, do you drive on the right or left hand side of the road?" I chose the middle.

I couldn't look back to see what the car of thugs was doing. I had my hands and eyes full just trying to keep control of the car which was

201

picking up speed in reverse. We even passed cars who were going the same direction as we were, only facing forward.

When we got a couple of blocks from the change in direction, I whipped the wheel and backed into the side street between the bowling alley and the fire station. Then I turned around and started going forward down that street, with my lights out. I ran through one stop sign and then another. I turned down one street and then another. I pulled into a driveway but decided it was too conspicuous a place.

As I started down the street again, a police car sped around the corner, turned across the road and blocked my path. He turned on his revolving red light on top of the car and quickly got out of his car, with his hand on his pistol.

As he approached the car, cautiously, he said: "Please get out of the car and put your hands on the roof."

I immediately got out and blurted: "I know this looks funny officer, but. . ."

He interrupted, somewhat more forceful this time: "I said. Place your hands on top of the car and spread your feet. You, too.", he said, motioning to Ronnie.

We did as he said. Then he said: "Now, carefully and slowly hand me your license."

I reached for my billfold and handed it toward him. "Remove it from the billfold, please."

He looked at the license and then instructed both of us to get in the back seat of the patrol car. While we sat there, he radioed in my drivers' license information and the tag number of my car. While he waited for a response, he said: "Now, would you like to tell me what's going on? I got a call from the fire station on Peoria who said there was some drunk doing about fifty down Peoria, going backwards! Was that you?"

"Yessir. I guess it was."

"Have either of you boys been drinking?"

"No sir!" we both answered quickly.

"Well, son. What would prompt you to do something crazy like that? It's not only crazy, but stupid and dangerous."

"Yes sir, I know." I replied. "But I didn't have any choice."

"How so?" he said. So I told him the whole story, trying to look as angelic as I could, sprinkling the narrative with an ample number of "sirs" and a high degree of respect, mingled with fear and relief. I was about to ask if he could call for a motorcycle escort for us to get home safely, but thought that might be a bit over the top, so I just stopped.

About that time the dispatcher came back and said the car was not stolen and there were no outstanding warrants out on me.

"Well son. You broke about a half dozen laws back there, but I didn't see any of it and I doubt that any of the firemen want to make a court appearance to testify. My advice to you is to get back in your car and drive straight home. Do not go back to Pennington's. And in the future, I don't want to hear of any more crazy stunts like that. Understand?"

"Oh, yes sir!" I had no problem doing exactly what he suggested. I didn't want my car seen on the streets anymore that night. No telling where the thugs might be cruising. It was at least a month before I drove my car back to Big Pennington's.

* * * * *

On one of the trips over to Big Pennington's one night, we were cruising down Peoria when a group of 4 or 5 girls came running across the street in front of my car. I almost hit them. They had come shooting out of the Plaza movie theater toward the parking lot across the street.

One of the guys in the car said: "Hey! Wasn't that the two Ann's and some of their friends?", referring to a few of the more popular girls in our class.

"It sure looked like them", I said, promptly turning right to come around the block and intercept them.

As I pulled up to the parking lot, the girls were piling into a car we recognized. It was indeed this group of class pillars. The problem was, they were coming out of the Plaza where the notorious movie, "And God Created Woman", starring that new French sexpot sensation, Brigitte Bardot, was playing. This movie had caused quite a stir upon its release, not only because of its sexual theme (very mild by today's standards), but because of a scene in which the nude Bardot could be seen standing on the other side of a filmy curtain, in low light—nothing more than a silhouette. It had been banned in several towns. Everyone was talking about the movie, but no one would admit seeing it or having seen it (except the boys in conversations among themselves, only). But certainly, no "nice" girl would go see this.

Obviously, curiosity had overcome these girls and they picked what they thought would be a perfect night to go see it. Our basketball team, with a strong winning season going (eventually culminating in the state championship) had a game. No one in school wanted to miss this. So, the girls felt they would run little chance in being seen.

However, our little group of guys left the game early and decided to cruise our favorite spots to see what was going on.

As we approached the girls' car they looked up in shock and total surprise and all started talking, very nervously, at once.

"We've just been to the Crosstown Grill (pointing to the little café which shared the parking lot with the Plaza) to get a Coke!", one of them yelled. (We knew that these girls would not be caught dead at the Crosstown Grill—a 24-hour a day dive in the not too great section of town. If we went anywhere besides Pennington's at night, it would have been to Bishop's Restaurant, downtown or maybe Howard Johnson's. Never to the Crosstown.)

"Yes", said another. "We've been to the basketball game. Wasn't it great? We won!" They thought this would be a safe assumption, adding to their "alibi", as it were. Actually, this was the first game our team had lost in many outings. That's why we left early.

So, here the girls were—busted on two counts. "Sure! Sure!", we said. "We know where you've been. So what did you think of the movie?"

They continued to try to protest but finally broke down. "Please don't tell anyone you saw us here!", they pleaded. (Are you kidding? This was simply too good to keep a lid on. After all, one of these girls was the daughter of the Superintendent of Schools.) We knew that this minor incident would do absolutely no damage to any of these girls' reputations. It would only make them seem more human and down to earth, which it did.

After they broke down, they admitted that the movie was somewhat a disappointment and not what it was built up to be. We feigned surprise (although we had all seen it already).

Chapter Fifty Seven

A Pretty Girl is Like a Melody

My junior year in high school started off busy and didn't ever change. It was somewhat different from the sophomore year. For one thing, I was driving my own car to school which meant that I could leave the school grounds for lunch every day. Usually I took a whole car full of guys and we went to Coney Corner, Harden's Hamburgers, Town Talk Drive-In, Brownie's or one of several other places. We rarely went to Pennington's for lunch, even though their food was great. It just wasn't a lunch place. It was a place you went at night.

Al's dad still had the printing company, so I decided to run for a class office again. When I went to the office on candidate sign-up day, there were several classmates there. I was trying to decide what to run for and was discussing it with Al. Some of the girls heard me talking and said: "Why don't you run for president?"

"I've already done that. Twice. I don't think so."

"We think you'd make a great president. Why not go for it again? Third time's a charm, you know."

Well, that was enough for my fragile ego. So, I signed up to run for president.

I really worked on my campaign speech hard. Did a good job of giving it. Plastered the school with even more great posters and got everyone in most of my classes to wear my campaign badge.

We ran a great campaign. This time it was different. Not just a landslide. It was a veritable stomping. I lost. A guy named Mike won (same Mike).

* * * * *

Oh well. On to other things. The next event was the junior class play. I signed up to audition, as I had done every year. Because of my size, I almost always played one of the kids in whatever family was the center of the play (every play centered around a family) or I had the comedy lead. This play had a great comedy lead which was a teenage boy. I felt I was perfect for it. I couldn't believe it when I didn't get the part, especially since I had met a new girl during the tryouts and thought she was really neat. She got a part in the play, so I volunteered for one of the backstage committees—props or costumes or something—so that I could be at rehearsals with Virginia.

Virginia didn't have a car, so I offered to pick her up and take her home from each play practice. We usually went to Pennington's after rehearsal. By New Year's we were going steady. (This technique seemed to work pretty well. Two years later I used the same approach with a girl in college—Coke dates after play rehearsal. In that case, by New Year's we were married.)

I think the drama teacher, Miss Niles, felt sorry for me since I didn't get a part in the play. So she asked me if I would like to consider being the emcee of the assembly to introduce the queen candidates. At Will Rogers, instead of having Yearbook Queens or Beauty Queens we had what was known as Round Up Queens. The Round Up was the all school talent show. The Queens were paraded in one scene in the Round Up and then their pictures were also in the yearbook. It was a nice honor, since the student body voted on the queens. They weren't picked by some committee or group of judges.

Miss Niles called me and a boy named Homer into her office and announced that each of us was to write a speech of introduction for the queen candidates. We were to say something about the contest, the event and each girl. Whoever wrote the best speech would be the one to emcee the assembly.

Fantastic! This was right up my alley! I considered myself a better than average creative writer and was sure I could write a dynamite speech. Homer, on the other hand, was a tad on the shy side and had a hard time putting two spoken sentences together. There's no doubt he was a very intelligent guy. He made perfect grades. All the teachers loved him. He was the epitome of a nerd--wore his pants (not Levi's) up nearly to his armpits. He shuffled his pudgy body from class to class without saying much to anyone. Everyone knew him. No one disliked him. He was just a classic outsider.

We had a week to prepare our entry speeches. I created a masterpiece. I assigned each of the twelve candidates a fictitious title or award. "Donna was voted by the all the boys in sixth hour gym class as the girl they'd most like to do the bop in a telephone booth with." Or, "Darielle was selected by the football team as the girl they'd most like to have in the middle of a huddle." Stuff like that. Oh, it was great. Couldn't lose.

Homer's on the other hand, was, as might be expected, very well written, but straight forward and dry. He even called each of the candidates "Miss", as in "Miss Hyatt is a majorette in the band. English is her favorite subject." Or, "Miss Polite is a cheerleader and would like to be a nurse when she graduates." Ho hum!, I thought, arrogantly.

Miss Niles started to read my speech but about half way through put it down and looked up to say: "This won't do at all. We can't have things said about these girls which aren't true. No, this is just not acceptable."

"But Miss Niles", I protested. "Everyone knows it's not true and that it's just a joke. That's the point."

"Makes no difference", she said. "Homer, we'll use you and your speech on the assembly."

I thought this was patently unfair and that she was totally out of touch. Again, I discovered that you can't win against or even reason with the establishment. So, I just accepted it and left.

The assembly came when Homer was to introduce the model candidates. The whole student body was in place in the auditorium. After the Call to the Colors by the trumpet trio, the Pledge of Allegiance, the American's Creed, the singing of the Alma Mater and the announcements by Dr. Knight, the Principal, Homer was introduced. The orchestra was in place, ready to play "A Pretty Girl is Like a Melody", "Sweet and Lovely" or something like these while each candidate was introduced and walked across the stage.

Homer stepped up to the microphone, front and center and pulled out his notes. There was no podium or lectern. Nothing between him and the audience except a skinny microphone stand. He said a few words of greeting, rather haltingly and low keyed. Then, someone in one of the front rows noticed that his knees were knocking together and mentioned it to those around her, while pointing. The word spread throughout the auditorium and the laughter started. Homer looked down and saw his knees knocking as well. It was like something out of an animated cartoon. They weren't just shaking. They were literally knocking together. Each was moving several inches back and forth.

Trying to talk above the laughter was futile. He just stood there, hands at his side with a fistful of notes, looking obviously uncomfortable and strangely like Jackie Gleason's "Poor Soul" character. Finally, as the laughter started to die down, Homer said. "I can't help it. I can't make them stop." He reached down and held one of his knees. The other one continued to move back and forth. He shrugged and then straightened up to continue.

The laughter finally subsided and a wave of what appeared to be sympathy swept over the crowd. The students broke into applause and a group started to chant: "Homer! Homer! Homer!"

Homer stepped back up the microphone and started his speech back at the beginning, as if he had just been introduced. He recovered admirably well and it really went quite smooth after that, albeit a bit dry, in spite of the knocking knees, that went still about the time the second candidate was introduced.

Bill Haley and his Comets, of "Rock Around The Clock" fame.

Chapter Fifty Eight
Long Live Rock and Roll

Probably no element of twentieth century culture changed the face of our society on a more widespread basis than rock and roll music. Until that idiom came on the scene, the music which young people listened to and danced to was the music of their parents. The big band music of the thirties, forties and early fifties was the only widespread popular music available in the mainstream. Of course there were other types of popular or secular music which were followed by small segments of the population, such as country, rag time, Dixieland, jazz, etc. But the music of the movies, most radio programs and dances was the music of Benny Goodman, Glenn Miller, the Dorsey Brothers, Woody Herman, etc. and it was shared by young and old alike. The individual stars were singers like Frank Sinatra, Perry Como, Kay Starr and Tulsan Patti Page.

In late 1954, Bing Crosby's oldest son, Gary, had a hit record with the song: "I've Got My Eyes On You." It was not true rock and roll, but was different from most of the music until that time, with more of a small group sound and a more definite beat. Many music historians credit this as the first white rock and roll song. It wasn't black rhythm and blues or country and western with a beat. It was a unique sound. Then, in 1955 the movie "Blackboard Jungle" was released and the main theme, "Rock Around the Clock" burst on the scene and took America's youth by storm. There was no stopping the wave then.

The term "Rock and Roll" is generally attributed to a disk jockey named

Alan Freed. Whether or not this is true, there's little doubt that Freed was a pioneer in the field and helped propel the music to the forefront, both on the radio and in several movies, in which he was featured.

Rock and roll generally had its roots in several camps. Country and western music (or "hillbilly") was the primary platform from which artists like Carl Perkins, Bill Haley, Johnny Cash, Jerry Lee Lewis and a youngster born in Tupelo, Mississippi, named Elvis Presley sprang. This form of music was generally called "Rockabilly".

The other primary platform which produced and influenced rock music to a great degree was rhythm and blues, especially that from the black artists. Much of this music had its early roots in black gospel music. At first the black artists were not played by the mainstream white radio stations. This meant that some of the pioneer white rock and pop singers got a huge boost in their careers by recording some of these great songs which were originally recorded by black artists (this is called "covering" the song). Songs like "Hound Dog" by Elvis Presley, "Tutti Frutti" and "Ain't That a Shame" by Pat Boone were written by and first recorded by black artists.

But this was not all bad for the black artists, either. It provided a forum to have their music, even if in watered down versions, heard and accepted by the mainstream market. It wasn't long before the kids demanded the music from the originators and most stations started playing early black rock and roll artists, such as Little Richard, Chuck Berry, Fats Domino and the groups such as The Charms, The Coasters, The Drifters and The Platters.

The main program which showcased popular music on early television was "Your Hit Parade". The top ten songs of the week, based on record sales, jukebox plays, etc. were performed by the stars of the show. Unfortunately, they were not performed by the original artists (except in rare, guest appearances). This was acceptable for most of the music up until 1955. However, when rock music hit the scene, the public (especially the kids) wanted to hear the song the way they had come to be hooked on it. No one wanted to hear Snooky Lanson sing "Hound Dog" or Giselle McKenzie sing "Rock Around the Clock". It just didn't compute. It wasn't long before "Your Hit Parade" was history.

Of course, the thing which characterized this music more than anything was the electric guitar. When the first rock bands hit the scene, many people asked: "Where are the horns?" "How can they do some of that music without violins?" Many rock bands didn't even have a piano!

I came to the realization that if I was still a pound shy of being a football star; and if I couldn't beg, borrow, steal or buy my way into the class presidency; and if music featuring the trumpet player was dying, then probably the best way to impress the girls was to become a rock star. This meant learning to play the guitar.

My early experience with the ukulele carried over well when I graduated to six string guitar. During the very early days of rock and roll, my dad took me down to buy my first electric guitar and amplifier. It was a Rickenbacker and the little amplifier was no bigger than a bread box. We bought it at Craig Music in Tulsa and Mr. Craig himself was demonstrating the new rig before we walked out of the store with it. He knew a few chords and was showing them to me. When he passed the guitar over to me and I played a dozen or so chords immediately, following his lead, he was astounded. He asked if I had ever played guitar. I said I had not, but I did play ukulele and had learned to finger the fret board for certain chords from that instrument. (The four strings on a uke are the same as the top four strings on a guitar. Only the low "A" and "E" strings are added on the guitar.) However, my chords on my new guitar were somewhat confined to those four strings. I was not able to take advantage of the full range of the chord or the bottom notes, as yet.

Of course I was very anxious to develop my prowess on the guitar, but didn't want to fall into the same trap with guitar lessons as I had on the piano. I didn't want a classical or conventional teacher. I wanted someone who could teach me rock and roll. Unfortunately there were precious few players around in 1956. Rock and roll had only come on the scene about a year earlier. Many of the guitarists came out of the country and western field.

Fortunately one of my friends at school had formed one of the first rock bands in Tulsa and had become quite proficient on the guitar. His name was David Gates. I asked David if he would like to give some guitar lessons to a potential competitor for his band. I think he weighed the trade off between immediate funds and the unlikely situation of my really forming a band which might enter the developing market which he almost monopolized. He chose the quick money. So, for five bucks a lesson, David would come over to my house one or two afternoons a week and show me chords, licks and little secrets to playing the guitar.

David's guitar that he played on gigs and taught me on was this gorgeous, but huge, Epiphone. This was a full-sized, hollow-body instrument, with a metallic green finish. The neck was so large I couldn't get my hand around it. But, neither could he. So he had adopted a technique of fretting the low E and A strings with his thumb, curled over the top of the neck from

211

behind. He passed this along to me. Even though the neck on my guitar was smaller and I could have reached those strings with my index finger, I started fretting full chords from both sides of the neck. Most players use what is known as a bar chord, where the index finger lays across all six strings, like a bar, to set the root key for the chord and the other fingers actually form the chord. To this day I still finger chords the way David taught me at age 15. But, so does he.

(Apparently this technique did not hold David back, since he has achieved a high degree of success in the music business. In addition to numerous accomplishments, he was the founder, lead singer and primary song writer for the group "Bread" who had numerous gold records in the seventies, such as "If", "Make It With You", "Baby I'm-A Want You", "Diary", "Everything I Own" and many others. He also wrote and sang the title song in the Neil Simon movie "The Goodbye Girl", which starred Richard Dreyfuss and Marcia Mason. I don't know who he angered in the Motion Picture Academy, but the song was passed over for an Oscar nomination that year. The nominated songs were mostly worthless pap, in my opinion. Even the winning song was very forgettable—in fact, I don't even remember what it was (see?), except that it was nowhere near as good as "The Goodbye Girl".)

David never forgot our early days competing for the dance gig market. In the early 1970's, "Bread" recorded their first album and got a gold record out of it. I was in California on business, staying with the Gates in their home and went with him to pick up the actual gold record. He signed a copy of the first album to me, inscribing it with these words: "To my fiercest competition."

* * * * *

The market for local rock bands was mushrooming in 1956. There were precious few bands to satisfy the demand. David had his band, called "The Accents". I named my band "Little Joe and the Strangers". We were the two bands playing most of the more upscale, "soash" type jobs for the social clubs. Then bands like Gene Crose and the Rockets, Dudley Murphy and the Fadeaways and the Johnny Cale Band (who later made a big name for himself as J.J. Cale) entered the market, playing not only the teenage dance jobs but some of the local clubs.

My band consisted of two guys named Jerry. One played guitar and the other played bass. Our drummer was named Gary and he didn't own a full set of drums, so he played our gigs using a snare drum, a tom-tom and one or two cymbals.

There are those who feel that Jerry, our guitar player, was more of a Fonzy than even Daryl. He certainly had a world-class ducktail hair style and a black leather jacket. What's more, he drove a really cool motorcycle—a Mustang—which had been souped up by his dad. Jerry was (and still is) a real rarity in the music field—a super musician with almost no ego. He's contented to play either lead or rhythm. He's happy to front the band or stay in the background. He'll sing or stay silent. Solo or no solo—either way is okay with him. He just wants to play. And he's good.

Our first appearance was more of an audition than a gig. One of the girls' social clubs was planning its big Fall dance and I told some of their members that I had a new band and we'd love to play it. She invited us to one of their meetings to play for the members.

Social club meetings were held at a different member's house each week. This week it was at Patricia's house. The problem was, Gary, our drummer, couldn't make it. Oh well. We'd go and audition anyway. So the two Jerry's and I showed up, hauled in our small guitar amps and the big upright bass. The house was not very large and the meeting was being held in the living room, which was wall to wall with girls. Some of the girls scooted over and made room for us to come through. We found a place to plug in our amps and tuned up. We didn't have a microphone or vocal amp, so I cautioned the Jerry's to play fairly softly so the vocals could be heard.

Jerry the bass player stood in the curved part of the grand piano which was in their living room. The other Jerry and I sat down on the piano bench. So, we kicked off with one of the popular rock songs. We played about three or four songs and the reaction seemed to be quite good. Lots of applause. Lots of "You guys are really good!" type compliments. But, The Accents got the gig. I decided not ever to audition under unfavorable conditions again.

* * * * *

It wasn't long before we started breaking into the market and playing quite a few gigs. Then David told me something which I was sure was going to rule him out of the market and make it possible for Little Joe and the Strangers to have all the gigs we could handle.

David told me that he and the guys in his band were going to join the musicians' union. I couldn't understand the logic behind this. Part of it probably stemmed from the fact that the father of David's bass player,

Gerald, was some sort of local union official-- not in the musicians' union but in some more prominent union and Gerald was so pro-union that one day something incomprehensible to me happened. Gerald and I, as well as the piano player for the Accents, Russell Bridges (who later became famous as Leon Russell) were at my house, sitting in the breakfast room and eating some of my Mom's world class chocolate chip cookies, still warm from the oven. Now, everyone knows there is nothing better with chocolate chip cookies than a glass of cold milk. So, I asked the guys if they wanted a glass of milk. Of course they did. Russell went to the refrigerator and took out a quart bottle of milk as I got the glasses from the cabinet. He looked at the bottle, then held it up for Gerald to see.

"Do you want it?", Russell asked Gerald. "It's Meadow Gold brand."

Gerald looked up and simply shook his head no.

"Why not?", I said. "It's fresh. The milkman only delivered it this morning."

Russell looked at me and said: "Meadow Gold is a non-union dairy. Gerald won't touch it."

"So what?", I said. I was unfamiliar with this concept. But I had to admire Gerald's resolve and the fact that he stuck by his principles in the face of what I thought was unparalleled temptation.

The ramifications of joining the union were primarily economic. We charged forty dollars to play a dance and we split the fee evenly—ten bucks each. Not bad for three hours of doing something I loved to do. Remember, I had just come off a job where I had to work twenty hours drawing mugs of root beer to make ten dollars.

David's band was slightly better known, so he got by with charging fifty dollars in most cases. However, when he became a union band, he would have to charge union scale. Scale for four pieces for a three-hour dance was a whopping $92.50! The Accents were just about to price themselves out of the market! I could hardly wait.

They joined the union and I didn't notice any perceptible drop in the level of their bookings. What was the deal? I started to understand the law of supply and demand, so we raised our fee to sixty bucks.

Chapter Fifty Nine-
Playing the Venerable Cimarron Ballroom

In the early days of rock, there were two radio stations in Tulsa jockeying for the number one position in what was called the "Top Forty" format. The eventual winner in this battle was KAKC, 970 on your AM radio dial.

The management at KAKC were masters at promotion. They made stars out of their disk jockeys. They had remote broadcasts, giveaways, special interviews with stars and they sponsored concerts.

They called their original lineup of disk jockeys the "Big 5 Deejays". This was soon expanded to the "Big 7 Deejays". The kingpin of this group was a deejay named Chris Lane.

KAKC started hosting a series of hops at the Cimarron Ballroom, a gorgeous, big, art deco style facility which had seen frequent appearances by the top country acts like Bob Wills and the Texas Playboys, Leon McAuliffe and the legendary Hank Williams. Only the famous Cain's Academy in Tulsa had seen more artists and stars, but the Cimarron was more upscale.

The KAKC hops were broadcast live on Saturday nights and featured the current top records plus a guest appearance by one or two of the local bands. Appearance at the KAKC hop gave your band instant credibility and a certain degree of local fame and stardom.

David Gates and the Accents had played the hop once or twice but may have been restricted from playing there often. David had aligned his band with the primary DJ at the rival station, KTUL, who was sort of managing the Accents. When our band was asked to play the KAKC event, we were ecstatic! This may be the break we're looking for!

The other band appearing with us that night was called the Thunderbirds, as I recall. They featured a really good guitarist; a little Indian guy named Leo Feather. They were really good, but avoided playing the top forty stuff, going for more R&B and rockabilly. They might play Buddy Knox or Gene Vincent. We were more likely to play Buddy Holly and Chuck Berry. They played their three or four songs, and then started moving their equipment off the stage while Chris Lane talked a little and played a few records.

Then it was our turn. We were psyched and ready. We had decided to kick off our set with a Chuck Berry song, "Roll Over Beethoven". The song started with the high energy, classic Chuck Berry guitar intro. I was the one who played this intro and I also sang the lead on the song.

The mikes were in place, the amps were on and ready and the guitars were tuned, loaded and ready. Chris Lane went into his announcement. "And now, put your hands together and welcome. . . Little Joe and the Strangers!"

I struck down on the guitar strings with my pick, ready to kick right into the famous Chuck Berry intro. But, the guitar simply fell away from my hands! After the first striking of the strings I was picking at air. I panicked! What happened? I was holding the guitar at the low end of the neck with my left hand and the main body was just hanging straight down. Then it hit me: the strap which goes over my neck and shoulder and attached to the back end of the guitar had come loose. I reached back to grab it and slip it over the knob on the guitar, but discovered that it hadn't come loose, it had broken! I frantically looked around for a chair or stool—something I could put my leg up on to rest the guitar on my knee. There was none to be found. I could have used an amplifier, but then I wouldn't have been close enough to the microphone to sing.

Jerry immediately spotted what had happened, and being the great musician he is, picked up the intro without missing a lick. The other two guys did not falter, and so, to most observers, we were OK.

But then, who was going to play the rhythm guitar part, which was critical? It had to be me, but there's no way I could do it with the guitar hanging down like a pendulum.

Then Chris Lane himself spotted the problem and stepped around behind me. I felt a hand slip past my right side from behind as he grabbed the knob on the back of the guitar and pulled the instrument back up, parallel with the floor and close to my body. I continued to play and sing while he stood behind me, holding the guitar in place. The whole scene was surreal and I felt sort of like a ventriloquist dummy with my controller standing immediately behind me. It was not only an uncomfortable way to play, but very restrictive. About all I could muster was barely passable rhythm guitar.

At the end of the song, there was huge applause, screaming and whistling. It reminded me of Zip-A-Dee-Doo-Dah at the Rialto Theater. I started to take off the guitar in order to fix the strap or get another one. Chris whispered in my ear: "Keep going. We're live on the radio. You can't stop now!"

"How embarrassing", I thought. Not just breaking a strap, but having your guitar held in place by THE Chris Lane! Why didn't I just see if I could get Dick Clark to carry my amplifier? Or maybe Elvis to tune my guitar?

So we kicked off the next song and then the next and finally our closer. The reaction was great. The audience yelled for more. So Chris asked us to do an encore, which was almost unheard of. He took a short break for a commercial. This gave us about sixty seconds to figure out what we were going to do with a minimum of potential disruption with one and a half guitars. I didn't know the guys in the other band so didn't feel I could ask to borrow a guitar from them. Besides, there was sort of an unspoken rivalry there. This was the equivalent of a battle of the bands. Those guys were probably enjoying our difficulties.

About that time a guy who had been standing backstage came up to me and asked if he could sit in. There was a Hammond B-3 organ on stage—the epitome of rock and roll keyboards. His name was Doug. He said he would play organ and asked what song would we like to do. I suggested "You Win Again", a semi-slow song made famous by Jerry Lee Lewis but also recorded by others. He said, "Fine! I know it."

I said: "Can you take the solo?"

"No sweat.", he said.

So, he went over to the organ and got ready to play. Then I remembered something critical. The original Jerry Lee Lewis record was in the key of C. When I learned unfamiliar songs, I took them directly off the record and tried to play them in exactly the same key, so long as it was within my vocal range. The problem is, my hi fi played slightly fast. So, instead of spinning a 45 RPM record at 45 RPM's, it turned a little faster, making the song come out in a slightly higher key. This meant that I had learned "You Win Again" in the key of C-Sharp. I was not proficient enough on guitar to transpose to another key yet. C-Sharp is probably the most difficult key to play piano or organ in. A high percentage of the notes to be played are on the black keys. But it's the mixture of the black and white keys that is the killer.

Just before we were due to come back live on the air and kick off our encore, I looked over to Doug at the organ and said: "We do this in C-Sharp."

"C-Sharp?!" he said. I nodded. Then he just shrugged and said: "OK".

We kicked off the song, and the organ part added a completely new dimension to the band. We sounded fabulous. When the Jerry Lee Lewis keyboard solo part came up, Doug nailed it unbelievably well, even though the original was on piano, not organ. Probably better than Lewis himself could have played it.

We brought the house down, again, but stopped after one encore. I immediately got Doug's phone number. He said he was playing in a couple of bands but was open to playing some with us. I never added him to the band on a permanent basis, but he did play several gigs with us.

A few years later, Doug was on tour with a band when he was tragically killed by carbon monoxide poisoning from a faulty heater in a third rate motel.

Chapter Sixty
Pranks and Papering

To say that the mainstream at Will Rogers High School in the fifties was tame—nearly squeaky clean—is certainly one of the understatements of that decade. Golly, gee whiz! Richie Cunningham, Potsy and the Fonz had nothing on us. That's not to say that there weren't a few transgressions, but most of them were low key and harmless by standards of the sixties or later.

However, one little prank got out of hand and created an episode which resulted in quite a furor. A girl named Lois, who I had dated some, had a brother, Bobby, who was a senior when I was a junior. He was a little on the wild side, but basically harmless. One afternoon Bobby got a pass to go to the restroom. He went to the boys room on the fourth floor. He then took a cherry bomb, which is a firework about the size of a marshmallow, only bright red in color, with a fuse. The unique thing about cherry bombs is that they are waterproof. Even the fuse is wax coated and continues to burn underwater. They were also quite powerful, and were outlawed sometime in the sixties, after taking off hundreds of fingers and hands which held the devices a little too long before throwing them.

Bobby decided to light a cherry bomb and flush it down the toilet in the boys' room. The theory was that as the cherry bomb traveled through the plumbing and exploded, it would be heard all over the school. A great

219

prank, in his estimation. Bobby figured that the sewage pipe was probably a fairly straight shot down from the bathroom and would be empty from lack of use since nearly everyone was in class.

So, he lit the fuse and held it for a few seconds. Then at just the right moment, he dropped it in the water and flushed the toilet. In about five or six seconds, as the water was gushing down, the cherry bomb exploded. It was thunderous. No doubt most people on the west end of the third and fourth floor heard it.

Unfortunately, Bobby underestimated the power of the device, the concussion it would produce within the confines of the narrow pipe and the weakness or brittleness of the old plumbing and the porcelain toilet fixture. When the cherry bomb exploded, it must have blown out the entire sewer pipe between the third and fourth floor. It shot a column of water straight up through the toilet, cracking the bowl and starting a stream of water spewing out onto the floor. It wasn't long before the bathroom floor was flooded and the water was creeping out into the hall. Water was leaking down into the third floor.

Bobby panicked. He wasn't sure what to do. He had told several friends of his plan, so he knew it was only a matter of time until the authorities knew who was responsible. Bobby did not return to class. I'm sure he was feeling just what I did in the sixth grade after the Lik-M-Aid incident. He went straight out to the parking lot, got in his car and started driving.

He decided to not go home. Facing his parents would be about as bad as facing the Principal or Boys Counselor. He didn't show up at home for dinner either. His parents were becoming quite worried about him when bedtime came and he had not returned.

Bobby didn't return home all night. Finally, late in the afternoon the next day, his folks received a collect phone call from Bobby. He was somewhere in Mississippi or Alabama. He had simply started driving and not stopped. After a conversation with his folks, he turned around and came home. While I'm sure the school officials were not very happy with him, most of his friends harbored a certain level of awe—even envy. It was, after all, a pretty funny episode.

* * * * *

Many of the guys waited until the last week of school to pull off some sort of super prank. Some would plan these things all year. Generally, these stunts were the purview of the graduating seniors and took place during Senior Week, which was the last week of school, when Seniors were excused from classes while the underclassmen continued to attend. There were some dillies in '57 and '58. (More about these later.)

The most common prank or bit of minor vandalism in which most people partook was papering houses—in some cities, they call it "rolling" a house. The paperer throws the toilet tissue roll into a tree and lets it cascade down, leaving a long stream of paper hanging from the tree. We generally papered the houses of our friends as a sort of perverted sign of fondness. Someone said: "The only thing worse than getting papered is not getting papered."

It became a weekly occurrence for some of us, even if we had a date on Friday night. We would meet at Pennington's about midnight and before going home, go by Food Town, the only 24-hour supermarket in town, and buy as many rolls of paper as we could afford. Then we'd choose who that week's victim was going to be. Some of our papering jobs were pure works of contemporary art.

One night we papered the house of a girl who had, until recently, been my girlfriend, Francine. She had the perfect house to paper. Huge trees, some of which hung over the street like massive awnings. We started papering, and went through about a dozen rolls. A neighbor heard us, opened his front door and yelled at us. We ran to our cars, down the street, drove away and then decided we had too good a job going, so we went back. We ran out of paper, so we went back to Food Town and bought some more. We absolutely saturated the trees with paper. There were so many streamers hanging down, you couldn't see through them. At one point, a car turned the corner and started coming down the street. It was a taxi cab. We ran and hid behind bushes. As he approached the wall of paper streamers which were hanging down from the overhanging trees, he slowed to a crawl. As he entered the wall, his cab started to disappear. Soon, he was totally engulfed and then slowly emerged from the other side.

I couldn't resist phoning Francine first thing on Saturday morning. Of course, she knew who was responsible. But I wanted to see what she thought about our masterpiece. She tried to feign anger, but grudgingly admitted that it was the best job she had ever seen. Francine had a great sense of humor and a delightful laugh which I can still recall clearly.

Chapter Sixty One
Who died?

Any other pranks or practical jokes I was involved with were pretty tame. My friend Charles, who lived a couple of blocks from me, was going to Cascia Hall, the Catholic boys school and he had a good friend named Mike who was a great practical joker and creative guy. Mike suffered from a rare disease which made his bones very brittle and stunted his growth severely. He was confined to a wheelchair. His parents were relatively affluent so they hired a young man to live with them and act as Mike's companion and chauffeur. His parents bought a Cadillac limousine which had a very wide door and a lot of space between the back seat and the front. Juan, Mike's companion, could simply wheel the chair into the back of the limo and then take off. (I heard that after Juan got out of college and left the Tulsa area, he ended up in Albuquerque where he became mayor of that city.)

Mike was a brilliant guy. His grades were top notch and his sense of humor was keen. He used to sit around and think up practical jokes we could pull.

Mike kept a spotlight in the Cadillac which plugged into the cigarette lighter. Juan would use it to spot addresses or signs. Some nights when we were driving around, we would pull up to the curb in downtown Tulsa directly across from the Ritz or Orpheum Theaters, just before the change in movie times. Mike would plug in the spotlight. Two or three of us would get out of the car and Mike would lean out the window shining the light in the gutter and around on the sidewalk. We would then start diligently looking around in the gutter and on the sidewalk.

As soon as there were several people within earshot, one of us would say: "Describe it again."

Mike would yell: "It has a large center diamond with rubies on each side and a heavy platinum mounting. It is inscribed 'To M.S. from J.R.' We just have to find it!"

A bystander would invariably ask: "Did you boys lose something?"

"Yessir. His dad lost a very valuable ring somewhere down here. He's offering a five thousand dollar reward to anyone who finds it."

This revelation, coupled with the fact that we were in a new Cadillac Limousine, lent great credibility to the story. Before long, there would be 5 or 10 people looking. Then it might swell to 20 or more. Everyone wanted to know what it was and where was he when it was lost? Five thousand dollar reward? Really? People would be digging through sidewalk trash receptacles or on their hands and knees with a cigarette lighter trying to peer down through the grating in a storm drain.

As soon as we felt we had milked it enough, we would hop back into the car and Juan would speed away, leaving this crowd of people still looking, hoping for a great prize. Most of them were going to be late for the movie, of course.

Occasionally we would even drive through Pennington's and Cotton's in the limo. One night as we were pulling through Cotton's, to a chorus of whistles, jeers and cat calls, some guy leaned out of his car and yelled: "Who died?"

In order to support some of our Friday or Saturday night activities, we would sometimes create a fake scavenger hunt. We would sit in the back of the limo and write down a list of items like those which might be in a real scavenger hunt. Starting with frivolous items like a piece of red thread, a matchbook with any restaurant's name on it or an ad for Pepsodent toothpaste torn from a magazine, we would then add the stuff we really wanted: an unopened, full roll of toilet paper, a quarter minted in an even numbered year (but we'd take the odd numbered year in a pinch), a balloon (for making a water bomb) or an egg. After hitting the houses in just a couple of blocks, we usually had enough money to buy a round of Cokes and some French fries for the entire car and enough toilet paper to do a respectable job on a house. We could also water bomb or egg a rival's car pretty well, if we felt so inclined.

Sometimes we would take the limo to the drive-in movie. We could get about six or eight people in the car and we would get a speaker for the front and one for the back. There were two ways to get into the drive-in without paying. One was to get as many guys in the trunk as you could cram in. The other was to drive in the exit with your lights off and hope they didn't spot you. This latter method was not feasible at the Admiral Twin Drive-In, the one featured in the movie "The Outsiders", since the exit was near the ticket booths, and you couldn't get by without being seen. However, at the Airview or the Sheridan, the exits were around to the side, slightly, and it could be pulled off, if you were careful.

One night at the Riverside Drive-In, we were there in the limo, watching the movie, parked somewhat near the back. The back row was, of course, the row for those who cared nothing about seeing the movie. The Riverside was especially good for this group since the lighting at the back was almost non-existent. On this particular night, we were just watching the movie and chatting when all of a sudden: "WHAM! CRASH!" We looked around and discovered that a car full of guys in about a '46 Ford had come barreling in the back exit with the lights off, swerved slightly to get out of the mainstream and melt into the crowd of cars before being seen and plowed right into the side of this couple in a '53 Chevy, which the driver could obviously not see, since his lights were off and the black Chevy was on the darkened back row. Not exactly the ideal end to a perfect date.

We never tried that approach to the drive in, especially in the limo. However, the Cadillac had a huge trunk and we could get four guys in it, if they were small. The problem was extricating the stowaways at the right moment, when they were not likely to be seen. The limo was not exactly an inconspicuous vehicle. So Juan had to jockey it into position and sit and wait for a few minutes while people went back to watching the movie or whatever. These minutes seemed like hours if you were in the trunk. "Nobody move. Nobody laugh. And most of all, nobody fart."

Chapter Sixty Two
Social Clubs

Much of the social life at Rogers revolved around a group of social clubs—especially the life of the "soashes". There were several girls clubs—Damsels, Highlanders and Emanon. But there was only one boys club, Vikings, until my senior year when a group of younger guys decided to form another club they called Cavaliers.

I was asked to pledge Vikings, which was a nice sign of acceptance. I had several friends in Vikings, including some of my buddies who were a year older than me and were in the band.

It was the social clubs who had most of the good parties. They could do much more than an individual since they had collective funds to work with. So, they hired halls, bands and often had themes for their parties, much like college fraternities and sororities.

The pledge period was the better part of a semester and wasn't too bad. You had to put up with a little verbal abuse, especially on meeting night. And you had to carry a big selection of gum and mints for the members, which you offered to them whenever you saw them.

At the end of each weekly Vikings meeting, which was held at a member's home, on a rotating basis, everyone went out into the front yard. The pledges would line up and "assume the position" (bend over at the waist). Each member then took the pledge's wooden paddle and gave him a swat on the rear end. Most of the members did not hit the pledges hard. The last one to go down the line and deliver the final swat was the

225

president. He was obligated to give each pledge a healthy swat, and not hold back. When I pledged, the president of Vikings was none other than William Henry Diffendaffer Burgess IV. That's right. The great left handed baseball pitcher. This meant his arm was well developed and we felt it.

Once a month (every fourth meeting) Vikings and Highlanders held a joint meeting. This set up the worst and most humiliating experience of the month. All of the pledges hated it. After this joint meeting was over, everyone went into the front yard—both the boys and the girls. All the pledges would assume the position again and the members would give us our swats, while the girls watched. The main problem is that many of the members felt that they had to take this opportunity to show how hard they could hit. Even those who might normally just give a little tap would take some sort of perverse pleasure in seeing if they could lift a pledge off the ground with a swat.

Before the first of these joint meetings, I was in my bedroom quietly engaged in what I felt might thwart some of the pain I was about to experience. My mother looked into my room and saw me with a needle and thread and a pair of my underpants.

"What in the world are you doing?", she asked.

"Oh, nothing. Just putting a little padding into my underpants." I had gone to my dad's drawer and "borrowed" a half dozen handkerchiefs. I folded them to the right shape and started sewing them into my shorts. The problem was: how much padding to put in. I wanted to put the maximum amount in, to protect my sensitive bottom, but not so much that I looked like some deformed Quasi Moto whose hunchback had sunk.

I went to meeting that night and tried to always stand with my back to the wall. We went out into the yard after the meeting, and I felt I was as ready as I could be. I bent over and starting taking licks. The padding didn't seem to make one bit of difference. It felt like I was standing there totally bare-bottomed. Each lick stung like crazy. I decided that next time I was going to try to sew in a metal plate.

Finally, pledging was over and we were to be initiated into full membership in Vikings. The initiation was not too bad. Very little hazing and a fairly serious ceremony. However, after the initiation, which was held out in the country, in a field, some of the guys started drinking beer. Vikings did not necessarily promote drinking nor was it offered at parties. Some of the guys were simply prone to have a beer now and then and would have imbibed whether or not they were in Vikings.

One of these guys was named Bob. He was a really nice guy. Very smiley. Everyone liked him a lot. He took pride in his ability to chug-alug a whole quart of beer at a time. He brought quite a stash with him that night and it wasn't long before he was really drunk.

After a while, many of the guys had left, and only a few of us remained. I did not drink, nor did a couple of the other guys. We were just enjoying the afterglow of the initiation and the beautiful night. Finally, Bob ran out of beer and was totally "wasted". One of the guys said that we would have to take Bob home. I suddenly realized that "we" meant "me"—I would have to take Bob home.

"C'mon you guys! Why me?", I said. He could hardly walk. Two of the guys said: "C'mon, we'll go with you."

So we helped Bob to my car. We couldn't get him in the back seat, so we dumped him in the front. Good thing we did, though. He opened the door and barfed twice on the way home.

Bob's parents were considerably older than the parents of most of us. He was obviously a late-life baby and was an only child. On top of this, his parents were very conservative. I had only met them once, but they weren't my idea of a really fun couple.

By the time we got to Bob's house, he had totally passed out and reeked of beer and vomit. It took all three of us to drag him up the sidewalk to his front porch, and up the three or four steps to the front door.

"What are we going to do now?" I whispered. "I don't even know where his room is. Besides, we'll make too much noise if we take him inside."

"Well, we can't leave him out here.", one of the guys said.

About that time the front porch light came on and the front door opened to reveal a tall, Nordic looking, quizzical father in robe and slippers.

We all froze. We looked down at Bob then up at his father, then down at Bob then up at his father again, in total silence. I didn't know what else to do, so I blurted out: "Hello, sir! Uh-h-h, Bob's not feeling very well." Then we just dropped him into a pile on the front porch in front of the screen door, turned tail and ran to the waiting car at the curb.

As we drove off, we looked back to see Bob's father trying to push the screen door open with this lump of humanity he called a son lying up against the door.

The Vikings' parties were generally held at a member's home. We didn't have as much money as the girls' clubs. One of the members, Charles, had a great house for parties, with a large family room and his parents were gracious enough to open it up to us. However, there was more than one occasion when we would have a party at Charles' house and he would end up being a solo host—no date, which makes for a pretty dull party for him.

He couldn't even leave early to go to Pennington's or cruise around.

This situation was brought about by the fact that Charles was dating a classmate whose schedule was unpredictable. Her name was Anita Bryant. She had already started to make her mark in the show business arena and would be called to New York or wherever to appear on the Arthur Godfrey Show or some appearance with Bob Hope, leaving Charles high and dry. It's not difficult to see why some show business marriages don't last.

Chapter Sixty Three
The Metronomes

While we were reaching a certain degree of success and notoriety as a rock band, school administrations would still not engage private bands for school dances or functions—especially rock and roll bands. This was a market both David Gates and I desperately wanted to open up.

Whenever there was a sock hop or mixer in the gym after a football game, for instance, the Will Rogers Dance Band, called the Metronomes, would generally play it. I'm not sure who it was that came up with the name for the band, but I sort of put it in the same category as the "Offbeats" as a stupid name. I doubt that a handful of kids even knew what a metronome was (an object which keeps time or tempo for musicians to rehearse to). Some probably thought we were supposed to be leprechauns from the big city (Metro – gnomes), which would have been a little incongruous since our leader was 6'7", our lead trombonist was 6'5" and several others came in at six foot or better.

Even the members of the band disliked the name. We just referred to it as "Dance Band". I played trumpet in the dance band as both a junior and a senior. I was just a mediocre trumpet player and probably would not have been able to make the band as a junior (since there were at least three trumpet players better than me in school, and three trumpets was all the dance band used), were it not for the fact that my good friend Ron was selected as the student director of the Dance Band by Mr. Barnett, the band director and head of instrumental music at Rogers. Ron was an excellent

229

trumpet player. But since he would be fronting the band, this left an extra chair open in the trumpet section and I jumped in, behind Leonard and Bobby.

The Dance Band was almost like a little fraternity. We were all good friends and really enjoyed rehearsing and playing together. We started playing the teen canteen type of dances and small town schools throughout Northeast Oklahoma. The reaction was totally unexpected. We were big stars in some of these little towns. We'd blow into town, wearing our white dinner jackets and the girls would mob us, asking for autographs, hanging around like groupies. We didn't know what to think. The boys in these little towns didn't much appreciate it, of course.

The problem is that we played nothing but big band music and a lot of songs the kids didn't even know. I doubt that many of the kids had ever heard songs like "My Lean Baby" or "Harlem Nocturne", even if they did know some of the Glenn Miller stuff. The chaperones and faculty members loved us. The kids were so-so, when it came to the music. "Can't you do anything by Buddy Holly or Elvis?", they would ask. Sorry. If it's not printed on sheet music, we don't play it.

We could have played almost anything they wanted, had the school allowed it. After all, we had three members of the Accents in the Dance Band—David Gates on guitar, Russell Bridges on piano and David's bass player, Gerald. I could have also played guitar and the drummer, Pete, was very good. However, since we represented the school, we were to stick to the music in the folder, wear our bow ties and act properly.

At one of these small town dances, the boys at the host school were feeling especially antagonistic toward these guys from the city who were commanding so much attention from their girls. We took a break and were at the back of the room getting something to drink when a bunch of the local boys wandered back and started making snide remarks, making fun of our jackets, etc. We were getting pretty fed up. Ron, the leader, was (and still is) 6 ft. 7 inches tall. He was taking a drink of water when one of the locals said: "How's the weather up there?", which all his buddies thought was hilarious. Ron turned and sprayed a mouthful of water all over three or four of this cackling group and replied: "Wet. How is it down there?" We then went back up and played our next set.

Chapter Sixty Four
New car, new house

Mid way through my junior year I still loved my little black Ford. It wasn't fancy but it was a great car for a 16-year old. But I was about to lose it. I had started to bowl in the adult leagues in Tulsa at this time. Occasionally I even filled in for a team in the premier Classic League on Friday night, which featured all the best bowlers in town. One of my dad's teammates was the leading salesman at the largest Ford dealership in town. One Friday night he told Dad that he had just taken in a beautiful 1955 Ford Fairlane convertible on a trade. It was very low mileage and in perfect shape and he could let Dad have a real good deal on it.

The next day, we went down to look at this jewel, and it was gorgeous. Snow white with a dusty pink and white interior. And. . .it was stick shift! (Automatic transmissions were for family cars and old folks. No teenager wanted anything but a standard transmission—a stick shift.) That was it. I wanted this car.

I drooled over the car while my dad and Frank talked about the deal. In less than an hour I drove out in this gorgeous machine. No doubt about it. I had the coolest car at Will Rogers High School.

On top of this, my folks decided that it was time for me to have my own room. We were still living in the two bedroom duplex which we had moved into temporarily, eight years ago. My little brother was about five years old now. They found a lovely two story house in the Florence Park area, about three blocks from my favorite house where my grandmother lived when I was in kindergarten.

We moved into this house, and my bedroom and bath were located on the second floor. No other rooms were up there.

* * * * *

The acquisition of a convertible opened up another perceived business opportunity for me. What if I got a paper route and threw papers from the car with the top down? Man, I could zip through a route in fifteen minutes. But, wouldn't it be better if I had a partner, so one of us could drive and the other could throw papers from the back seat? So I approached Jerry and suggested that we get not one, but two paper routes. One in his name and one in mine. Hopefully we could get them adjacent to each other and just treat them sort of as one route.

What luck! There were two routes open next to each other. They were in neighborhoods right adjacent to the high school. This meant we would be throwing the houses of several of our classmates. We got all signed up, got the information on the routes—which houses to throw and which ones to skip and when we had to collect (the worst part). Then the route supervisor dropped the bombshell: since this was the morning paper, every newspaper had to be on the front porch, next to the door. My experience with paper routes to this point had been in helping my friend Charlie. We threw his route from our bicycles, but it was an evening route. Anywhere within a half mile of the front door was okay for those. We just tried to hit the yard somewhere if we could.

Jerry and I were nonplussed. How were we going to hit the porch throwing from a car going ten or fifteen miles an hour? Some of the houses had very small porches—nothing more than a step.

We made a valiant effort. We showed up the first morning to pick up our papers. The bundles were delivered to a parking lot at Eleventh and Pittsburg at about 4:30 in the morning. That was tough enough. Being a musician and a bowler, both of which are very late night activities, early mornings were not my best times. I used to say that if I was up at 5 o'clock in the morning, it was because I was STILL up.

The only thing that made the mornings bearable was the fact that there was a coffee shop in the little strip center where we got our papers. Oh, it wasn't open then--but one of the bakeries delivered several dozen fresh donuts to the shop and left them next to the door so that when the proprietor arrived, he could take in the fresh donuts, ready to serve. One of the paperboys regularly took it on himself to requisition a dozen or so of the donuts as soon as the bakery truck left and passed them all around among the paperboys as we sat and folded our papers. It wasn't long before they traced down the regular disappearance of the coffee shop's supply, and this activity had to cease.

The first thing that would happen when the paper truck arrived and they threw these bundles of newspapers off, bound with wire like a hay bale, was to see how many pages the paper had that day. A small number of pages brought a cheer. A large number of pages brought a groan.

The second thing we would check are the slips of paper on top of the stack. Occasionally there would be a piece of paper about four by six inches keyed to your route number with a significant message. They were called: starts, stops and kicks. A start was a new customer or subscriber. It came on green paper. A stop was a cancellation. It came on pink paper. A kick was a complaint or request. It came on yellow paper. Kicks were usually a complaint that a customer had not received his paper the day before (usually not the carrier's fault, but we got blamed), or that the paper was not on the porch. Sometimes it was a request such as to throw the paper on the side porch.

Getting up at 4AM every day and walking two paper routes, then collecting from all the subscribers, house to house and going on solicitation (sales) calls to non-subscriber houses, as we were required to do a couple of times a month, got old fast. Jerry disliked it as much as I did. The first day it was so cold I though my toes were going to freeze off, I told Jerry I'd had it. We quit the next day.

Chapter Sixty Five
Water nymphs

The families of both my friends Al and Bobby had boats and lake cabins and I started going up to the lake with each of them from time to time. We would even go to the lake during the fall, when it was starting to turn cold, and would occasionally ski. It was brisk, to say the least.

Many people named their boats, even their small, 14 and 16 foot ski boats. They usually named them after females (either in the family or fantasy) or came up with clever little puns or plays on words like "Play Daze" or something like that. Al's ski rig didn't have a name painted on it and people kept asking his dad what the name of the boat was. So, one weekend when I went up there, I noticed a name had been painted on the stern. It was: "Damifino". I asked Al what it meant—it looked like some Italian name to me (but Al's family was Scottish). He said every time someone asked Al's dad what the boat's name was all he could say was: "Damn if I know!" So that became the name.

Bobby had a hot Chris Craft inboard which was fun to ski behind and had a beautiful throaty sound to the engine.

One fall Saturday, several of us decided to go up to Bobby's place on the lake and take a boat ride. We invited several girls to go with us. My girl friend at the time (who shall remain nameless) came along. She was a gorgeous blonde with a very sweet, fun loving personality and two other, very outstanding, points. She was quite healthy, to say the least.

When we had taken a boat ride and were back at the dock securing the boat, we started horsing around on the dock. It wasn't long before someone was thrown in the water. This was followed by someone else and soon everyone was pushed into the water. It was cold, but not unbearable. We were all fully clothed. Then, as we climbed up the ladder on the dock out of the water, I was helping my girlfriend up. She was wearing a white cotton blouse and as she came out of the water, the water had made the blouse transparent. My eyes nearly bugged out of my head. A couple of the other guys noticed it immediately, rushed over and said. "Here. Let me help you.", like they really wanted to help. The girl did not notice that she was basically nude from the waist up and thanked all the boys sweetly.

Then one of the girls screamed and came running to my girl friend. She gave her a bear hug, covering her front, and whispered in her ear what the situation was. My girl glanced down and turned white, then red. They called the other girls over who formed a tight wall around her like circling the wagons. They escorted her up to the cabin so they could get a towel and a robe for her. When wet tee-shirt contests became the rage in the sixties and seventies, I immediately grasped the significance.

Chapter Sixty Five
I Christen Thee "Kickback"

I talked my dad into buying us a ski rig. It was a 16 foot all wood boat with a 40 horsepower motor, the largest available at that time. I started hauling the boat up to the lake on a trailer every chance I got, to join my other friends. One Sunday I was preparing to go to the lake, towing the trailer, and my dad noticed the lights on the trailer were not working. I worked on them for ten or fifteen minutes but couldn't get them to function. I was anxious to get up to the lake, so I told Dad I would be careful and I would get them fixed as soon as I returned.

He reluctantly gave in but admonished me to return before dark. "If you don't have that boat and trailer back in the driveway before dark, I'm going to sell it tomorrow!" That statement was burned into my brain as I left.

I had a great day at the lake water skiing and being with my friends. Then, toward the end of the day, I was zooming through an area near the shore, hit something in shallow water and sheared a pin on the propeller. This meant the motor would still run just fine, but the propeller would not turn so the boat would not go anywhere. It was like blowing a fuse.

It was nearing sundown and few boats were still on the lake. I started paddling my dead boat across the lake making about a half knot. After a long time at trying this, I decided that maybe it would be better to abandon the boat and swim across the lake to the dock and get some help. Then another boater saw I was stranded and came to my rescue, towing me back to the boat launch ramp, where my car and trailer were.

236

By the time I got the boat loaded on the trailer and started back home the sun was nearly down and I figured there was about 30 minutes of twilight left before darkness would set in. "If you don't have that boat and trailer back in the driveway before dark, I'm going to sell it tomorrow!" Dad's voice reverberated in my brain.

I pulled up onto Highway 51 headed to Tulsa. It was normally about a one hour trip. 45 minutes if you really pushed it hard. I had to make it in half that time. I floored the little Fairlane and got up to about 90 MPH in no time. I had the top down and had to start securing everything I had inside the car—towels, clothes, etc. Then I had to go through the little town of Wagoner, speed limit 25 MPH. I zoomed through town at about 65, ignoring the single traffic light. As soon as I emerged on the other side, I hit it again. The speedometer climbed to 80, 90, 100 and nearly 110. I envisioned the boat and trailer flying behind me like a kite tail. The trailer wheels probably only touched the highway every few hundred yards before going airborne again.

Soon I saw the flashing red light in my rear view mirror, and then one in front of me. I was caught in the classic Wewoka Switch. I gave up and just let the highway patrol cars come to me. I was out of the car immediately, with license in hand. Maybe this wouldn't take too long.

The patrolman said: "Joseph," (reading from my drivers' license), "I don't know how fast you were going. I couldn't catch up with you enough to clock you. Do you know what the speed limit is here?"

"Yes sir", I said. "It's 65, but I have an emergency."

"Well, actually it's 55 if you're pulling a trailer. But exactly what's the big emergency that you would risk your life and that of others on the road along here?"

Uh-oh. I couldn't tell him there were no lights on the trailer, so I just said the first thing that came to my mind. "I phoned home to let my parents know I was leaving for home and found that they just took my mother to the hospital."

Showing concern, he said: "Was it an accident? Shall I contact them on my radio from here? Do you need us to take you into Tulsa?"

I felt myself digging a hole which I might not get out of, so I said: "Oh, no sir. That won't be necessary. I think it's something like appendicitis. But I feel I must get back as soon as possible. Someone has to stay with my little brother."

The patrolman relaxed somewhat, got a semi-disgusted look on his face and said: "Well I'm sure there's a neighbor or someone who will watch your brother while your dad takes your mother to the doctor. It doesn't sound like that much of an emergency. Now, I think you were going faster than this, but I'm going to give you a ticket for going 85. You must appear before the Justice of the Peace in Wagoner County two weeks from Tuesday. Don't let me ever catch you speeding with a trailer behind your car again, or you'll go straight to jail."

"Yes sir." I said. "Thank you, sir."

I got back in the car and took off for home. As soon as the patrol cars disappeared from my rear view mirror, I pushed it up to about 75. But it was dark long before I got home.

When I got home and went in the house, Dad didn't say a thing about its being dark or my being late. I certainly didn't bring it up, nor did I tell him about the ticket.

I phoned the Justice of the Peace's office in Wagoner to ask them how much the fine would be for a ticket going 85 MPH in a 65 zone. I was somewhat surprised when the judge himself answered the phone. I neglected to tell him that I was pulling a trailer. He said it would be 25 dollars plus 5 dollars per mile per hour over the speed limit plus court costs, which was another twenty dollars. That would be 145 bucks, if they didn't catch that I was pulling a trailer (and it was not noted on the ticket).

Where was I going to get 145 dollars? I started considering what I had that I could sell. The only thing was my guitar and amp. But that was out of the question. I had gigs to play.

I looked at my calendar to figure out what my income was going to be over the next two weeks. Pretty bleak. I had two gigs. That would be thirty bucks. Then I had allowance and lunch money, which was over and above the allowance—maybe another 15 or 20 bucks. It wasn't a sure thing that I would win at poker or at the bowling alley (we always made bets during league and then bowled pot games or match games for money after the league was over). But our poker games were penny ante and rarely did anyone win or lose over five dollars, so that didn't present much hope.

I had one possibility which probably offered more hope than anything else: liar's poker! The bowlers who did not participate in the pot games after league would often sit around and play dollar bill poker or liar's poker at the bowling alley. This game was played with dollar bills, using the serial numbers as your poker hand. The game was played by declaring the number of 4's or 7's or 9's or whatever was in the game, total on everyone's bills combined. Declarations or bids started low and then escalated around the circle. Either you believed the number bid by the guy on your right or you didn't. If you did, you bid higher. If you didn't, you challenged him. The winner of the last challenge, when only two players remained, won not only the two man challenge but the pot as well. Players could declare as many numbers as they wanted when it was their turn to bid. They didn't even have to have any of that particular number in their hand. The serial number on your bill might say 12345, but you'd start out by declaring three 6's in hopes of making other players think there were a lot of sixes in the game, thereby creating some inflated bids which you could challenge. Hence, "liar's poker".

A game which started with ten players could yield 25 to 30 dollars to the eventual winner.

I had watched some of these guys play the game for hours and pretty well knew the strategy of most. Which ones played conservatively. Which ones were liars. Which ones jumped out with lying calls, then pulled back.

Friday night, I showed up for Classic League and after league bowling was over, I suggested a game of liar's poker to some of the regular players. They were amenable and we soon had about a dozen guys in the first game. I had come armed with about ten dollars saved over the week, eating very meager lunches.

I played conservatively for the first few rounds. I won 2 or 3 challenges, but not the final pot, so I was ahead of the game, but far from my goal. All twelve players stayed for the next game, and I started playing more aggressively. I won not only several challenges, but the final pot, winning over thirty dollars. All right! Now I was on a roll. "One in a row!", as one of the guys was famous for saying whenever he got a strike.

A couple of guys dropped out and we continued going with nine or ten players. I did pretty well and won one of the next two games, so I was up over fifty dollars.

The number of players then dropped down to about six. I suggested that we play one game with five dollar bills. There was a bit of hesitation, but finally everyone agreed. We went up to the counter of the bowling alley and bought a bunch of five dollar bills for the game. If I could just do well in this game, I could get close to what I needed for the court appearance.

It was going well. I played fairly conservative. I was involved in only one two-man challenge, which I won, but I was surviving each round. It came down to the last two players, me and Doc. How apropos. Sort of like playing against the legendary gambler, Doc Holliday, although this Doc was a chiropractor named Jim who everyone called Doc. I knew how he played. I knew his favorite trick at this stage was to start out calling a couple of numbers of which he had none in his hand. His hope was that his opponent would count on these numbers being in the game and would add them to his own, coming back with a larger number. Doc would then pounce and challenge, knowing that his opponent would have to have every one of them in his hand—very unlikely.

For the final round, both of us drew new five dollar bills and studied our serial numbers. It was Doc's first call. He started out with a pair of 2's. This is the easiest opening bid to raise, since it was the lowest possible bid. I looked at my serial number again. I didn't have a single 2 in the series. I had him! I was sure he was lying and that he had none of them either. He was using his old ploy. So, I did something which was almost unheard of. I challenged on the first bid! And a pair of deuces bid, at that!

"I challenge that, Doc", I said. "I don't have any 2's and I don't think you have any, either."

Doc didn't even show his bill. He just blew up. "You peeked!", he said. "You saw that I had none. There's no way you could have known. I don't believe this!"

"No, Doc. I just know how you play. Give me the five bucks and put the other five in the pot."

He was still griping as he forked over the two fives. I grabbed up the sixty bucks in the pot, elated to have won about $120 for the total session. I would make it!

* * * * *

When I went to court in Wagoner in another week, I was armed with about $150, just praying that the trailer issue would not come up and another fifty bucks added to the fine. Al went with me to lend a little moral support.

I found it odd that the traffic court was not held in the court house on the square. I was directed to a small office which was behind the combination fire station/police station. The door to the office opened to the street. I walked in and instead of finding the traditional judge's bench, witness stand, etc. like I had seen on Perry Mason, I saw this fat guy in a dirty sport shirt sitting behind a desk in this tiny office with grimy walls. There were about three highway patrolmen standing around against the wall, including the one who had given me my ticket.

The "judge" asked my name. I told him. He looked down a list on his clipboard and said: "85 in a 65. How do you plead, guilty or not guilty?" There were no formalities--no "the court will come to order", no swearing in, no court reporter, no how ya doin'. I looked at the patrolman, who recognized me and he had a little grin of recognition on his face.

"Guilty", I said.

"125 dollars plus 20 dollars costs. Cash only, please." No gavel or pronouncement. Just "show me the dough".

I plunked down 7 twenty dollar bills and a ten on his desk. He opened the top left drawer on his desk and I saw that it was stuffed with more cash than the vault at the First National Bank, except it wasn't stacked neatly. It was crammed in there. Some bills were folded, some were wadded up, some were stacked. I saw very few one dollar bills.

The JP fished a five dollar bill out of the drawer, handed it to me, then crammed my offering into the drawer.

"Thank you", he said. "Who's next?"

Al and I walked out and got into the car to drive back to Tulsa.

"Well, that was interesting.", I said.

Al said: "I wonder what the patrolman's cut of your 145 bucks is? A third? Half?"

"What do you mean?", I asked, naively. "You don't really think he gets a kickback on that do you? I mean, what about the records? It has to go into the county or state treasury, doesn't it?"

"What records?", Al said. "I didn't see any records. I didn't see any receipt. I didn't see him write anything down. And that drawer didn't look like any state treasury to me. I didn't even see anyone official, except three highway patrolmen, and I don't think they were there just to guard the cash drawer."

As the realization of truth swept over me, I could hardly believe it. My faith in the legal system was just blown to bits. Those guys had quite a little racket going there. I wondered what would have happened if I had pled "not guilty". Would he have asked the patrolman to testify right then and run a little kangaroo court on the spot? Or would it have been moved over into a real court room?

Chapter Sixty Seven
Stag Nights every week

Virtually every weekend, on Friday or Saturday night or both, a bunch of us would get together, play poker, paper a house or two and spend the night at someone's house. Even if one had a date, he would join us after the date since the poker games went on until the wee hours.

One of the guys got a miniature roulette wheel for his birthday and we started playing roulette part of the time instead of poker. The problem was that at the first, no one wanted to be the bank or the "house". That was the dull job. Placing the bets in rather creative ways was the fun part. So, we made it that the host would be obligated to be the bank at roulette if we played. Then I started to notice that for some reason, the host seemed to win more than others when it came to roulette. What a coincidence, I thought. Charlie also noticed that, so he volunteered to be the bank every time. Soon, I understood why the casinos made so much money.

One of the guys in this poker group was my good friend Al. He and my other good friend Bobby (Be-Bop Bob) were having a little rivalry over a cute girl named Judy. Both were trying to date her and it was developing into quite a situation, especially since both Al and Bobby played in the dance band, we were all on the same bowling team and we often went to the lake together to water ski.

Pretty soon, the rivalry forced sides and members of our group had to line up on one side or the other, whether you wanted to or not. Basically, my close friend Jerry, and another good friend and member of our little group named Mike (not the class President) sort of lined up with Al. My friend Lamar, who I had worked with at Brownie's, lined up with Bobby, since Lamar's girl friend and Judy were friends.

The war started manifesting itself in various types of pranks, house papering strikes, etc. We decided to strike some sort of major blow against the other side. Bobby and Lamar along with their dates, Judy and Darlene, had already papered Jerry, Al and Mike. They hadn't struck me as yet and we knew I was likely to be next on the list. So, all week at school we let it be known that my parents were going to be out of town (true) and that I would be spending the night at Jerry's house on Friday night (not true), leaving my house totally unprotected. We made sure that both Bobby and Lamar got this message.

When Friday came, our group, including Jerry, Al, Mike, myself and a couple of the guys from Cascia Hall, Charlie and John, got to my house early in the evening to start playing poker. The guys parked their cars around the corner, away from the house. We then started filling balloons with water and stashing them in strategic places around the house—at each corner, behind bushes, on the porch, etc. We hooked up garden hoses to both sides of the house and strategically placed them, turning the water on but shutting off the flow at the nozzle. We hooked up spotlights on the front porch, ready to bathe the front yard in bright light. Then we ran a long piece of twine from the front window of the house, through the living room, dining room and kitchen and attached it to an empty ice tray which we placed on top of the refrigerator. One tug on the line from the front window lookout spot would bring the metal ice tray down to the floor as an alarm. We would be playing poker in the breakfast room, with the only light in the house being the fixture over the breakfast room table.

Each of us was then assigned a battle position. Two would man the hoses. One would hit the spotlights. Two would start chunking water balloons. We had a dry run so that everything would go like clockwork.

We figured that Bobby and Lamar and the girls would probably go to the movie first and then head to my house. It would probably be after ten o'clock. So about ten, we started rotating lookouts. Every 15 minutes, one of us would leave the poker table, go to the front window and wait in the dark, alarm line in hand, ready to alert the defense team.

Sure enough, at about eleven o'clock, in the middle of a spirited hand of seven card stud, the alarm ice tray clanked to the floor. We doused the breakfast room light and immediately went into action. Four went out the back door to take up their positions. I went to the front to hit the spotlights.

Jerry was at the lookout post and was ready to fire water balloons from the front porch.

We waited until the four aggressors had unwrapped a roll of paper each and started to fling them up into the trees. We gave them a few minutes to become engrossed in their nefarious project. When they were sufficiently far away from the shelter of their car, I turned on the spotlights. They were like deer in the headlights. Suddenly it was raining on them like a cloudburst as both hoses were trained on them. Then the water balloon barrage came. Whap! Whap! Whap!

We kept up the barrage for a few more seconds and then shut it down because we were laughing so hard.

The girls were shrieking and running toward the car. When the attackers all were back in Lamar's car they took off and the ambushers jumped in a car in hot pursuit. Bobby and Judy, sitting in the back seat, commenced to unroll toilet paper and let it stream out the back windows of the car in the hopes that it would accumulate on the pursuit car's windshield.

Finally we all stopped to reflect on the occurrence. Both Bobby and Lamar reluctantly admitted that we got them good and that it was a pretty good trick. The girls just wanted to get home and dry their hair.

As they left, there was a sharp edge to their farewell. "We'll get you for this!", they all said. "Just get ready!"

Perhaps in a stroke of some sort of justice, as I was cleaning the streamers of paper out of the trees in my front yard the next day, some of which had been thrown very high up in the trees, I was struck with this great idea. I decided to take a long pole, affix a wad of gasoline-soaked rags to the end, light it and burn the paper out of the trees. It was working beautifully. I discovered that if a touched the torch to the paper where it clung to the tree branch, it would let go and float to the ground. Seemed like a good idea at the time. Unfortunately, a couple of the flaming streamers drifted over to the neighbors' yard, landed in one of their beautifully manicured shrubs and caught it on fire. Before I could get the water turned on and the hose deployed, the bush was half destroyed. This created a doubly uncomfortable situation for me. Not only were the neighbors distraught, but my parents were embarrassed and very upset with me.

Chapter Sixty Eight
It's played on ice, but it's not hockey

We had a pretty good cold snap in early 1957 and some of the ponds froze over. The Braden Park lake looked like a Christmas card scene again, with all the family skaters. There was also a pond behind a drive-in restaurant about a mile from my house. For some reason, when this one would freeze over it attracted guys who were ready to rumble. It was the site of some legendary hockey games—or brawls. These generally started innocently enough. Eight or ten guys with hockey equipment would show up to play hockey in an organized fashion. Several of my friends were the sons of former players on the Tulsa Ice Oilers, the semi-pro hockey team. One of them even had a couple of hockey nets or goals. The goals would be set up at approximately the right distance from each other and at least one boy would act as the referee and start the game by dropping the puck.

Unfortunately, true hockey would only be played for about ten minutes. It wouldn't be long before others started showing up. Some would have ice skates and some wouldn't. Some might have a hockey stick while others might just have a broom. There was little chance that any of them would patiently wait for someone to drop out for a while to rest (or a line change) to go into the game. Newcomers would simply pick a team and join the game. It wouldn't be long before each team had 8, 10, 15 or 20 members or even more, several times the standard complement of five plus goalie. Of course rules went out the window. No one even kept score, nor did they care. It just became one big conglomerated game—sort of a combination of Ice Rugby, Ice Wrestling, Ice Keepaway, Ice Football, Curling and Ice Housekeeping (because of all the brooms). (The reader will notice that Ice Hockey is not one of the components listed.) Once the "game" got fully underway, there was little about it that approximated hockey. The object(s) of the game were unclear except to say that putting the puck into the other team's goal was not high on the list.

Invariably, there would be a couple of big ol' boys wearing tennis shoes and using a broom for a hockey stick. Once they got the puck you could just about forget it. A small guy wearing skates would simply bounce off these guys who would just move through the middle of everyone like some hulking iceberg wearing a football letterman's jacket. Typically, instead of pushing the puck in front of him like a hockey player, these guys would usually just cram the broom down on top of the puck, completely covering it with bristles, and scoot it down the ice. The poor goalie didn't have a chance. These hockey hulks would shuffle right into the crease, "check" the goalie to one side and shove the puck into the net. In spite of the fact that this bore little resemblance to hockey, which was the original intent of the activity, these games were fun. It was a distinct advantage if you had one or two of those abominable snowmen on your team, although even that made little difference since you couldn't tell who was on your team and who wasn't. One friend of mine switched teams continually during the course of these games. He just always wanted to be on the side of the team who had control of the puck. You just hoped that if you passed the puck to someone he was going for the same goal you were.

Chapter Sixty Nine

Mr. Cool becomes the drummer

A new guy moved into town and started to Rogers our junior year. We hit it off real well and became good friends. His name was Gary and he had moved to Tulsa from Southern California. He was cool personified. He was unlike anybody in our school. Very hip. Very worldly.

His dad was an executive with Douglas Aircraft and was a top notch baritone sax player—a well known jazz musician when he lived in California who was accepted almost immediately into the circle of jazz musicians in Tulsa.

Gary's folks were divorced and his mother still lived in Anaheim, California, along with his sister.

Gary had a great love of all types of music and was obviously musically inclined, having inherited it and lived around it all his life, although he had never played an instrument or taken a lesson.

Gary's dad, Marty, knew a lot of professional and famous musicians and I never knew who might be at his house when I went over there.

One day I was over at Gary's and I looked out to see a big white Cadillac convertible pull into the driveway, with the top down. There were three people in the front seat—all black. A big guy with a cool suede hat on was sitting in the middle. Behind the wheel was a gorgeous girl. Sitting on the passenger side was another.

As they got out of the car, Marty walked out the front door and yelled, "Hey, Diz!" The guy came up on the front porch and Marty and "Diz" embraced like long lost brothers.

"Who is that guy?" I asked Gary.

"That's Dizzy Gillespie" (the famous jazz trumpet player who puffs his cheeks out the size of grapefruits when he plays).

"Wow!", I thought. This is cool. THE Dizzy Gillespie! He was driving through Tulsa and decided to stop in and see his old buddy Marty. I was impressed. I just sat quietly while they talked about mutual friends and the music business. It was the first time I had ever heard real musician's jive talk spoken in a full conversation, not just occasional words sprinkled in.

"So. How's Bones doin' man?"

"Dat cat's blowin' with a bitchin' spade group on the coast! They're smokin'
on the pier and a coupla dives in da valley. Layin' down some groovy R&B licks."

"No shit, Shinola! Das cool. Piles of bread?"

"Rollin'. He cut me some slack when I needed a new axe. It was bitchin'"

"Das cool. Das cool. Far out"

I tried to imagine Marty trying to communicate like this with his fellow executives at Douglas Aircraft come Monday morning.

Another day I went by Gary's and there were several cars around the house. As I approached the front door I heard some great jazz music being played, obviously live. There was a heckuva jam session going on. These guys were really wailing. Gary was just listening to the music and occasionally getting a fresh beer for some of the guys.

When Gary got up to go into the kitchen, I went in and asked him: "Who are these guys, anyway? They're fantastic!"

"Oh, that's just PeeWee, Eldon and some of the other guys from the Johnny Lee Wills and Leon McAuliffe bands."

"But those are country and western bands!", I said, incredulously.

"Yeah. . .so?" Gary said. "They're just good musicians who love to play jazz but make their living playing western swing."

I went back into the living room and just watched them in awe.

After a couple of more songs, the drummer got up to go to the bathroom. "You want to play the next number?" he asked Gary.

"Sure!", Gary answered, and took a seat at the drums. He didn't do as well as the regular drummer, but he sounded surprisingly good. I had no idea he could play drums.

A great idea struck me at that point. I was losing the other Gary, who had been the drummer in the Strangers. I asked Gary if he wanted to play and he said: "Why not?" The problem was, he didn't own a set of drums. He didn't even own any drum sticks.

I remembered that Sonny Gray had a basement full of musical instruments. He owned at least one full set of drums which he kept in the rehearsal room so that his drummer wouldn't have to set up and tear down for each rehearsal. I thought I saw some other drums stacked in the pool room. So, I called him.

"I think I have a bunch of old drums." Sonny said. "You're welcome to come on over and look through them to see what there is."

Gary and I went over to Sonny's house that day and looked through what was in the basement. They were covered with a thick layer of dust, but most of the heads looked to be in good shape. We were able to put together most of a full trap set, except for cymbals. We had a snare, with stand, a floor tom-tom, but no mounted tom, and a huge bass drum. Drummers had gone to smaller bass drums, about twenty inches in diameter. This one was about 24 or 26 inches and looked like a big barrel. There was a high hat, but the pedal was broken, and a single cymbal with a chunk broken out of it.

It was a start, and Sonny said we could borrow all of it until Gary could get his own. Gary bought some sticks, brushes and a few extra accessories, like a drum key. Then he got an old duffel bag to load all the small items in, since there was no trap case. We were back in business as a band.

Gary proved to be a pretty good drummer, and he could also sing, so I pressed him into a couple of duets with me. This presented a real problem on one gig.

We had been trying to crack into the college market so we could play fraternity or sorority dances at the University of Tulsa. Most of the other Tulsa bands were into this market as well as a guy from Fayetteville, Arkansas, the John Tolleson band.

We finally got a booking, through the brother of Kay, the girl I used to date, who had heard us. We were to play a dance at the Sigma Chi house for the fraternity. This was our chance to show our stuff to this important market segment.

One of the songs we did was "All I Have to do is Dream", made famous by the Everly Brothers. When we did this song, Gary would get up from behind the drums and join me at the microphone for the two part harmony song. The song is a soft ballad and we didn't even use drums on it.

The room we were playing at the Sigma Chi house was not large and when it was full, the noise level was high, even when we weren't playing.

249

We were set up on the floor level—no stage or bandstand. Whenever I called a tune, I always called out the key it was played in to the rest of the band, having remembered the fact that I almost blew it at the KAKC hop with Doug at the organ.

I called the tune "All I Have to do is Dream" and Gary got up from the drums and came up to the microphone. I turned around and, above the crowd noise, said to Jerry and Jerry: "key of D". Jerry the guitarist thought I said "E", the most common key for a lot of rock and roll songs. Jerry the bass player thought I said "G". They were ready to play in those keys.

The song starts with a single D chord and the vocal picks up immediately. No introduction. The D chord I hit was low on the neck of the guitar, which means the highest note heard is an F sharp. That's the note Gary heard over the crowd noise.

So, I hit the D chord. We started the song with me playing and singing in D, Gary singing in F#, Jerry playing guitar in E and the other Jerry playing the bass part in G. It was a cacophony worse than a train wreck. After a couple of measures, everyone stopped but me. I felt it would be a disaster if we stopped the song after it was started—very unprofessional—so I just doggedly kept it going, as a solo. (So, how professional is that?) I thought for sure the other guys would pick it up and everything would recover just fine. But they didn't. Gary just stood there looking at me like I was an idiot. Jerry the guitarist had his arms folded over his guitar with a huge grin on his face. Jerry the bass player just rolled his eyes and looked at the ceiling.

Not only did I continue to sing (and some of the more inebriated members of the audience actually danced to it—or maybe it was those with a severe hearing impairment), but when I came to the end of the first time through, which would have been a natural stopping point where I could gracefully bow out, I just went right along, just like the record, and kept going. I thought to myself: "Why didn't you end it then, you idiot?"

Thankfully, the song finally ended, or should I say died a painful death? Gary went back to the drums and we tried to pick it up with one of our better rock tunes.

After we took a break and came back for the last set, it was going fairly well. There was another duet which Gary and I sang. I called that song and as Gary left the drums to come back up to the microphone. I heard someone yell: "Oh no! Look out! They're gonna do it again!" Not a great morale booster.

Chapter Seventy

Executive Privilege

One of the programs which the City of Tulsa and Public School System had put into place in Tulsa was the Youth Court. A representative of each high school was assigned to the Youth Court. It was quite an honor since the representatives had to be screened and voted on by both faculty and students. They took their positions very seriously.

The idea of the Youth Court was three fold: 1) Adjudicate minor infractions such as traffic violations, simple vandalism charges, etc. 2) Free up the mainstream courts for more serious or adult cases and 3) Teach some students about the judicial system.

When all the representatives were selected at the first of the year, each one was assigned a position or function. The principal position was Youth Court Judge, which rotated from school to school each year. In addition to Judge, there was Prosecutor, Public Defender, Chief Clerk, Bailiff and a couple of others. Youth Court representatives were considered the best Tulsa had to offer in the way of its youth.

As we approached the end of the school year, several of my friends who were a year older than me were thinking about graduation and starting to college in a few months. This was about to set up a conflict which created an uncomfortable episode.

One night four of us were riding around and had been to Pennington's. I was the only junior in the car. The other three guys were seniors, coming to the end of their high school careers. We were in Ron's (the tall trumpet player) car. Also there was Steve, our good friend, who played trombone in the Dance Band, and Andre, who played sax in the Dance Band.

Ron said he had to go by his girl friend Linda's house for some reason and would only be there a few minutes. Linda lived on a corner one block from the school. Ron pulled up in front of Linda's house and went inside. The three of us were sitting there talking, mostly about Steve and Andre going away to college next year. Suddenly Steve grabbed Ron's keys out of the ignition, got out of the car and went around to the back to open up the trunk. He fished around until he found a crescent wrench and some pliers.

I got out of the car and asked what he was doing. Steve said that he thought a stop sign would look great hanging on the wall of his dorm room at college next year. So he promptly went to work trying to take the two bolts out of the sign at Linda's corner to remove it from the pole to which it was affixed. The bolts were rusty and difficult to get, but he finally got them loose. Then he took the octagon shaped sign and slipped it under the mat in the trunk of Ron's car, out of sight, and replaced the tools in Ron's tool kit.

As Steve and I were getting back in the car, Ron was coming out of Linda's house, walking down the sidewalk toward the car. About that time, three police cars came racing up—one from each direction--and screeched to a halt, lights rotating. Apparently one of Linda's neighbors had spotted Steve's handiwork and phoned the police. At least three policemen approached our car and told everyone to get out. They were quite belligerent.

"All right, give us the stop sign you punks stole. We just hope that when someone goes through an intersection that has a sign missing, you're the one they hit."

They started getting very abusive verbally and we just stood there and listened to it. Then they started searching Ron's car, without asking. They instructed someone to open the trunk. They looked around and didn't find the sign. The verbal barbs continued.

Then one of them said: "I'll bet this isn't the only thing you've stolen. You're just the kind of trash who will be in trouble all the time." Then he looked at Ron and said: "I'll bet you know Kenneth [blank] really well." He had just mentioned the name of my former next door neighbor in grade school. The same guy who gave me five dollars of his birthday money. The same guy who tried to set up a cross-driveway communications system with me. The same guy with the crazy sisters. "Yeah. You're just as bad as he is, I'll bet!"

Obviously Kenneth was now well known to the police and qualified for full Juvenile Delinquency status, in his pre-prison days.

Ron said: "No sir. I've never heard of him."

"How about you?", looking at Steve. "You know this Kenneth don't you?"

"No sir.", Steve said.

Fortunately, they stopped asking before they got to me. Since I had not seen Kenneth for years, I probably would have denied I knew him anyway.

Then one of the officers said: "How about Youth Court? Have you ever been to Youth Court?" Both Ron and Steve drove with a fairly lead foot and had received more than one traffic ticket. They both nodded affirmatively.

"Yeah. I thought so.", the cop said. "You seem the types."

Then he looked at Andre. "How about you? Ever been to Youth Court?"

"Yes sir", Andre said.

"I thought so. What did you do?"

"I'm the Youth Court Judge", Andre replied.

This stopped all of the officers in mid sentence. They looked at each other and their whole attitude obviously changed. They looked at Andre's drivers license to assure themselves of who he was, then issued a short obligatory lecture, got into their cars and left. I realized that it was really true…there was such a thing as Executive Privilege.

Chapter Seventy One
The Big Flood of '57

The night of our Junior/Senior Prom in 1957 it had been raining for several days and had really been pouring down that day. The Arkansas River had crested the day before and to keep the flood waters from overrunning the Brookside area of town, crews were stacking sandbags along the bank at strategic areas. Truckloads of sand were delivered to the areas adjacent to the river. Then a crew would fill the bags with sand and tie them, passing them to the crew that was stacking them to make the dike. It was dirty, back-breaking work. The river was rising almost as fast as the levee could be constructed.

The banquet and prom, being held in the Mayo Hotel's Crystal Ballroom on the 16th Floor, was proceeding as scheduled. However, several of the guys didn't have dates to the prom and decided they would go down to the river and volunteer in the sand bag effort. Even some of the guys with dates felt obligated to join in the effort and talked their dates into staying at the prom as a group while they went to lend a hand.

I was not one of those who volunteered. There were numerous reasons. But one of them (really!) was the fact that my date to the prom was not my

254

girl friend, but just a good friend who was in my chemistry class, a senior (one year older than me). Her boy friend was attending an out-of-state college. It was his week of final exams, so he couldn't come back to take her to the prom. Everyone knew she had this serious boyfriend, so none of the boys asked her to the prom. JoAnn was her name, and her senior banquet and prom was really important to her. She had dreamed about this night for a long time and had bought her dress several months earlier. She just didn't want to go without an escort, so she asked me one day in class who I was taking to the prom. When I informed her that it was one of those rare periods when I didn't have a girl friend and had neglected to get a prom date, she asked if I would escort her. I was delighted to. She was a really cute and sweet girl and I envied the out-of-state boyfriend.

* * * * *

My good friend Ron had to play trumpet at the pre-prom ceremonies and banquet and his date, Linda, couldn't join him because she was in one of the preliminary events for the upcoming Miss Tulsa pageant, in which she was a contestant. (She went on to win that as well as Miss Oklahoma). Ron then had to leave the Mayo to go pick up Linda, planning to return by about 9 o'clock. The rain had not let up and 9 o'clock came and went and no Ron or Linda. 10 o'clock came and went and no Ron or Linda. 11 o'clock came and no Ron or Linda. The rain was still coming down hard. Unfortunately Billy had borrowed Andre's uncle's new Dodge Charger.

About midnight, in walked Ron, looking like a drowned rat. He and his white dinner jacket were thoroughly soaked. He explained that as he was headed to pick up Linda, about 8 o'clock, he was about to go under the railroad overpass at Peoria. As soon as he rounded the corner to go down the incline under the bridge, he spotted the high water and several cars at the bottom with water up past the windows. He immediately slammed on the brakes, but it was too late. The current of water which was pouring down Third Street to the makeshift reservoir under the train overpass simply swept up his car and carried it down to the bottom where he joined the other vehicles which had collected at the bottom. He managed to crawl out the window and get back up to higher ground, carrying his shoes over his head. There were no emergency vehicles available or tow trucks of any kind. They were in great demand all over town.

After a period of time in which he made calls and investigated various alternatives, Ron saw that it was hopeless trying to get his car out, so he decided to leave it and come back the next day. The problem was that his new trumpet was still in the car. It was a special order instrument. Not only expensive, but he had waited for it for months. This is what he planned to use as he started college to make his early mark in that new arena. He made several attempts to extricate the horn from the car, but to no avail. To make matters worse, the car was borrowed from our friend Andre's uncle—a brand new Dodge.

Ron was able to contact our friend Bill's (the trumpet player) parents who came to pick him up. He finally was able to collect Linda at about 11:45 and make it to the prom for the last part.

Some of the guys who had gone down to the river to help with sandbagging at about 7 o'clock returned about midnight. All of them looked like they had been rolling in a mud pit. They were unbelievably dirty and still covered with mucky, wet sand. White dinner jackets were the uniform of the day for proms in the fifties. No one wore black tuxedos and there were only a few of the pastel jackets, mostly powder blue. The wilder colors and styles had not yet come in. Since the guys were working in the rain, a lot of them just kept their jackets on while they worked with the sand bags. The problem was that virtually every one of the garments was rented. Al's Tuxedo Rentals was about to take a big hit.

* * * * *

The other big event which took place at the end of that year was during Senior Week. Everyone wondered what monumental prank or event the guys in the class of '57 had cooked up leave their mark during Senior Week. Well, on Tuesday or Wednesday of that week, at the end of the school day, the bell rang as usual at 3:30 and all the students poured out into the hallway. As the students came out into the main part of the third floor hallway, they were confronted with a floor covered with thousands and thousands of glass marbles. It was like trying to stand on an oil slick-covered mirror. Unless you kept your feet flat on the floor and just slid them along, you were in danger of ending up on your rear end.

Not a bad trick. The only problem was that it wasn't perpetrated by anyone in the class of '57. We found out later that several guys in the sophomore class (class of '59) had brought barrels full of the marbles to the school and overturned them just at 3:30. They made a clean getaway. This is the same gang from '59 who pulled off the infamous Gator Caper where they turned an alligator loose in the halls of the school. Said alligator, "Tuffy" had been gator-napped from the zoo.

Chapter Seventy Two-

Gunnison

The chance for Bobby and Lamar to get back at those who sprang the famous ambush on them during the aborted papering job on my house came early in the summer after our junior year. Most of my friends, including Al, Mike, Jerry, Lamar, Bobby, Tommy and several others, had signed up to go to band camp for two weeks at Western State College in Gunnison, Colorado. We all piled onto a chartered bus and headed for the mountains.

The campus and the setting were beautiful. We were billeted in the campus dorm rooms. Bobby and Lamar shared a room and took the opportunity to hatch this retaliation. Instead of just doing typical camp pranks, like short-sheeting a bed or putting alum in the toothpaste, Bobby came up with this diabolical plan.

Between classes at the camp, we would often hang around the Student Union on the campus and play pool. Bobby filled his pockets with pool chalk—the little cubes of blue, chalky substance which you rubbed over the tip of the pool cue to give it a little friction. He then sequestered himself in his dorm room at night and painstakingly scraped and chopped these cubes of hardened chalk into a little mountain of fine powder.

He and Lamar then snuck into the dorm rooms of all those on their hit list who had perpetrated the sinister ambush. They carefully turned back the sheets of the beds and scattered about a half a cup of this powder from about midway down the bed to the foot. Then they re-made the bed, carefully.

When each of us went to bed that night, we simply turned the covers down enough to get in, without noticing anything unusual about the top part of the bedding. We slept soundly, tossing and turning the normal amount, with each movement spreading the chalk more and more over the lower extremities of our bodies as well as our pajamas or underwear or whatever we were or were not wearing. The dye in that chalk is industrial strength.

The showers in the men's dorms at Western State are like many dorms—a large, community shower with shower heads protruding from the wall every four feet or so. As we went down to take our morning showers sporting blue legs, feet, buttocks or other parts, we caused quite a stir. Whistles, jeers and impromptu name calling abounded and our only comfort was in the fact that whatever the cause or malady, it afflicted several of us. It would have been an impossible situation if you had been the solitary blue boy.

It took several days to get the blue caste off your skin, but I don't think my mother ever got the blue out of that pair of undershorts I was wearing.

* * * * *

The main attraction about Band Camp at Gunnison was not the classes, the interaction, the mountains or even the overall experience, it was the girls. This is because the camp was not only open to band members, but they had programs for twirlers and majorettes as well. This meant that there were numerous groups of young lovelies running around the campus in their short, majorette skirts, practicing twirling and routines on the lawn where we sat around and watched and otherwise dressing up the place considerably.

The majorettes from Rogers went, but they were sort of like part of the gang. Nothing exciting about them, although some of them were quite cute. But, we were too familiar with them, having traveled on the bus with them to out of town football games, parades, etc. We knew their boyfriends. The thrill was gone.

While none of the band members from our rival, Central High School went to Gunnison, the entire Central twirling squad went. This was cool. My little group immediately zeroed in on this bevy of beauties and decided these were the ones we were going to team up with for extra curricular activities at Gunnison. There was Patsy, Doylene, Linda, Judy and a couple of others. All of them were cute, sweet and fun. What's more, we had a

258

day or so on the bus with them on the way to Gunnison in order to get the ball rolling.

However, once we arrived at Gunnison, I must admit that the selection of other twirlers from all over the country presented a very tempting diversion. In particular, the famous Kilgore Rangerettes, from Kilgore, Texas, were there. This was the most famous twirling squad in the country. They had been in numerous nationally televised parades, made network TV appearances, etc. However, they proved to be a bit aloof—even arrogant—and quite unapproachable. They walked around the campus, from class to class, everyday as a group, wearing their uniforms as if they were going to some sort of performance. They definitely wanted everyone to know that they were THE Kilgore Rangerettes, wearing their white cowboy boots, their fringed shirts and their cute little cowboy hats.

We marked them off our list immediately and went back to concentrating on the Central twirlers.

The opportunity for social interactivity was somewhat limited at the camp. We had no car and so the opportunities to spend time with the girls was limited to afternoons, just sitting on the grass in the commons area of the campus, or playing pool and listening to music in the Student Union. Sometimes they would have mixers at night in the cafeteria.

Then one day Tommy came bursting into the dorm where several of us were sitting. "Come outside and see what I've got.", he said.

We all followed him out the door and down the sidewalk to the parking lot. He walked directly up to a rusty old Jeep which looked like it had probably served one of Eisenhower's aides well for many years a couple of decades ago. This was about as basic a piece of transportation as one could ever imagine. The two front "seats" had no padding; in fact, had no leather or fabric. They were just metal slabs. The back "seat" was a metal bench. There was a windshield, but it was so pitted and etched, you could hardly see through it. It had a series of gauges, but Tommy informed us that none of them worked—speedometer, fuel level, oil pressure, etc. The tires looked like the original ones that had come on the vehicle. They were so old and brittle that you could break off chunks of dried rubber from the knobby treads with your hands.

We looked at him with the obvious question written across our faces.

"I rented it from a guy who runs a filling station in town.", he said. "Ten bucks for the whole week." Then he held out his hand and said: "I need three bucks from each of you guys.", which would give him a free ride and a two dollar profit, to boot. Well, that was Tommy's style, so we didn't complain. "I'll buy the gas.", he said.

259

"What are we going to do with this?", someone asked. "Just use it to run into town and back?"

"No.", Tommy replied. "I've got this great idea. We'll get the Central twirlers and all pile into this baby and go into the mountains for a picnic."

Well, that hit an immediate responsive chord. Grins all around. "When?", we all wanted to know.

"How about tomorrow?" This meant that several of us, as well as the girls, would probably have to cut at least one class. No problem.

There were five of us who would be going. With five twirlers, that meant ten people in this little Jeep. We started thinking about how this was going to work.

"Well. The girls are simply going to have to sit on our laps.", one of the guys said, seriously. No problem, we all thought without hesitation.

Tommy asked the guy he had rented the Jeep from where a good picnic spot would be, and he drew a map to guide us into the mountains and along a little stream. We arranged for food, lined up the girls and took off mid-day the next day.

It was a gorgeous day. The setting was unbelievably beautiful. The company was great. Even the baloney sandwiches tasted like a banquet. We ate, talked, walked around in the mountains, waded in the stream and took pictures. All in all, it was a fantastic outing, and was the highlight of the two weeks at Gunnison.

I felt a little guilty, however. I was dating Francine again, who was not in the band and didn't make the trip. But, we weren't going steady, so where's the problem? But when we got back from the outing, the mail had arrived, as it did every afternoon. I had received a box from Francine. It had a sweet note attached, saying how much she missed me and she hoped I would enjoy these cookies she had baked for me—my favorites, chocolate chip.

I opened the box and found about two pounds of cookie crumbs staring me in the face. The largest pieces of edible matter in the box were the chocolate chips which had not been crushed or broken up. The cookie portions had been reduced to granules.

Obviously Francine had simply loaded the box with cookies, stacking them in there neatly for mailing. The post office is not famous for carefully handling boxes of any type. I think most postal handlers think "Fragile" is an Italian word, pronounced "Fra-GEE-lay" meaning "throw freely". Well, it's the thought that counts. I told Francine that the cookies were delicious (as I'm sure they once were) and that I really appreciated the thought and effort.

Chapter Seventy Three
Partners with a Chevy Truck

After we returned from Gunnison, I was somewhat at a loss for the summer. I didn't want to go back to work at Brownie's. Then a new opportunity came up.

Bobby's dad owned a chain of home appliance stores and he had contracted with Bobby to deliver and install window air conditioners and water coolers over the summer. Bobby needed helpers, so he approached his buddies. Jerry, Lamar and I all worked in this endeavor. Al was still a little too much a rival of Bobby's and they still hadn't fully settled the Judy affair.

Bobby was paid fifteen dollars by his dad for every installation. He was very open with me about it. "I get fifteen bucks for the installation. We will split it evenly." That sounded like a fair deal to me--$7.50 for each installation. We could do about four a day. Thirty bucks a day was good money.

"OK, I said. Seven fifty each."

"No." Bobby said. "Five bucks." What kind of strange math was this? This is splitting it "evenly"? I thought Bobby wanted to be an engineer. He was going to have a tough time if he thought half of fifteen was five.

"How is this an even split?", I asked.

"Five bucks for you, five bucks for me and five bucks for the truck.", as serious as he could be.

"The truck?" Bobby had acquired an old black Chevy pickup truck for this job, which we would use to haul the units and the tools.

"Sure", he said. "We have to have the truck."

I guessed there was a certain amount of logic in this reasoning, although I wasn't sure the truck was worth a full share. I doubted that the truck would be helping to carry a heavy air conditioner up two or three flights of stairs. In essence, Bobby was getting a double cut, of course. But so what? It was his gig and his truck and the money was still good at five bucks a throw.

Most of the installations were pretty dull and straight forward. Some of them, however, were like something out of a movie—sometimes out of Abbott & Costello or the Three Stooges and sometimes out of Tennessee Williams or John Steinbeck.

We went into all sorts of strange houses and situations. I had never been exposed to anything outside of what I thought was a normal house—neat, reasonably well furnished, habitable, etc. But whoah! I saw some places that made me think there must have been a hidden camera to get our reactions.

In one house, we were installing a big water cooler in a very large kitchen which had a big table and several chairs in the middle. A water cooler is a big square box which hangs outside the window. A water hose is hooked up to it and water trickles down the packing in the wall—sort of a porous, straw excelsior material. A fan then blows across the saturated material, projecting cool, damp air into the room. They are exactly opposite of an air conditioner, which contains a compressor for keeping gas (usually freon) chilled. Air conditioners dehumidify the air. Water coolers humidify the air.

Jerry and I were installing the water cooler in this large kitchen and were just about finished. The man of the house was watching our every move, standing there in his sleeveless undershirt and bare feet. "I'll sho' be glad when you gets my cooler in.", he kept saying. "It's been powerful hot this summer!" We agreed.

The final step before turning the unit on was to hook up the water hose. We had put the "T" fitting on his outside hydrant and run the line to the unit. However, we didn't have the right fitting or a washer to complete hooking the line into the unit. We informed the customer that we would have to go get another fitting and washer and since it was late in the day, we couldn't get back until tomorrow.

"Oh, no!", he said. "I gots to have my coolin'. I don't think I kin stand another night like las' night. What kind of fittin' and washer does you need?", he asked.

We informed him that it was a standard pipe nut and washer, probably similar to the ones he had on his faucets at the sink, which we motioned toward.

He promptly grabbed one of our wrenches, walked over to his sink, and proceeded to take apart one of the valves. He removed all of the components and laid them out in his hand, holding them up in front of us.

"Will any of these do?", he asked.

We selected the parts we could probably use, and said: "These will probably work."

"Well, go ahead.", he said. "And hurry!

 The problem was that when he removed the valve and all the parts from the tap, a stream of water was shooting into the air like a huge fountain. It was squirting about six feet across the room, landing on the linoleum floor next to the kitchen table. The kitchen floor was rapidly becoming flooded. He calmly walked over to the back screen door and opened it to let some of the water escape. But some of it was running through the other door toward other rooms in the house and some was running under the stove, under the refrigerator and elsewhere.

"We'll go out and turn the water to your house off at your meter to stop that", we said.

"Oh, no!", he protested. "Then I won't get no water to my cooler. I gots to have my coolin'! Jes keep on keepin' on."

So we installed the hose to the cooler, turned it on, made sure it was running properly and got the heck out of there as soon as we could. As we were leaving, we could see him just sitting in a chair at the kitchen table, holding a big glass of iced tea and facing the cooler with his eyes closed, enjoying the cool breeze while the water continued to spew into the room and land beside him. He was probably imagining that he was in Hawaii.

* * * * *

Another time we had an air conditioner to install in an older house not too far from the downtown area. When we arrived, we were greeted by two teenage girls, both of whom were kind of cute. They showed us the window where the unit was to be installed.

As we went out to the truck to bring the unit up, we both remarked that the house had a very peculiar odor to it. We simply put it down to lack of air conditioning—too much heat and humidity had made the house musty.

When we started the installation, I asked one of the girls if I could use the restroom. She directed me toward the back. "Just go through the kitchen and out the door. It's across the little porch."

I headed toward the kitchen where she pointed. When I opened the door to the kitchen, I thought it was a joke. There were dirty dishes, dirty pots and pans, partially eaten food and no telling what else, everywhere. It was stacked on every surface and nearly every square inch of floorspace. The oven door was open and the oven was crammed full of utensils, plates, pots, etc. As I walked past a small table I saw pots with substances which probably were food several weeks or months ago. There were half sandwiches with bites taken out of them which were now covered with green fuzzy mold, left on top of mounds of pans, opened cans, etc.

I just about turned around to get out of there quick, but my need to find a toilet overcame me. I turned the handle to go out the back door and pushed the door open slightly. As soon as I did, the biggest creature I had ever encountered jumped up at the crack in the door, growling, snarling and drooling all over the place. I don't know what kind of dog this was but he was as big as a horse. Then I heard a female voice yell at me from the living room: "Don't mind Fred. He won't hurt you."

Easy for you to say, I thought. I edged the door a little more and could see that poor Fred was cooped up on this little porch that was about four feet square. There was a door to the outside, which was locked. He had a water dish, which was empty, and a dish of some sort of stuff which was dry and crusty. This poor guy wasn't vicious, he was just starved for attention.

I spoke a few kind words to him, patted him on the head and stepped across his cell to enter the bathroom on the other side. Only a powerful need was sufficient incentive to stay long enough to relieve myself in this facility. I beat a hasty retreat, but not before refilling Fred's water dish. No more will be said about it.

When I returned to the front room, where we were installing the air conditioner, I said to Jerry: "You won't believe where I have just been." He looked at me with obvious curiosity and expressed a desire to go see for himself.

"I wouldn't do that, if I were you.", I said. Trust me." He didn't. He promptly got up and announced that he needed to go to the restroom as well.

Jerry took a significantly longer amount of time on his sojourn than I had. When he returned, he was grinning and said something like: "There's some really cool stuff in there!"

I couldn't imagine anything in there which could be classified as even approaching "cool" in the vernacular. I decided then and there that Jerry must be sick. Too much work in the hot weather had gone to his head.

After we finished the job and were back in the truck, Jerry said: "We've got to come back to this place. We'll tell them we have some adjustments to make, or something. I've got to think of what we can do with some of that stuff in the kitchen. What a tremendous source for some great pranks! All we have to figure out is what we're going to do and who we're going to do it to." I know he was thinking back to the time we spread the decayed minnows on Mimi's window sill.

I did go back there one more time, ostensibly to check the air conditioning unit. But Jerry was not with me. I had told Lamar about this place and he just had to see it. We went over there, and Lamar made his own trek to the bathroom, to see for himself. He couldn't stop talking about the experience for days.

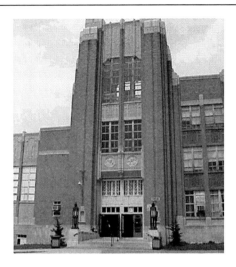

Chapter Seventy Four
Kings of the Hill

When our senior year started at Rogers (affectionately known as "Will on the Hill") we were flying high. We owned the world and I think most of us knew it was a special time and a special place.

The first order of business was, of course, election of class officers. I decided to NOT run for president. I'm not that much of a glutton for punishment. A guy named Mike won (same Mike). This guy should have succeeded JFK in the White House. He couldn't lose. He went to West Point from Rogers and on to Columbia University. How I ever thought I could win against him in the early races is beyond me.

What I did decide to run for was Senior Class Treasurer. When I signed up as a candidate, no one else had entered that race. Then, at the last minute, one of the most popular girls in the class, named Sandy, decided to run. Even worse, she was one of my favorite people. I didn't want to oppose her. Well, what the heck? I decided. We were nearly adults. Surely everyone would see that this election was not a popularity contest. Perhaps I could be elected based on my platform and what I would do for the class if elected treasurer. (Can you believe I thought this?)

The primary campaign thrust is the campaign speech, which was given at the first Senior Class Assembly. My speech was first. I was sincere, serious and well grounded. I would make such a great treasurer. I would work hard with Mike to really institute some great programs. We would work closely with faculty and administration, etc. etc. etc. What a load of crap! I received polite applause.

Then it was Sandy's turn. She brought out an easel with a big chart on it. Uh Oh! This was a bad sign, already. Then she proceeded to talk about fiscal matters as shown on the chart. But the chart was upside down! She went over to turn it back up and knocked the whole thing over. Then she tried to hold it up with one hand while speaking to the numbers. By then the audience was rolling in the aisles with laughter. It became sickeningly apparent to me that the whole speech was a put on. I must have been the last person in the place to realize it. She gave a five minute stand-up comedy act which made our contest look like Lucille Ball versus Boris Karloff. She was hilarious. After flustering about at the end, she just walked off the stage, in a sort of daze. She didn't ask for their votes or anything. I was dead and I knew it.

The election was closer than I would have thought. I lost by only four votes. I was proud of myself, in defeat.

When I got into band class that day after checking on the vote totals, I was talking to my friends in the trumpet section and discovered that at least five of my closest friends had not even voted! I could have won the election if they'd only taken the time to vote! After my anger and frustration had subsided a little, all I could think of that I wanted to say to them was "Why didn't you vote? You got some splainin' to do, Lucy!"

* * * * *

The fact that we were in a special school and situation was confirmed to us before long. Will Rogers High School was selected as the recipient of the Bellamy Flag Award, which recognized the outstanding high school in the United States. We were all bursting with pride when the committee (whoever they were) showed up and presented the award to Stanley Davis, president of our student council.

Chapter Seventy Five

Can you cash this $3,000 check?

I had already started my senior year busier than I wanted to be. My band was getting very busy and we were playing almost every weekend. Then, I had started bowling in professional tournaments, which required quite a bit of weekend travel. I sort of charted out my own pro bowlers' tour, based on how long it would take me to get to the city where the tournament was and when I could get back, assuming I made the cut and had to stay until the last squad bowled. This meant I could probably go as far as Kansas City and St. Louis to the North, Little Rock and Memphis to the East, Dallas and Ft. Worth (but maybe Houston) to the South, and Oklahoma City, Wichita and Amarillo to the West. I was starting to miss quite a few Fridays at school and occasional Mondays.

On one of the trips to Kansas City I won a tour event called the "Carl Richard Open". Carl Richard had been a prominent and very popular professional bowler from Kansas and they had named the tournament after him. I won $3,000 in this tournament. This was about six months' salary to the average working man in 1957—a huge amount for a high school kid.

As soon as I got back to Tulsa I had the prize money check Photostatted. This was in the days before Xerox machines. A Photostat was a picture of the document, but in reverse—that is, the paper was black and the writing was white. Other than that, it looked identical. I had all my prize checks Photostatted to keep in my scrapbook.

One morning I got to school and happened to have the copy of the $3,000 check. Two girls from TU were set up at a table in the front hall, near Soash Corner. They were selling tickets to TU's all school talent review, called Varsity Night. They were twin sisters, Jan and Judy, who had graduated from Rogers just four months earlier. Everyone knew them.

I walked up to the table and asked what they were doing. They put the sales pitch on me about Varsity Night and wouldn't I like to go and take a date?

"How much are the tickets?" I asked. I was informed that they were two dollars.

"I'll tell you what", I said. We have about 800 members of our senior class. I'd like to buy them all a ticket to Varsity Night. I think they would really enjoy it."

Jan and Judy just laughed at my little "joke" and asked once again if I would like a couple of tickets.

"I'd like 800 tickets", I repeated. I then got out the copy of the check, thrust it in front of them and said: "Can you just give me my change in cash?"

They looked at the photostatic copy and their eyes popped out of their heads. It looked like a real check, even if it was white on black instead of black on white.

"Is this real?", they asked.

"Sure!", I said. Look at the bank it is drawn on in Kansas City. "This was first prize in a bowling tournament."

They hastily conferred with each other and then excitedly said: "OK. 800 tickets will be 1600 dollars. We don't have that many tickets with us, but I'll stay here and Judy will go back to school (TU was just a half mile away) and get the tickets and the change for your check--$1,400 in cash."

Of course I had already cashed the real check, given half of it to my sponsors, spent some and had a minor portion left. I strung the girls along for a few minutes more, and then burst their balloon. I hated to do it, and I really did think that it might have been fun to buy the whole class a ticket to Varsity Night. The girls enjoyed a few minutes on a real high.

Chapter Seventy Six
Dropping Acid

One of my best friends was named Tommy (the one who had rented the Jeep at Gunnison). He played in the band and occasionally joined us in our poker games. All the girls thought Tommy was "really cute".

Tommy wasn't exactly the perfect student. He was too busy having fun. He studied just about enough to get by, but is a very intelligent guy.

That's why it was a total surprise to everyone in our little group when Tommy volunteered to be the lab assistant in Mr. Setliff's senior chemistry class. This was a brown-nose job. Sure, you'd get extra credit and probably come out of the class with an E. But you could do that fairly easily without doing all the extra work.

Being lab assistant meant you had to clean up after experiments were done. You had to wash the beakers, put away the Bunsen burners, secure all the chemicals, etc. Tommy had chemistry sixth hour, the last class of the day, which meant he would have to stay an hour late or more, every day, to perform his chores.

In a way this worked out great. He was not in the dance band. We rehearsed right after school. Tommy didn't have a car, so I would frequently give him a ride home. When school had been out for about fifteen minutes, he would say: "That's okay, Mr. Setliff. I can handle everything from here. I'll clean up and put everything away. Why don't you go on home?" The elderly Mr. Setliff was tired of spending every waking hour at the school, and was more than glad to turn the dirty work over to this cooperative, young assistant. I'm sure he thought Tommy was quite a find.

270

After dance band rehearsal one day, I met Tommy at the main entrance so I could take him home. His arms were loaded with paraphernalia, jars, beakers, test tubes, etc.

"What the heck is all that stuff?" I asked.

"Shut up, and hurry!" Tommy said. As we went to the car he said: "I'm building the greatest home chemistry lab you've ever seen! I'm even gonna make my own nitroglycerine."

Tommy explained that he had a book on how to make nitro, how you had to control the temperature, not only of the substance, but the ambient temperature and atmosphere. He said you'd know if you had a good batch if you put a drop of it on an anvil, hit it with a hammer and it blew the hammer out of your hand.

"What in the world will you do with it?"

"Lots of things!", he replied rather sinisterly.

Of course, by the time rehearsal was over and Tommy and I left school, the building was nearly deserted. The janitors were working in some parts of the building, but we rarely saw them. Even the people in the office had gone home.

Each day when I met Tommy after rehearsal he was taking more components for his lab home. Then one day I was waiting at the door for Tommy when he came flying down the stairs on a dead run—feet hardly touching the steps—but he was empty handed.

"Let's get the hell out of here, quick!", he said.

"What happened?" I asked.

"I dropped a full quart beaker of pure, concentrated hydrochloric acid at the top of the stairs on the fourth floor! C'mon. Let's get outta here!"

"Wait.", I said. "We'd better clean it up first. That stuff could be dangerous."

"I already tried that", he said. "I grabbed a mop from the janitor's closet and tried to mop it up. It just ate up the mop head as soon as it was touched. It's already eating through the marble floor. There's a spot about 15 inches in diameter there. The smoke and fumes are coming up like crazy."

I couldn't think of anything else to do, so we left.

The next morning, the first thing I did was go to the fourth floor to check out the spot where Tommy had dropped acid (a term which took on an entirely different meaning about ten years later). Sure enough, the spot was there, although it was now dry. The terrazzo was a dull, grayish white, instead of the maroon with multi-colored flecks in it. The janitors had put a tent sign over the spot that said "Caution. Wet Floor". I guess they were trying to figure out what to do with it and how to repair it. (They never replaced that section of flooring. When we had a class reunion in the building about twenty years later, I went up to the spot and you could still see it, but only faintly.)

Tommy was never able to make nitroglycerine, a fact for which I am still grateful, as would his neighbors be, if they had only known.

* * * * *

Tommy had become good friends with a police officer who lived across the street from him. The officer worked juvenile (how convenient) and was a very sharp guy. He was in his early twenties, good looking and non-uniformed, most of the time. Al would even sometimes join us for poker games, when we played at Tommy's. We all liked him a lot.

One night Tommy was hanging out at Pennington's with Lamar and a guy named Dave (who later became a police officer). Dave and Lamar said they knew this really cute girl they could pick up and maybe get lucky with. So, they headed off toward her house in Dave's Ford. It was a Wednesday night. This is the only night her dad would let her out of the house. He suspected that she was a bit on the wild side and couldn't say no to the boys. But Wednesday was church night and church was only two blocks away, so she could get out for that reason, and that reason only.

Dave, Lamar and Tommy were waiting at the end of the block to intercept her on her way to church, with no pangs of conscience, I'm sure. When she got there, Dave hopped out and asked her if she would like to go get a Coke. She got in the front seat of Dave's car and they went to Pennington's. Then they drove around while the boys tried to put the make on her. But she was having none of it that night. She said her dad had been beating her nearly every night and she was really afraid of him and he had really put the fear in her, so she was strictly on the straight and narrow.

After another hour or so of no luck, they took her back to her church and let her out. Her dad was there, having gone up to the church to check on her. He came storming toward the car and Dave peeled out of there leaving nothing but dust.

The guys returned to Pennington's empty handed and were back in their old parking place. Before long, a police car pulled in and two officers got out. They walked directly to Dave's car, went around behind it with a flashlight and checked the license plate. Then they asked who had been in that car earlier in the evening. Dave, Tommy and Lamar all said they had, believing that they had done nothing wrong.

"You're all under arrest.", one of the officers said. "Please get in the patrol car."

"What for?", one of the guys asked.

"Statutory rape of a minor."

Under great protest, the guys got in the car and were taken downtown. When their drivers licenses were checked and they were found to be under 18, they were turned over to the juvenile division (where Al worked). Darn the luck! That's like Brer Rabbit being thrown into that nasty ol' briar patch.

Al was on duty that night and when Tommy, Lamar and Dave came walking in, escorted by the uniformed officers, Al said: "Thanks, officers. I'll take it from here."

Al took them into his office, got a copy of the complainant's report and read it. Then he said: "All right. Tell me what happened."

Tommy relayed the events of earlier that evening and assured Al they had not raped the girl. They had hardly touched her, but not for lack of trying.

Al said that she told her dad she had been forced into the car, taken out to the country and raped. He also informed them that she was only 14 and dangerously close to being jail bait. It became apparent that this was nothing personal against the guys. She was just trying to protect herself from another beating at the hands of an abusive father. The boys explained this to Al and he told them to go on home. He'd do a little checking, and if it appeared true, he'd see the whole thing was dropped and never appeared on their records.

About a week later, Tommy, Lamar and I were downtown. My car was parked at a parking meter. As we were coming back to the car, the guy who was parked in the space in front of mine backed up to leave his place. In so doing, he crashed into the front of my car, bent the grill and broke out a parking light. We yelled at him but he turned and saw us and sped off. We got his license tag number.

Tommy said: "C'mon. We'll go down to Al's office at the police station. They'll run a trace on the tag number and give us the name and address of the owner immediately."

So we headed down to the police station, a few blocks away and up to Al's office on the second floor. The juvenile department had a single secretary who sat in the front area and worked for the officers who had small offices around the perimeter. She was about twenty years old and was one of the prettiest girls I had ever seen in my life. Large, dark eyes and dark, flowing hair down past her shoulders. I fell in love immediately.

Then, one of the most humiliating things I had ever experienced happened. As we walked in, there were several people standing around in the large open area of the office where this pretty girl's desk was. There were a couple of more matronly women with file folders in hand and one or two men. We walked toward the goddess' desk, following Tommy. Suddenly she turned toward Al's office and in an impish voice said, quite loudly: "Al. Your little rapists are here again." I wanted to crawl under the nearest desk. Even though I was not one of the "little rapists", the others in the room didn't know this. We were all being painted with the same brush. Of course, Miss Gorgeous thought it was hilarious. The others in the room just looked at us like we were scum.

OPENING ROUND PIN WINNERS—Joe Welling, Jr., and Lois Owens had a good reason to display big smiles in the above photograph. They rattled the bowling pins for huge scores to win the Tribune "Bowler of the Week" honors last week. Young Welling tossed a 699 and Mrs. Owens posted a 670 series to top their respective divisions.

Clipping from the Tulsa World

Chapter Seventy Seven
The Hustler

Not only was I now an alleged rapist, even if only among a small handful of people who I didn't know, but I was starting to become a hustler. When I had decided to try my hand at professional bowling, on a part time basis, it became painfully apparent that if you didn't place fairly high in the money, you weren't likely to make enough to pay expenses. I had acquired three sponsors, but this was both good and bad. The sponsors made sure you could get expenses covered, but they also wanted a piece of your winnings, and the expenses came off the top.

My sponsors were the King Louie Bowling Shirt company (I had met their representative when he called on the bowling alley where I sometimes worked part time), Crystal Bowl (the bowling house where I worked) and my dad. They all felt I was sort of a rising star in bowling ranks (at least that's what the newspapers had said on more than one occasion), and that's what justified their kicking in expense money each week when I traveled.

It soon became apparent that I was not yet in the same league with the true professionals. These were guys who practiced for hours every day and could read lane conditions like reading the daily newspaper. They had the capability to adjust their deliveries, not only for various types of lanes and conditions, but could even adjust from the first to the last of a three game set as conditions changed over the period of a couple of hours. Some of them had nerves of steel, total concentration and did not choke under any circumstance. I, on the other hand, would still choke under the most low pressure circumstances. I never had a sanctioned 300 (perfect) game because I would choke in the last frame after 9 strikes in a row.

I might win an occasional tournament (like the Carl Richard Open) but it would probably be luck, or a fluke. So, the only way I was likely to make any money when on the road was as a hustler. Several of the pros did this, in order to cover expenses, and I learned well from them. Unlike the locals, the pros would rarely bowl against each other in match game or pot games. What was the point? We just ended up trading our own money and the only winner was the house, who got paid for the games bowled.

The way to be successful as a hustler was to get fresh money—new blood. The pattern was almost the same in every town. The locals would come out to watch the pros in the tournament. The locals who considered themselves hot shots would pick a pro they thought they could beat— hopefully a wounded duck (someone off his game)—then challenge him to a match, supposedly for the "thrill" of seeing if they could beat one of the pros.

The pros, on the other hand, would bait the locals. If it looked like you were not likely to place high on the money list, then you started throwing off the last game or two. Maybe you'd miss an easy spare or two or not string strikes when you had an opportunity to. My composite average was 212 but if I was in my hustling mode, I'd try to shoot my last game in the 180's. Enough to be semi-respectable, but still look very beatable.

At the end of the last game of the last set, you would go ahead and start taking off your bowling shoes, as if leaving. But you would usually be approached by two guys—one older guy and one pimply faced kid. It's amazing how similar many of these were from town to town. The old man would approach you first while the kid hung back.

"You're a pretty good bowler.", the sugar daddy would often start off by saying.

"Well, thanks.", I would say. "But my timing is really off tonight. Maybe next week."

"Listen, how about bowling my boy here in a two game match? He'd like to just bowl against one of the pros for the fun of it. We'll make it interesting for you." His "boy" was not his son. It was a business arrangement. He covered the kid's losses but split the winnings, if any, with him.

"Oh, I don't know", I'd say. "It's not a good night for me. Is the kid any good?"

"Oh, he shoots OK in one of the leagues but he's only been bowling a couple of years. His goal is to get a lot better and maybe go on tour. It would be a big boost to him if you'd bowl a couple of games with him."

Finally I would "reluctantly" give in, put my shoes back on and the older guy would get a couple of lanes assigned. We would throw a couple of warmup balls and then the stakes would be set. "How about 5, 5 and 10?" , the backer would say. This meant five dollars for the winner of each game of a two-game match and ten dollars for the total pin count of both games, added together. The loser would also pay for the bowling lines for both players.

"That sounds OK to me." , I'd say.

We would start and I'd just coast along, getting the feel for how good the kid really was, whether he had the temperament or the killer instinct. Generally I'd let the kid win at least one, if not both games. Then I'd pay off and start to take my shoes off again.

"How about one more set?", the old guy would invariably ask. I'd protest, but he'd say: "Just one more. Then we can wrap it up. 5, 5 and 10 again?"

I'd acquiesce again and we'd bowl another set. Again, I'd lose some if not the whole thing. I had them hooked now.

Then, the old guy would beg for one more. I'd say something like: "Look. Some of the other guys are waiting for me to go get something to eat. I need to go." More begging. Then, almost perturbed, I would say: "Alright. But this is the last one." They would nod in agreement. "But if we're just bowling one more set, let's make it more interesting. How about 50, 50 a hundred?" Suddenly both of them would straighten up, eyes wide and hem haw around.

"Just a second.", the older guy would say. Then he and the kid would have a private little conversation where he was undoubtedly asking the kid something like: "Do you think you can take him? How do you feel?", etc. The kid would invariably answer with bravado on what a piece of cake this was going to be. They would come back and say: "OK. Let's go."

Generally you wouldn't start too hot. Toy with them a few frames, but not let him get too far ahead. And then, at the right moment, strike! In most cases, you didn't have to bowl 250 to win. Usually a turkey (three strikes in a row) would be enough to get the kid shook and he would start choking or making stupid mistakes. Some thought you had probably finally corrected your timing or whatever trouble you'd been having. The smart ones knew they'd been had, and this made it even harder for them.

If this wasn't working, a little verbal psyche job would generally do the trick. Usually a comment like: "Boy! That left alley sure seems to be getting a lot slower, don't you think?" (which means the ball is going to hook or curve more than on a fast or slick alley and you need to adjust), or "Wow! I almost fell on the right hand approach. It must have something slick on it.", or "I didn't notice, but how many steps do you take in your approach, 4 or 5?", or "Which foot do you start your delivery on, the left or the right? (this is an automatic movement which most bowlers never think about). Anything to get him thinking about his delivery, the alleys or whatever. Some kids would totally cave. Others would try to maintain their cool, but there was usually always some effect.

After the last match, I'd collect my money, settle up with the house and get out quick. Even at age 17, I realized that this was not a way to make a living, or even to earn extra money. I was happy to give it up.

Chapter Seventy Eight
Another New Car

I had only had my beautiful little Ford convertible about a year when my dad and my grandmother asked if I would like to have a new car for graduation. I hadn't even thought about it. But Dad had a good friend who was the Pontiac dealer in Nowata, Oklahoma, a little town about an hour North of Tulsa.

In February of 1958, about three months before graduation, I said goodbye to my cool little Ford convertible and drove off in this brand new, shiny black Pontiac Chieftain Convertible. It was not stick shift, but at that point I didn't care. It even had what Pontiac called a "Sportable" radio. You pushed a button in the glove compartment and the radio could be pulled out, complete with a disappearing handle and built in speaker and battery, for taking to the beach or whatever. The problem was that this radio was stolen out of my car so many times that the insurance company stopped covering it.

The first thing I did was to take some of my winnings from the bowling tournaments and do a slight amount of customization on the car. I had full length "Lakes Pipes" installed (external, chrome exhaust pipes which bypass the conventional exhaust pipes and mufflers and are attached along the side of the car, at the bottom (along the rocker panel). It was illegal to run with lakes pipes open (without a muffler) on the public streets.

Then I took the car over to King Dave, the pinstriping pro who had also become the pro at scallop and flame jobs. I didn't want a flame job—I didn't think that would be compatible with the lines of the car. Flame jobs were better on cars such as customized '50 and '51 Fords and Mercuries which had been nosed and decked and had very little chrome. A scallop job is a set of contrasting color trims designed to be compatible with the lines of the car, existing chrome, etc. They were often painted with the tips of the teardrops or trailing edges fading into another color. The scallops which King Dave put on the Pontiac were basically candy apple red which faded into silver at the tips. Each of the scallops is outlined with pinstriping. It certainly made the car distinctive and unique.

The main problem with a scallop job is that if you have a wreck, no matter how minor, and need to repaint a fender or quarter panel, it's almost impossible to match the scallops or duplicate what was there. Unfortunately, that's exactly what happened a couple months after graduation during a trip to California. That necessitated re-painting the entire car when the fender was repaired. But before that happened, the vehicle was definitely a show car unlike almost anything seen in Tulsa.

* * * * *

Every Sunday afternoon at the Tulsa North Airport, they had drag races. You could go out and enter in various classes and compete for trophies. There were some regular winners, like a guy named Jerry who had a fuel injected '57 Chevy Impala which was the hottest stock car in town.

I entered the Pontiac on two or three Sundays, but never won. A convertible was simply too heavy and not aerodynamic enough to compete against others in the same class of horsepower and displacement.

However, I did better in the private drag races. Often on Friday nights, someone would challenge somebody else to a drag race. Rather than risking a ticket and fine by dragging on high traffic, public streets, we picked a location which would serve this purpose better. There was a one mile stretch of straight, flat, two lane street on the North Side, near Mohawk Park. It was seldom traveled at night. There were no houses there and it really led to nowhere interesting.

Word would spread that there was going to be a drag race at the Mohawk strip at ten o'clock, and everyone would empty Pennington's and head for the site. A couple of cars would park at each end to keep any stray traffic from entering the combat zone. We had long ago marked off a quarter mile and painted a starting line and finish line across the street. We even had the official starter for the Sunday afternoon drags, a guy named Dave who went to Rogers.

The two opponents would take their places while Dave stood in position, raised the starting flag and kicked off the race. I won most of my competitions. The winner received nothing but bragging rights.

There was one guy at Rogers I was never able to beat, for some reason. A guy named Bill had a '54 Olds 88 with a J2 engine. It was a hot machine and tended to nose me out every time. I always held out hope that I would beat him someday. I never did.

Chapter Seventy Nine
The Great River Race

As we approached the end of our senior year several of us decided that instead of pulling some sort of sophomoric prank during senior week, why not do something which was more fun and even somewhat constructive?

Within an hour of Tulsa is a beautiful section of the Illinois River. There are several canoe concessionaires along the river where you can float down the river—3, 5, 10 miles and it is a very scenic trip. There are even semi-tame rapids in some areas, depending on how high the river is.

Flowing into the Illinois River is a clear water tributary called Spring Creek. It is not as wide or deep as the river and in order to traverse its entire length, you might have to get out, carry your craft and ford part of it. We decided that the thing to do would be to have a race down Spring Creek.

We set the day and the rules, which were simple--only one: no motors. Your vessel could be anything, as long as it floated and was propelled only by human power, with or without a paddle.

You could use a manufactured boat, canoe, etc. or make your own. It could be as big or as small as you want. It could be for one person or a whole crew.

We decided that everyone would pay an entry fee and the winner would take the entire pot. We each put in two dollars. There was no entry form. Just show up, pay your two dollars and go for it.

Word of the function spread throughout the class and it started to become a bigger deal than the prom. It was mostly boys who planned to take part as contestants. But most of the girls wanted to be there. Six of us decided to enter as a team on a single vessel. We designed a boat on which the flotation came from inflated inner tubes. That way, if we capsized, it would be no big deal. We would still float and there was no such thing as right side up. One side was just like the other. Al, who was into dragsters, decided what we needed was graduating sizes of inner tubes, not all the same size. He said it would be best if we put a large, truck tire tube in the front, with succeedingly smaller inner tubes going back. His uncle was a local Chrysler-Plymouth dealer and we could get whatever size tubes we wanted.

We then took large, one-by-twelve planks about 12 feet long, and lashed them top and bottom over the tubes, like a large sandwich. It looked pretty rakish and we got six double bladed paddles like those used with kayaks. We surmised that the way to navigate our vessel was to straddle the planks. When we were in deeper water and needed to make speed, we would pull our feet up and rest them on the bottom plank. When we needed stability or had to ford over shallow water or rocks, we could simply stick our legs out the bottom and walk with the entire craft between our legs. Seemed like a good idea at the time.

The big day for the race came. Launch time was to be 10 AM and the course was about eight to ten miles. We figured we would finish by early afternoon, depending on how much shallow water we ran into.

We hauled our craft up in Al's dad's pickup truck with the thing sticking over the top, probably illegally, since it was twelve feet long. Our girl friends packed picnic lunches, as did many of the girls, and rode up with us. They would drop us off and watch the start and then drive to the finish and wait. Then we would all have a big picnic.

When we planned the event, we expected 20 or 30 entrants. Maybe 50. We selected a relatively narrow part of the creek to start at, primarily because it had a large rocky bank area, sort of like a big beach, and accessibility was good.

The morning of the race when we got to the launch site, there were hundreds of people there. There were probably scores of entrants in everything from fishing boats to rubber life rafts. One guy named David had just driven up to watch but got so excited he wanted to enter. No one had a place for anyone else on their team, especially a 240 pound lineman from the football team. David, who liked to work on the engine of his '46 Ford, had pins installed on the hood of his car so he could pull the pins and

283

take the hood completely off in 30 seconds. David had this great idea. He popped the hood on his car, pulled the pins out of the hinges and took the hood off, turning it over. It resembled a black, metal bathtub. He dragged it down to the water and got in to test it. Sure enough it floated and he was ready to go.

I'm not sure how many final entrants there were, but it was well over a hundred. We decided to pay three places. First place was going to get about $150—a sizable sum.

The next problem was what format would be used for the starting which would be fair to all entrants. There were way too many to just stretch across the creek in a straight line. We toyed with starting in waves and timing the starts and finishes, then decided that would be too complicated. Finally, one of the geniuses in geometry said we could line up on the bank but the lineup would have to be at an angle—LeMans style. Those closest to the water would have to be further upstream. He sat down and figured what would be the equi-distant point for each entrant—what the slope of the starting line would have to be in order to give everyone an equal chance of reaching the same point about a hundred yards down the stream at about the same time. We pointed out that this was going to create a huge bottleneck. He acknowledged that but asked if anyone had a better suggestion. No one did, so we proceeded.

Those with large or heavy vessels, like ours, were given positions closest to the water but much further upstream. One-man, light weight vessels, such as kayaks, small canoes and surfboards would be furthest away from the water.

Everyone lined up in their positions and the line stretched clear into the woods. By the time we did all this, it was closer to 11 o'clock. One of the guys had a whistle and volunteered to act as a starter. He stood out in front, counted down and blew the whistle, and the race was on!

Everyone raced for the water with their crafts in tow. This was quite a race in its own right. The first ones in the water had a huge advantage. By the time the bulk of the guys were there, it was like trying to get a football team into a washtub. What a mess!

Even though we were one of the first in the water, our craft was so big and cumbersome and the creek was so shallow at that point, we couldn't make enough forward progress to get out of the way before the rest of the flotilla hit us. As new craft entered the water, we were simply pushed more and more toward the other bank, instead of downstream.

It took at least 15 or 20 minutes to get everyone launched and into the water going the right direction. By then, we were already close to being in last place. Then, when we reached deeper water, where we thought we could really make some speed, a fundamental design flaw emerged. The concept of putting the large tube in front and the small ones in back was exactly opposite of what it should have been. The large tube acted as a big resistance against the water and the tail end kept trying to pass the front. We had to spend most of our effort just trying to keep the dang thing pointed the right direction.

Then disaster number two struck: as we turned a bend and the creek narrowed, someone had stretched a couple of barb wire strands across the creek, probably to keep cattle from straying. By the time we spotted it, it was too late. The lower strand, which was just above the water, caught our lead, truck inner tube right across the center. It was punctured in 3 or 4 places and started losing air fast. In a few minutes it was only about 20% filled and was more a hindrance than a help. We extricated the wounded tube and tossed it aside. We then decided to turn the craft around, the way it wanted to be in the first place and started going down the creek small end first.

In a couple of hundred more yards, we ran into one of the girls in our class who was standing in shallow water holding a nearly flat inner tube. She too had been a victim of the barb wire booby trap. She was going down by herself on a tire inner tube when she struck the barb wire and was completely flat in a couple of hundred more yards. She then asked if she could just join us, since our craft was so big. Well we were still afloat with six of us even without our primary flotation tube. We also realized by now that we weren't likely to finish in the top five or the top fifty, probably. So we just told her to hop on. What the heck? We'd just enjoy the ride.

By the time we reached the finish, we were close to last. Some had already eaten their picnic lunches and some had gone home, but most were still there.

First place winner was a guy on a surfboard. Second place went to his buddy who was also on a surfboard. Third place went to a guy in a kayak. The kayak was actually the fastest of the three but he took more time getting in and out when he had to ford, losing precious seconds to the surfboards.

Even though we weren't a serious contender, the whole experience was a major league blast. It was definitely one of the most fun events I had ever participated in and the day was thoroughly enjoyable.

* * * * *

When we got back in town, we discovered that there had, indeed, been a prank perpetrated on the school in the name of the senior class. We didn't know who did it, but we did know it was not one of the several hundred kids that was with us at Spring Creek.

What happened was that when students poured out into the hallway after the 3:30 bell, instead of confronting thousands of marbles, what they were confronted with was a live, four foot alligator. Pandemonium ensued of course and the zoo was called to collect the animal.

Later we found out that the prank was pulled off by those wascally wabbits from the class of 1959. One of their ringleaders was a cherub-faced friend of mine named John who played sax in band and was one of the school cheerleaders.

John recruited a few of his buddies into slipping over the barrier and into the alligator pit at the Tulsa zoo. Taking a snake catcher with a loop on the end, they captured about a six foot, 100 pound alligator and turned him loose in the front hallway at school.

I think they may have thought this appropriate since we were about to leave the school and a very popular song by Bill Haley and the Comets had been "See You Later Alligator".

Three of the perpetrators, Gary, Jerry and Jerry, were taken to court over this—not by the school, but by the zoo officials. The judge actually chuckled when reading the charge in open court: "The defendants did willfully, acting in concert, with stealth, steal from the Tulsa Zoo one alligator, named 'Tuffy'". In view of the lack of previous records for any of the defendants, the charges were dismissed.

Chapter Eighty
Chuck Berry

Graduation went fairly uneventfully and we entered a new era and a new mindset. For example, David Gates was going off to OU to major in pre-dentistry. I didn't know where I would be going. Several other guys were spreading out. Suddenly we were no longer competitors or rivals. While we would still play gigs, we had more important fish to fry, so we even started collaborating and playing some gigs together.

In the summer after graduation, one of the girls' social clubs, Damsels, hired the legendary Chuck Berry for a concert. It was to be held at the Arena Roller Rink. Chuck Berry's fee was $750 for himself or $1500 if he brought a band. The girls elected to hire Chuck by himself for the $750 and contacted David Gates to play with his band for a couple of hundred bucks.

David put together a pickup band of several guys who had not been in the Accents, since some had already hit the road or were otherwise not available. Russell Bridges was not able to play, so to fill the void of the missing piano, David hired a great guitarist named Tommy Crook. (This is a guy who guitar virtuoso Chet Atkins told Johnny Carson on the Tonight Show, in the late sixties, was the best there was.)

They had moved in a temporary stage for the gig and set up folding chairs on the floor of the roller rink. The band was all set up and was warming up about 3:00 in the afternoon, running a sound check. A gold colored Cadillac pulled up outside the front door, right up on the sidewalk, and in walked the man himself, Chuck Berry, accompanied by what must have been his manager. His diminutive companion was about five feet two inches tall and was wearing a tuxedo with a ruffled shirt. (Remember this was about three in the afternoon.) He also had a pinky ring with a stone (assumed to be a rhinestone) about as big as a grape.

The two of them came up to the stage and David introduced himself. Then they sat down in the first row of the folding chairs. "Do you boys know any of my music?", Chuck asked.

"Yes sir.", David answered. "We know everything you ever recorded."

"Well let's hear something."

The band cut loose with something like Maybelline or Johnny B. Goode. David sang the lead and Tommy played the guitar solos. Tommy played up to his usual, brilliant standard.

"That's pretty good.", Chuck said. "Let's hear another one."

So the band played another. We noticed that in the middle of the song, Berry leaned over the said something to his manager. Then he got up and walked out while the band was still playing.

At the end of the song, the little guy in the tux stood up and said. "You boys will do fine." Then he pointed at Tommy and said: "We don't need you." And he walked out to join his boss, recognizing that Tommy's playing would have far outshadowed the star's.

Chapter Eighty One
The origin of an urban myth

When I graduated from high school, I didn't have the slightest idea where I was going to college. I had received a couple of scholarship offers as a result of the fact that I was a National Merit Scholarship Finalist and also one of five selected to submit a science project for the Armco Foundation—looked good on paper but didn't mean a thing. I decided not to major in geology (which I had put down on some applications since my dad said that petroleum geology was where the money was). My interests and apparent talents seemed to lean more toward the arts. So I turned down or didn't respond to any of the offers or inquiries. My grandmother had already told me to select whatever college I wanted and not to worry about the tuition. That was not a good idea. It only meant that I would procrastinate in my choice of a college.

Gary decided to go back to Southern California after graduation and live with his mother for a while in Anaheim. He got a really good paying job at PG&E. He suggested that Jerry and I come out and spend three or four weeks with him. There was plenty of room in his mother's big house and he could show us all around. We could also go to Tijuana and have some fun. So, in late July, Jerry and I hopped into the Pontiac convertible and drove the 1500 miles to visit Gary.

This trip could comprise an entire book in its own right. However, there is one story connected with this trip which is too good not to pass on.

Everyone knows someone who knows someone who knows the subject of one or more of the urban myths which float around from time to time. They swear they know the Ski Cat of the water skiing urban myth fame, or the fat lady who dropped the shoplifted ham from beneath her dress ("Who froo dat?") or the family who had the rug stolen off their motor home in Mexico with the dead grandmother rolled up in it.

But I really did know the participant in the following story, and it is a classic.

When Jerry and I arrived at Gary's house in Anaheim, there was a steady stream of kids coming over. Some were Gary's friends and some were his sister Karen's friends. One was an unusual guy who was Gary's cousin. His name was Rodney.

He always walked over to Gary's since he didn't live too far away, and then rode with us whenever we went out in the evenings. One day Gary asked Rodney when his car was going to be ready and he said it would probably take another week or so. Gary then explained that Rodney had a really "cherry" '53 Olds that was gorgeous but had recently been nearly totaled.

I asked Rodney what happened, and this is the story he told us. I'm not making this up.

Seems that Rodney's car died one day on one of the main residential streets in Anaheim. He couldn't seem to get it re-started again. The engine would crank a little, but not enough to start. Apparently he had either a generator or starter problem.

He got out of the car and lifted the hood to have a look. About that time, a little old lady in a big Buick Roadmaster pulled up beside him and asked him if she could be of any help. "Well, actually you could.", Rodney said. "Would you mind giving me a push to get started?"

"Not at all.", the little lady said, and proceeded to back her car up to get behind Rodney's car for a push. Rodney closed the hood and got in his car to steer, then remembered something important. He got out of his car and went back to the little old lady and said: "I've got an automatic transmission, so we're going to have to get up to about 25 or 30 miles per hour before it will start." The little old lady nodded with apparent understanding.

As Rodney was getting back in his car, the little old lady pulled out and into traffic and drove off, turning right at the next corner.

Rodney was baffled, but decided she must have changed her mind about giving him a push. So he got back in his car and decided to wait a minute or two before cranking it again to see if he could get it to turn over just enough to start. He turned off the radio and other electrical accessories.

Just as he was getting ready to try to start it again, he glanced up into the rear view mirror and spied the little old lady in her green Buick Roadmaster bearing down on him from behind at about 30 miles per hour. She had obviously gone around the block to build up her speed to the 30 MPH Rodney said was required. He didn't have time to do anything but brace himself before she hit him square in the rear end.

The Roadmaster weighed about six thousand pounds and was a tank. It took nearly three weeks to fix Rodney's car. The little old lady's car was damaged rather severely as well, but not as bad as Rodney's.

When the cops arrived, they started to give the little old lady a ticket. Rodney started to talk him out of it by telling him the complete story. The cop was laughing so hard he forgot the ticket. While they waited for the wreckers to come and tow Rodney's car off, he heard the cop on the police radio telling the story to the dispatcher.

* * * * *

Jerry and I both turned 18 while on the California trip. We got back to Tulsa about two weeks before the school year started for the colleges in the area. We both went down and enrolled at the University of Tulsa.

I had no idea what was in store for me at TU, including meeting the love of my life. This same time next year, I would be married, with a family on the way, highly active in a fraternity and trying to decide on a career path.

However, whatever avenues I would choose, I was heavily influenced in my decision-making processes by the first 18 years of my life and the events, episodes and people who are chronicled in this book. While my life since then has certainly been interesting, rich and full of fascinating people and events, most of them cannot match what was experienced in my youth.

But that's another story.

Joe and "BeBop" Bob

Joe's Dad and the car he had when Joe was born.

Joe's parents, vacationing in New Orleans.

Joe, in Tulsa Boy Singers.

Joe's father, standing next to the Chickasha Junior Chamber of Commerce "calaboose." Also pictured on the cover.

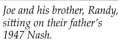

Joe and his brother, Randy, sitting on their father's 1947 Nash.

The neighborhood studs, sitting in Joe's basement.

294

Joe's father.

Joe with Mother, Christmas, 1950.

Joe in uniform at Wentworth Military Academy.

Tribe of fierce Indians, visiting Wentworth Military Academy

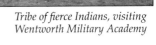

The neighborhood babes, sitting in Joe's basement.

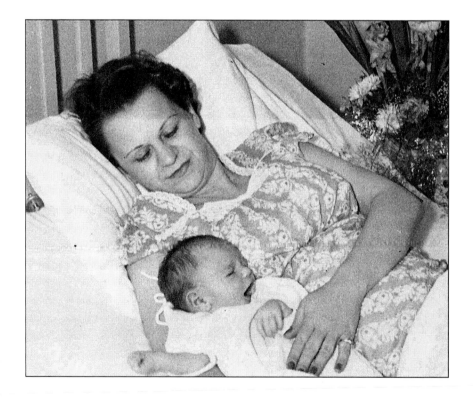

First photo of Joe. August 5, 1940.